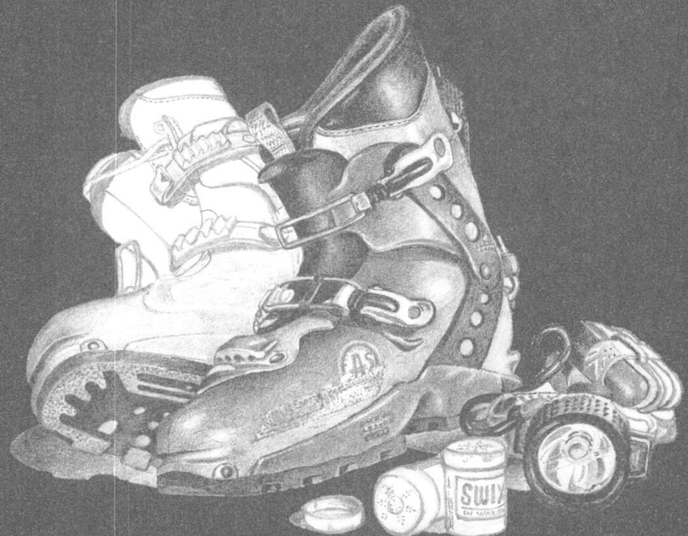

Enjoy the stories!
Lynn B 2006.

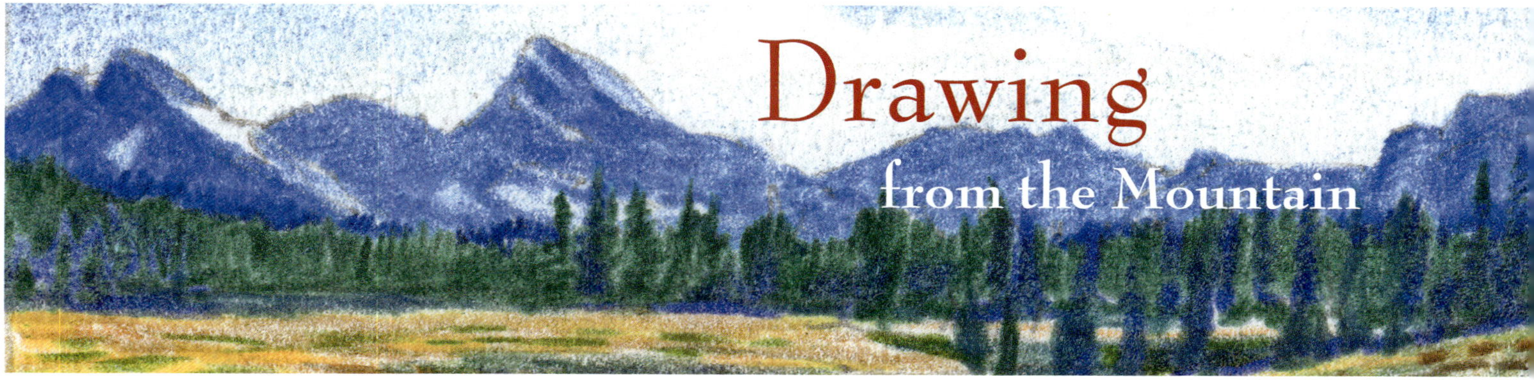
Drawing
from the Mountain

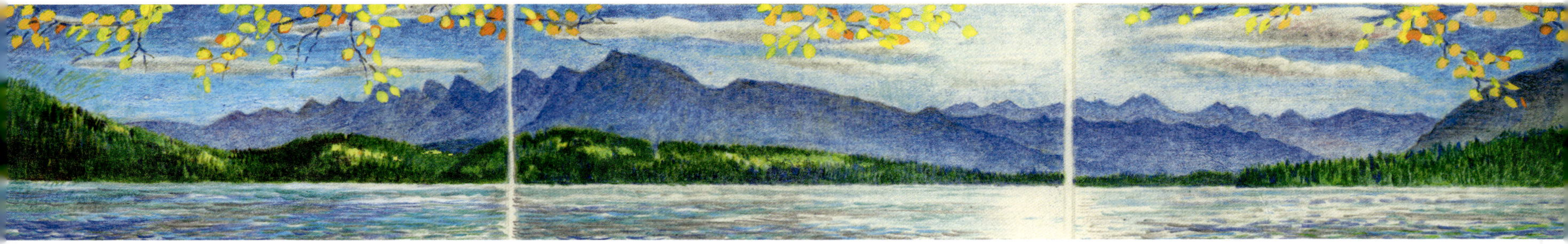

Mar. 1/2007

Dear Valentina —
It is a joy to have you in our lives. May this tale bring you some comfort in your life.

Claire L.

An Illustrated Journey | Lorne Perry

Drawing from the Mountain

Rocky Mountain Books

CALGARY • VANCOUVER • VICTORIA

The setting sun abandoned us high on the wall. Clipped in to safety lines, Ron and I were trying to find a little rest in a tiny bivouac. Literally cheek by jowl on a sloping ledge, every movement edged us toward the precipice. The right side of my face rested comfortably against Ron's pillow-like down jacket. My left, on turning over, was creased by the rocky edge of a nightmarish void. Should I awaken disoriented, it would be wise to remember there was no night table with shaded lamp, no book turned face down just beyond reach in the blackness. Rather, a trap door at my bedside sat silently drawn open.

Throughout the interminable night, we were serenaded by the continual high-pitched buzz of rocks zinging down. In the cold and wet and darkness, we watched the twinkling lights of the Lake Louise townsite float far beneath—like peering down from a midnight flight. As the nightlife got underway below, activity increased: lights going on here, cars parking over there. We even imagined we heard music starting up. Hours later, still awake, we watched in helpless envy as, one by one, cars slowly moved off and the scattered lights were doused. Partygoers pairing up, no doubt, to spend the rest of the long night together in warm, dry beds.

First edition

Rocky Mountain Books
#108–17665 66A Avenue, Surrey, BC V3S 2A7
www.rmbooks.com

LIBRARY AND ARCHIVES CANADA CATALOGUING IN PUBLICATION

Perry, Lorne
Drawing from the mountain : an illustrated journey / Lorne Perry.

ISBN-13: 978-1-894765-81-7
ISBN-10: 1-894765-81-8

1. Rocky Mountains, Canadian (B.C. and Alta.)—In art.
2. Perry, Lorne. I. Title.

N6549.P467A2 2006 760.092 C2006-904255-1

Edited by Judy Millar
Proofread by Marial Shea
Book design and layout by Jacqui Thomas
All photos and art by Lorne Perry
Printed and bound in Hong Kong

The Canada Council for the Arts | Le Conseil des Arts du Canada

Rocky Mountain Books acknowledges the financial support for its publishing program from the Government of Canada through the Book Publishing Industry Development Program (BPIDP), Canada Council for the Arts, and the province of British Columbia through the British Columbia Arts Council and the Book Publishing Tax Credit.

BRITISH COLUMBIA ARTS COUNCIL
Supported by the Province of British Columbia

Contents

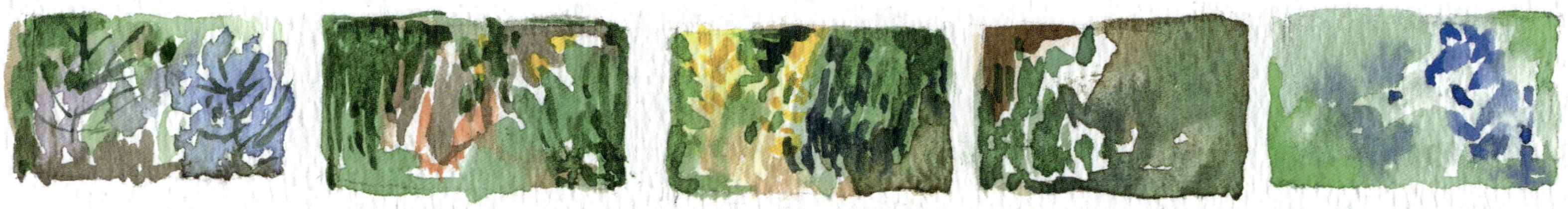

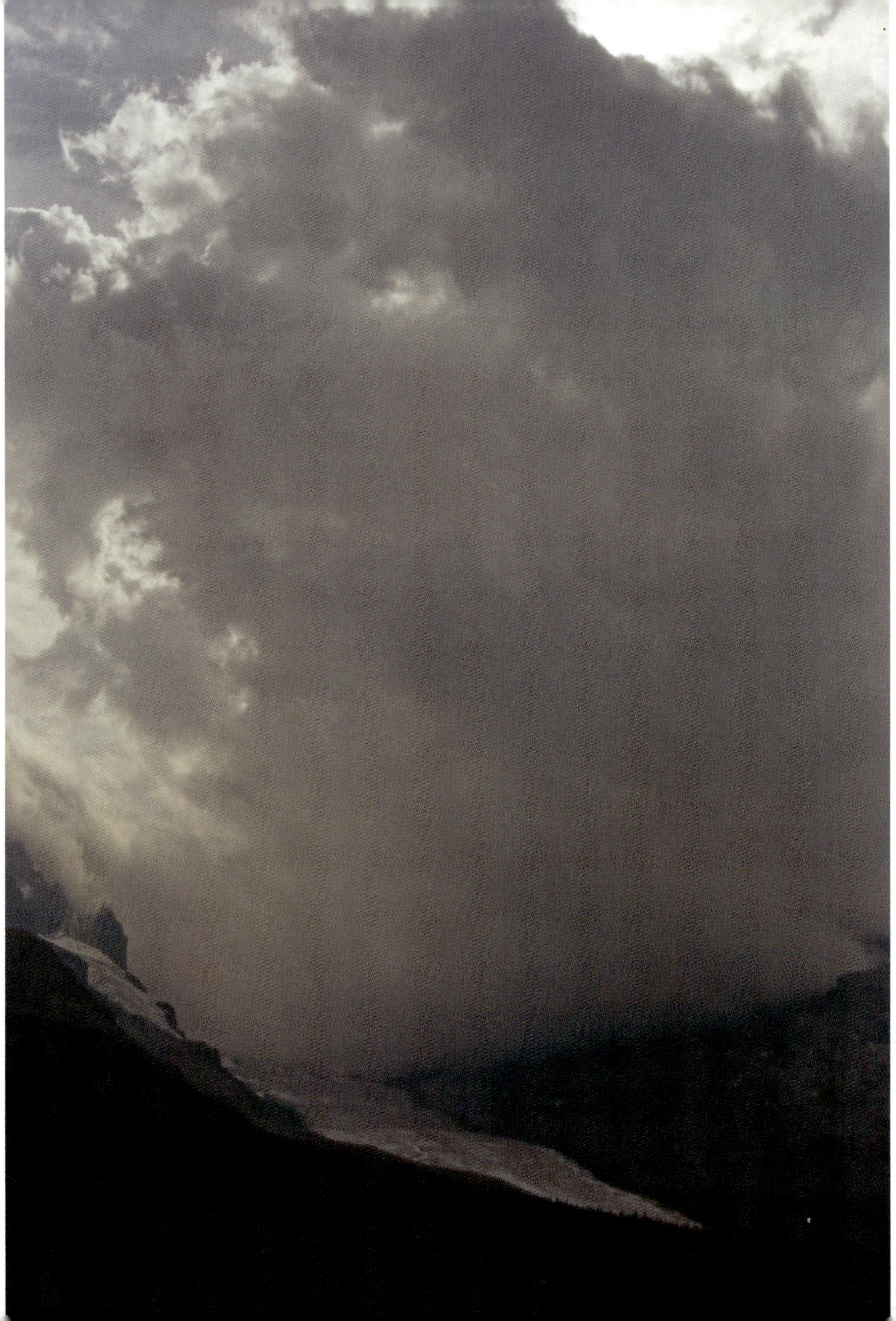

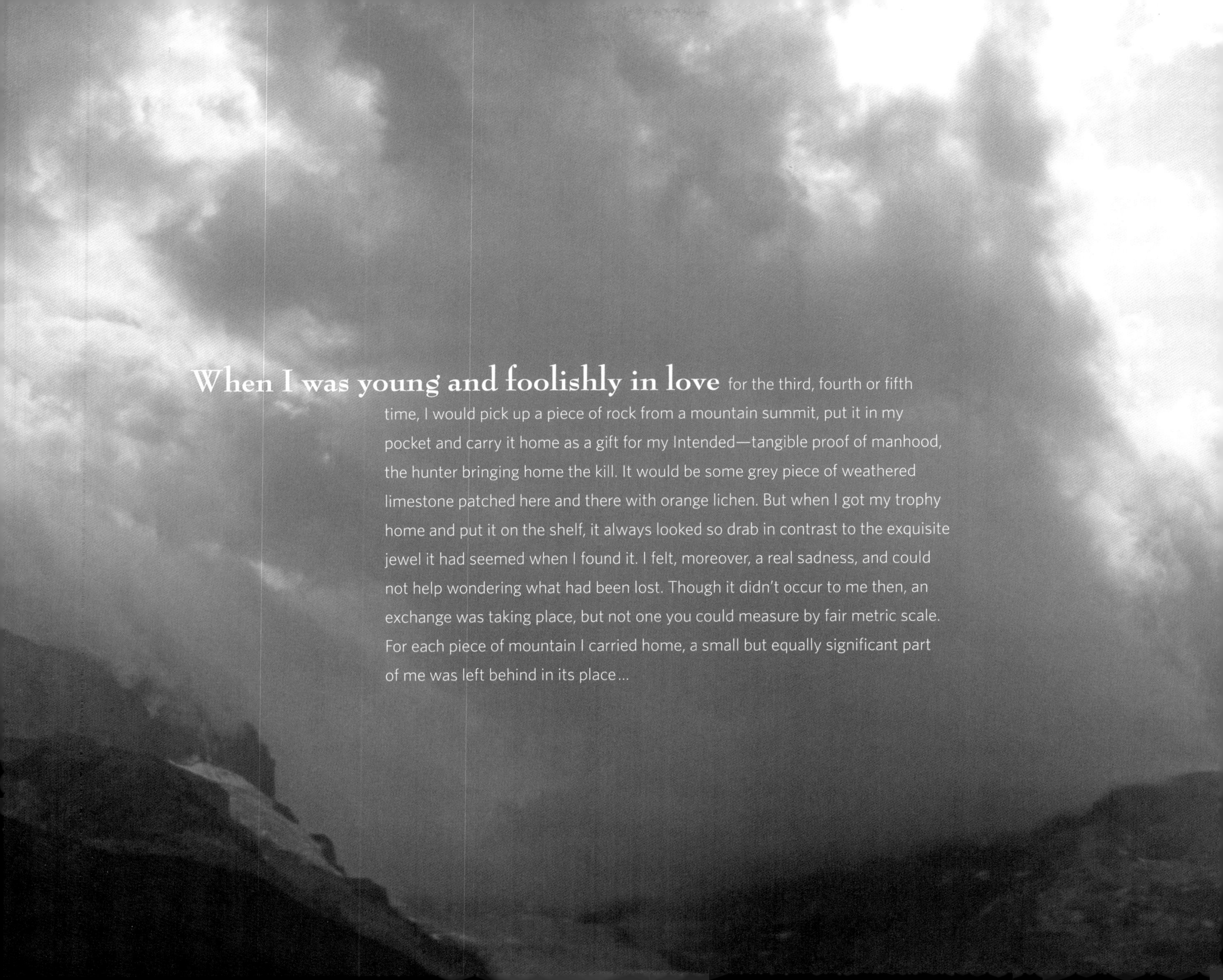

When I was young and foolishly in love for the third, fourth or fifth time, I would pick up a piece of rock from a mountain summit, put it in my pocket and carry it home as a gift for my Intended—tangible proof of manhood, the hunter bringing home the kill. It would be some grey piece of weathered limestone patched here and there with orange lichen. But when I got my trophy home and put it on the shelf, it always looked so drab in contrast to the exquisite jewel it had seemed when I found it. I felt, moreover, a real sadness, and could not help wondering what had been lost. Though it didn't occur to me then, an exchange was taking place, but not one you could measure by fair metric scale. For each piece of mountain I carried home, a small but equally significant part of me was left behind in its place…

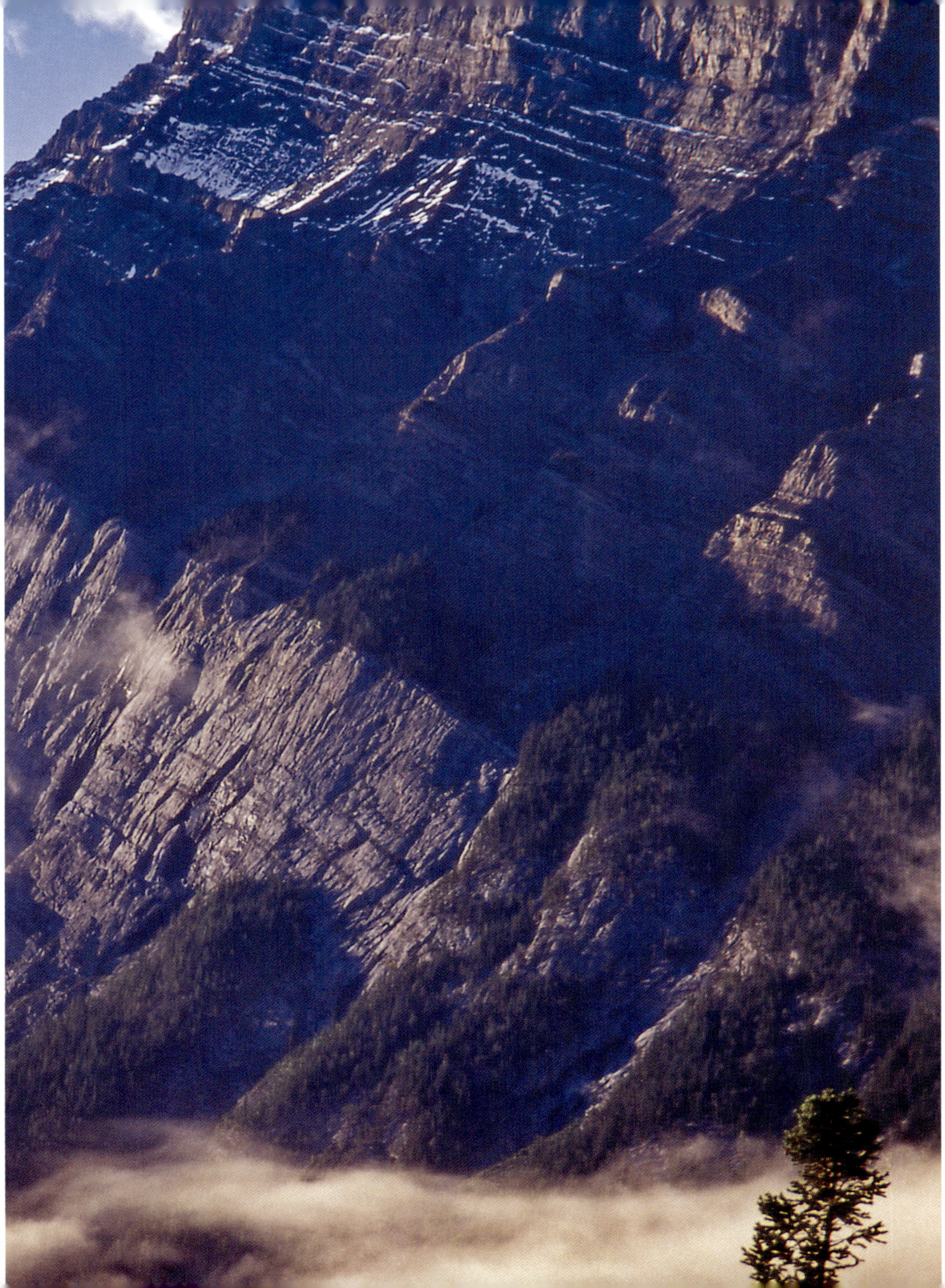

Seen from a point just a few minutes walk downstream of the town of Banff, the upper ramparts of Mount Rundle catch the early mountain light.

CHAPTER 1

Beginning with trees

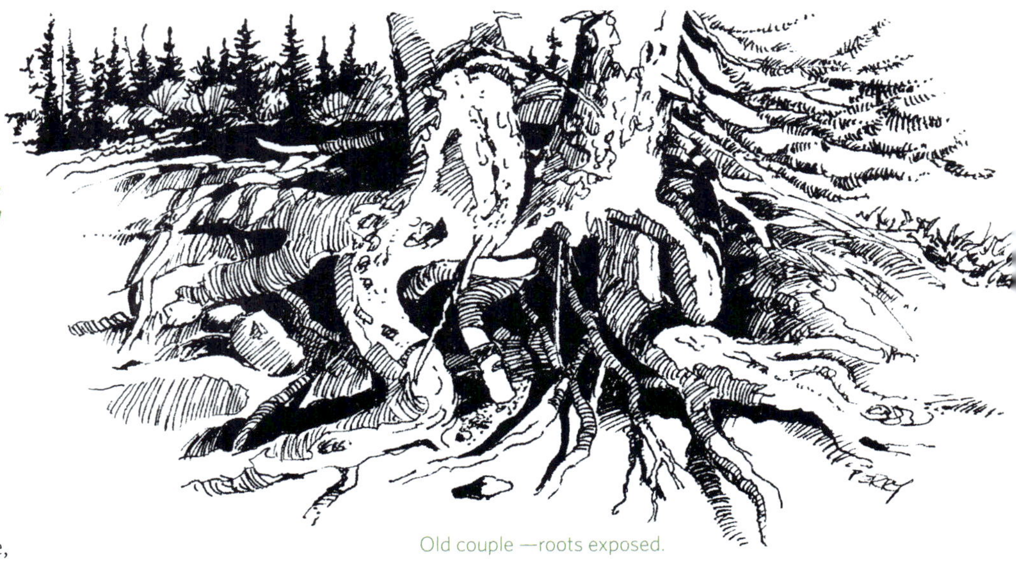

Old couple —roots exposed.

Its adaptations sequester it in the narrow zone, a lonely last high place for trees where persistence and resilience measure survival, grudge, and fitness on bare rock, in thin soil, its competence unquestioned (it has no competition): it does not scrabble on its knees . . .

JON WHYTE — FROM "LARIX LYALLII," *MIND OVER MOUNTAINS*

Dawn. A breath of wind stirs the sparse grass. Out of the haze, mauve light reveals a range of peaks. From one of these, a long ridge slopes to valley bottom in a green oblique. Over that shoulder, north to south, a thick mantle of trees stretches out of sight. Just below where the forest gives way to wind-riven limestone outcrops, clings a single spruce, its woody, calloused knuckles jammed in cracks of shattered rock. Gnarled survivor of frigid alpine storm, summer heat and fire, its fibrous root fingers dug into meagre earth, this rugged centurion lives on the periphery, at the physical limit of its kind.

The rising sun paints each branch a bright yellow, warming the needles. Tiny slits arranged in rows along each needle begin to open. Released from its nightly torpor, the tree inhales the day's first deep breath. At its head, in the top reaches, perches a Canada grey jay, queen of her universe. At its foot, in the thicket of low branches, a spruce ptarmigan coos contentedly.

AS A CHILD GROWING UP IN BRAGG CREEK, then a tiny village in the Rocky Mountain foothills, my life was played out against the ever-present backdrop of trees. The great forest stood in silence over my playing, singing, laughing, loving. From our home—a brown, log house adjoining the only store in town (my parents, the owners)—it was a dusty ride to reach the first peaks of the Rockies. My earliest life memory is driving home at night along a rough, gravel road in the old Chevrolet sedan, drifting happily in and out of sleep. The headlights washing the upper branches of the spruces illuminated a cavalcade of silhouettes against a star-pricked, indigo sky.

Outside our store stood a bright red, solid metal fuel pump with a clear glass cylinder on top where amber gasoline swirled and gurgled down through a heavy rubber hose to the tanks of the giant lumber trucks. For a kid they were all knobby tires, mud covered chains, wide fenders and heavy bumpers. I loved the smell of the drivers' cigarette smoke mixing with the sweet oily vapours on a hot day. Pounded into the grit at our feet, flattened bottle caps read "Grape Crush" and "Hires Root Beer" in bright purple and black.

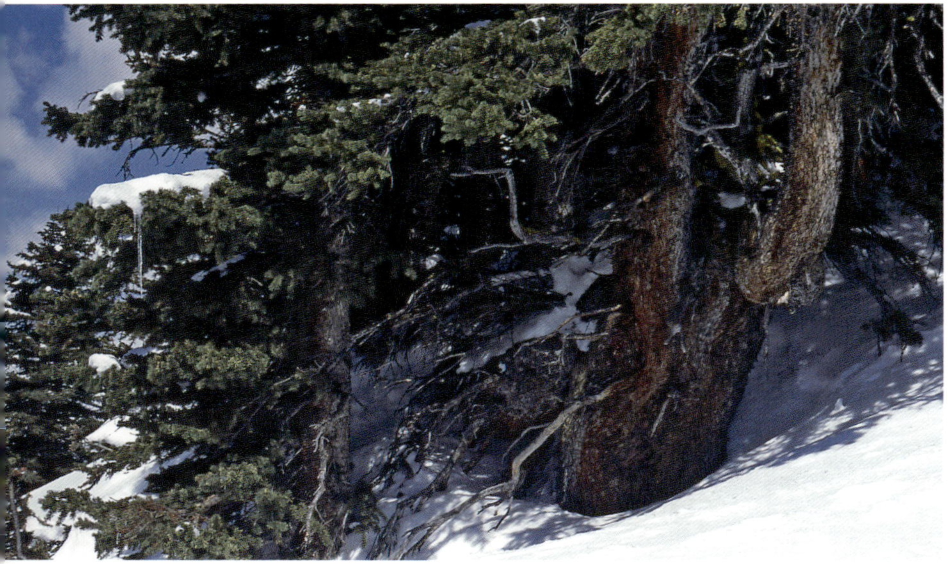

When I ran—I never walked—out the back door, screen door slamming behind on the log wall, a few minutes would bring me through a sun-dappled, spruce forest to the banks of the Elbow River. There, I spent whole afternoons engineering side streams into a fantasy world of grand canals, high dams and thundering spillways. Bent at the waist, and up to my knees in the chill water, I played and played, repeatedly stubbing toes beneath the deep water of my new reservoir. My fingers were pink and wrinkled, my feet hollow and numb. Climbing out of the creek to stand on a flat rock warm with sun, I felt the excruciating pleasure of returning sensation, watched my wet, dark footprints vanish before my eyes. Toe by toe, then arch, then heel, the little water stains would disappear—a parable of transience.

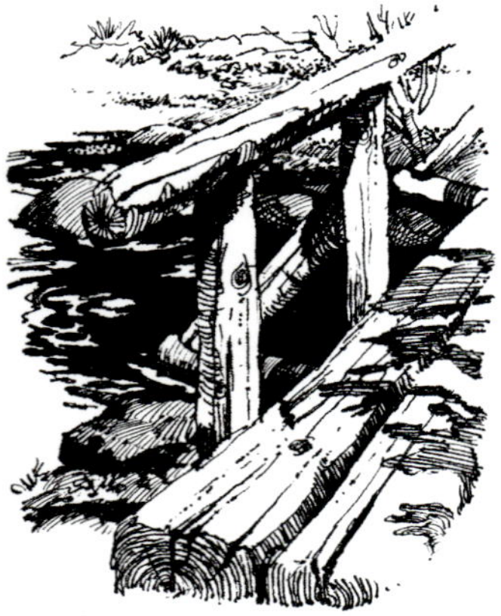

But the trees remained. In those days, trees were objects to be scaled and conquered. As I went higher, the trunk grew smaller and smaller in diameter, until there was a danger it would break and send me plummeting to the ground. I struggled past magpie nests so well hidden among the thickest branches they were invisible from below, even as I repeatedly circled the tree. A magpie's nest is itself a marvel of engineering, a tough ball of interwoven twigs around a thick mud bowl lined with soft down and dried grass. I clung to the uppermost branches, my fingers stuck with pitch, my hands abraded from gripping the sharp needles and rough bark, gently swaying with the tree in the wind. The reward was an eye-popping panorama, horizon to horizon, that made my world on the ground seem so small. The view to the end of the earth was ominous and haunting, but full of sweet longing.

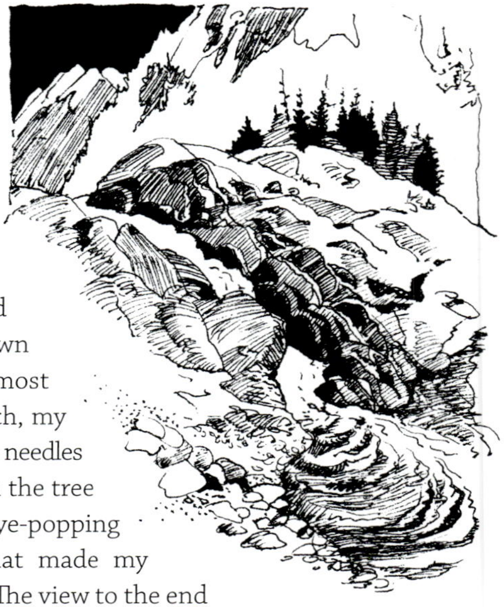

Back on the earth, games of "hide and seek" and wild rounds of "kick the can" were played out in these giants' shadows, heaps of giggling participants darting under their boughs, folding into their hidden places. In the evening, we would snap off dead branches near the base and collect fallen trunks to build fires. The fire hot on our faces in the cool night, we inhaled the acrid/sweet scent of pine smoke, roasting hot dogs and marshmallows. Firelight danced on rough woodbark while the night lit up with friendship and laughter. Wood turned to ash, and red embers shot up in a brilliant river of stars to die out among the treetops.

TIMES CHANGED. Towns got bigger, cars faster, distances smaller. Behind the hissing, roaring paving machine and its road crew, a giant scroll of black asphalt unfurled. The tiny general store with its bright green saws, red-painted wooden-handled axes, rows of canned goods and paper-wrapped Oh Henry! chocolate bars became just a memory. Who knew that, 45 years on, plenty of city-weary people would crave a

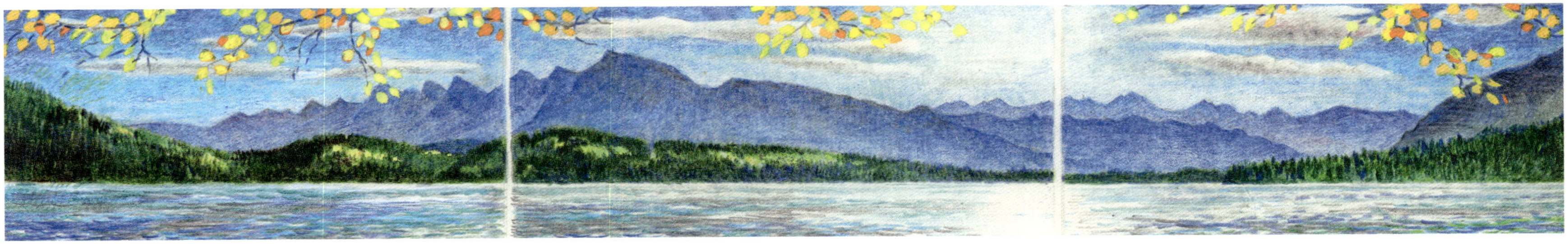

drive to Bragg Creek for a walk along the river and fresh cookies from the bakery? But back then, the locals drove to Calgary for groceries, bypassing our store, likely saving a few dollars. My parents gave it up, sold out and moved to town.

So began the pattern of "five and two," five weekdays given over to feed the body with urban employment, two weekend days to feed the soul on mountain air. From the city we embarked on family picnics near Lake Minnewanka north of Banff. And it was a big deal: a long trip on a winding, two-lane highway. The men talked about jacks and chains and stowed spare gas and Coleman stoves in car trunks smelling of rubber mats and oil. My father drove a 1952 Chevrolet. The big blue sedan was heavy, built like a streamlined turtle, and just about as quick. In the local garage owner's words, "she'd do 70 mile an hour easy if you could just keep the son of a bitch on the road!" A baseball hitting the metal side of this tank made a solid "thunk." You could slide down the fenders when nobody was looking. Light reached the soft, dark interior through small, thick windows. From the murk below the dashboard burst the occasional religious invocation as my father installed the first direction indicator available, allowing the driver to signal without sticking out his arm.

The women, laughing in the kitchen, made sandwiches, packed picnic baskets and poured thermos flasks full of hot coffee. My mother filled a tin with oatmeal cookies, folded a thick wool blanket and placed it in the back seat. The wise traveller carried something extra to keep warm at night, in case there was a breakdown. If something went wrong, a tow truck would be a long time coming. More likely, the men would be obliged to find the problem and fix it with whatever was at hand.

We would set out early on a Sunday morning, travelling in caravan. The cars passed through tiny towns—Cochrane, Seebe, where the high-tension wires sang and the penstock thrummed in the dam. Then on to Exshaw and Canmore, past Banff and finally to the national park picnic site, set in a pine-rimmed meadow on the shore of Lake Minnewanka. The lake, a man-made reservoir flanked north and south by high peaks, was so deep that the record lake trout that hung gaping, its mouth full of raked, needle teeth, on the wall of the musty Luxton museum on Banff Avenue was as thick as a telephone post. Some fish! That monster was longer than I was tall. It looked as though it could have snapped one of the black Labs right off the floating wharf where they paced, barking and sniffing and barking some more, sticking their noses in everywhere, checking out the day's catch.

Everyone trooped into the picnic shelter maintained by the park service. Built of thick logs with long open windows on all sides, the structure smelled of the wood stain used on the tables and charred wood in the big metal stoves. Beyond the windows, under the eaves where barn swallows built their clay nests, past the brown log ends, waggled golden aspen leaves against a deep blue sky. Down the valley was the great uplifted piece of the earth's crust known as the Rundle massif, its shape already defined by new snow patches hung on its ledges.

Someone split wood into kindling and, with some crumpled newspaper, started the fire. Dad assembled the gas stove, with its round copper-coloured tank and blackened grating, pumped the pressure knob and lit it. The burner would splurt and fuss, hiss and fume, gulp once or twice, then roar to life. Soon the crisp mountain air would carry the wonderful aroma of roast beef sandwiches and fresh brewed coffee. My father would take a horsehide blanket he kept in the trunk, lay it in the shade of a big aspen, stretch out and fall asleep. From time to time, leaves of gold and green drifted down without a sound.

My mother's directives followed us into the woods as we set off to explore. "Keep your eyes peeled! You might see a bear! Be back in a while for dessert, it's cookies and Kool-Aid. And remember there's no spare clothes if you fall in the water. Now, you be careful up there!"

We ran and played in wild abandon. Up, down, then back up again. We climbed trees, fell out of trees and skinned our knees. We scaled cliffs and tackled each other on the hard, pine-needle-covered ground. I remember the feel of the limestone boulders, warmed in the sun, rough to touch. The view down through the russet trunks of the pines was a Walter Phillips painting. Between the dark shapes of the branches glittered an aquamarine lake.

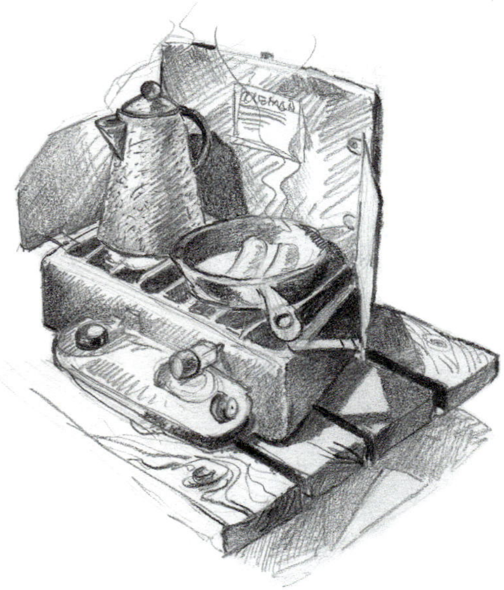

AS A YOUNG MAN, fresh from rock climbing school, most of my ascents began somewhere at a road clearing high in the thick spruce forest. My climbing buddies and I would wind our way upward, heavy climbing boots thump, thumping on exposed roots in the trail. As the way steepened, we brushed the low limbs of spruce, grabbing the small trees for purchase. Fragrant pitch stuck to our fingers. Pine needles and shreds of black wolf lichen tangled in helmet and hair. One day, years later, I would at last take the time to stop and have a closer look through the ten-power magnifying glass in my breast pocket. The lichen's surface was smooth, alien and untree like, similar to that of a bright green mushroom. Their shape was reminiscent of some

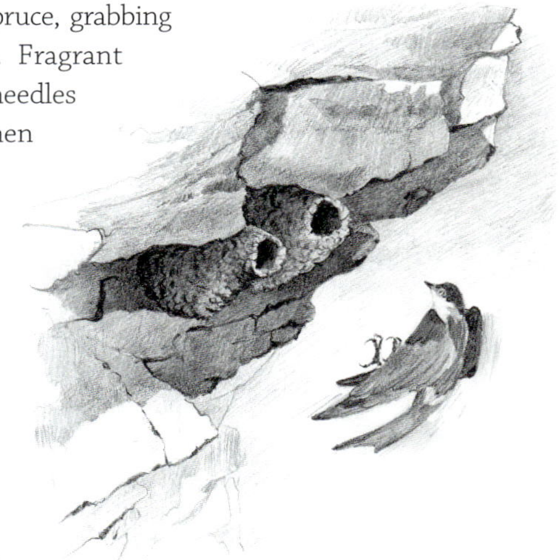

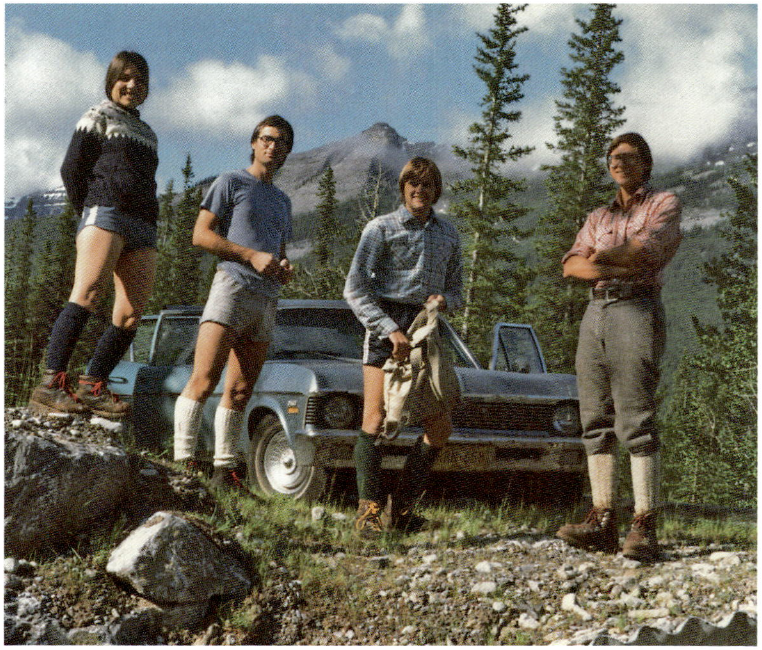

branched corals. No needles or leaves protruded from their finger-length stems because lichen are freeloaders; they do not produce their own food by photosynthesis. The lichen I held was attached at its base to the dead spruce branch by a little flat "foot" the size of an oatmeal flake.

I spent most of my free time in my early 20s hiking, climbing and skiing. Completely consumed as I was, relatives, female company, career, the pursuit of material wealth all came second, actually dead last, to an inner drive to explore the high places. I often carried a camera, and sometimes drawing materials, in response to an undefined need to record what I experienced.

Later, I worked as an archaeological photographer and illustrator in Ethiopia and Sudan, climbing a few of the big equatorial peaks on side trips. Those dry, high plateaus offered a dramatic counterpoint to the Rockies. Subsequently, back in Canada, I continued as an illustrator hunched over a drafting table into the wee hours, and variously worked as a fire spotter, mountain hostel coordinator, ski instructor, bus driver and outdoor equipment salesman.

These chapters drew to a close and I took on the serious professions of designer, husband and father, based in Calgary at the tip of the huge piece of country I call the limestone triangle. I continued to hike and ski on weekends, still carrying the sketch book, still taking the photographs and scribbling in the diary—sometimes with rain dripping off my nose onto the page, sometimes in a cloud of mosquitoes—not knowing to what end. Finally, it dawned on me that my viewpoint was at odds with the popularly held conception of mountaineers. I had no death wish. In fact, meeting and conquering fears and expending every last ounce of human energy to reach a grand summit was wonderfully life affirming. I revelled in a wild freedom and lightness of spirit. I was less interested in adrenaline-laced adventure (though there was some of that) than in the pursuit of sanctuary. The mountains were not proving ground but refuge. I found, on completing a demanding ascent, that I loved every rough rock, tiny black ant, blue shadow, mountain face, olive patch of kinnikinnik and puffy white cloud with a deep intensity. The alpine world was a living relic of a time when the earth was very, very big. I could hear its silent music.

IN VIEW OF THE LOCAL EFFECTS OF CLIMATE CHANGE, vanishing glaciers and unrestrained urban expansion, it is impossible at times to avoid the

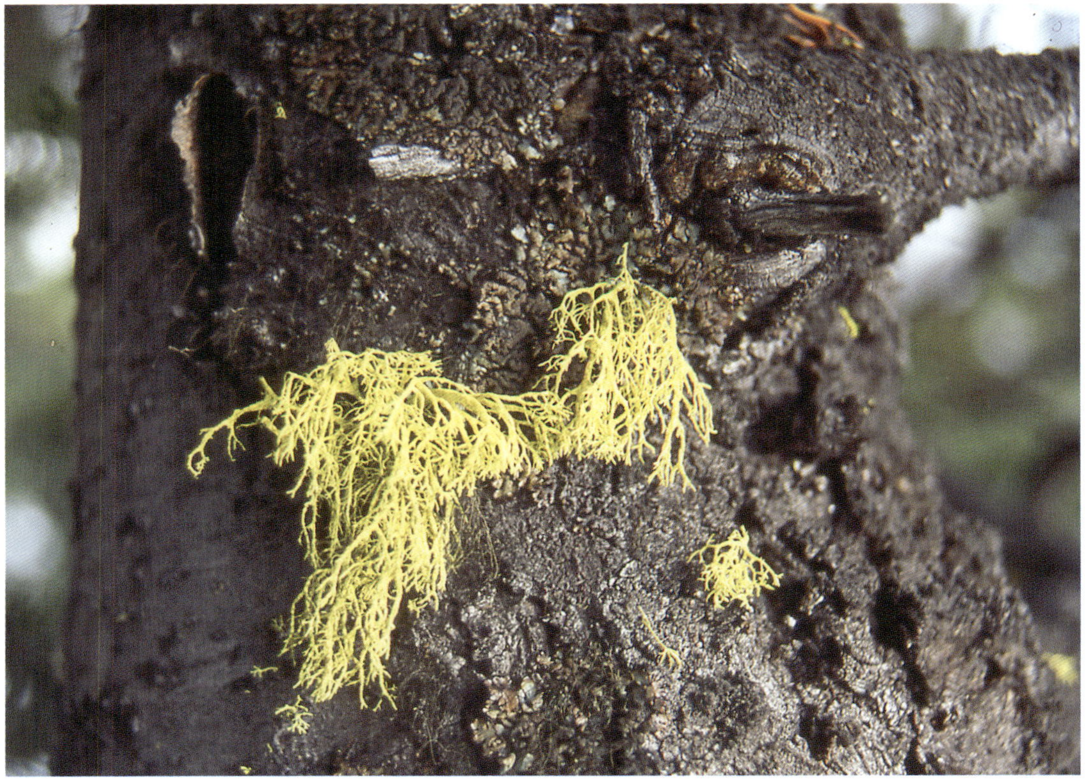

Grasp, Hug, Nip, Sniff

IF YOU TRAVEL ALONG THE BOW RIVER that cuts the great limestone wedge in two, leaving aside for the moment the magnificent peaks, you cannot help but be awestruck by the sheer immensity of the forest—all those trees! The conifer forests of Russia and Canada are the largest in the world. Trees and more trees everywhere: tall and slim, short and squat. Trees that drop their leaves come winter, trees that don't. Trees (like the subalpine larch) that look like they should keep their needles, but don't.

The species, its altitude, location in sun or shade, the soil in which it grows, age—all influence the shape of the tree. In extreme conditions such as exposure at high altitude, the struggle for survival so twists and stunts some spruce and fir, they've acquired their own name. *Kruppelholz* (German for "crippled wood") trees stand no taller than your waist. Seeking shelter from roaring wind that blew the rain sideways, I've burrowed in under their tightly knit branches and gotten a close-up look. The junction of branch and trunk is like nothing so much as the arms and body of some strange, dwarfed creature in a storybook. At the other extreme, some Douglas firs, growing on sheltered, moist north-facing slopes are huge and old enough to have sheltered parties of spear-carrying hunters following mountain trails that vanished several hundred years ago.

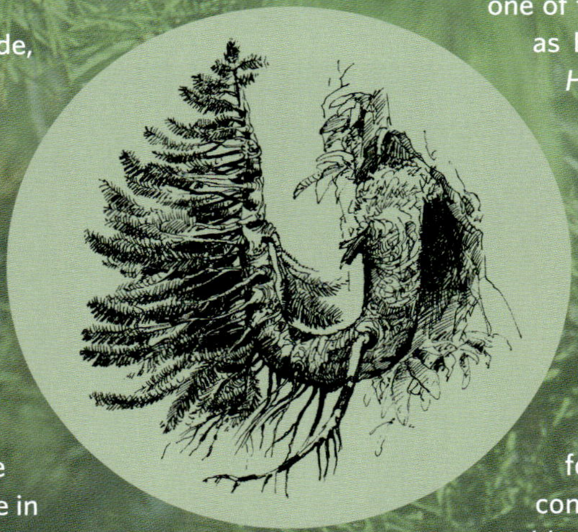

The Eastern Rockies and the limestone triangle are home to many species of trees, but most are one of the following: trembling aspen, lodgepole pine, Engelmann spruce, alpine fir or subalpine larch.

What follows is Perry's fourfold path to easy tree identification: the Grasp, the Hug, the Nip and the Sniff, which, all together, could be termed the Test. Employed with sensitivity, this "hands-on" approach can lead even the neophyte to sensual arboreal enlightenment. I have been surreptitiously performing the Test for years, striding ahead on the trail to avoid the suspicious glances of fellow climbers. Lately, mindful of contemporary trends in a liberalized society, I am getting in touch with my holistic and intuitive side by actually doing it *in front of people.* The instantaneous sensual approach can be quite gratifying for people like me, who don't easily carry a scientific database in their head. I also highly recommend taking the time to read one of the many excellent guides to the Rockies, such as Ben Gadd's comprehensive and very readable *Handbook of the Canadian Rockies.*

Trembling aspen, a svelte deciduous (loses its leaves) tree that lives on the lower, gently angled slopes of the montane forest, is found at the interface between prairie grasses and spruce forest. Go ahead, give it a **Hug**. The bark is a lustrous silvery green, marked with black splotches here and there. A mature aspen's trunk rises up to several times your height before it branches out to form the crown. Unlike the resinous zing of conifers, a gentle **Nip** of the fresh bark in spring yields a fresh smell but bitter taste. **Grasp** its broad flat leaf in your hand; feel the leaf stem. Flat, not round, this stem allows the leaf to vibrate in the wind, giving the tree its characteristic shimmer and rustle.

Be respectful, these are your elders. In his handbook, Gadd reports that, since groups of aspens are often really a single plant that propagates partly by cloning, some groves are an astounding 11,000 years old. Alive and growing since the end of the last ice age—before the Greeks, well before the Romans. Nearly three times farther back in history than the great pyramids of Mycerinus, Chefren and Cheops at Giza. Alive in a time before steel or the written word.

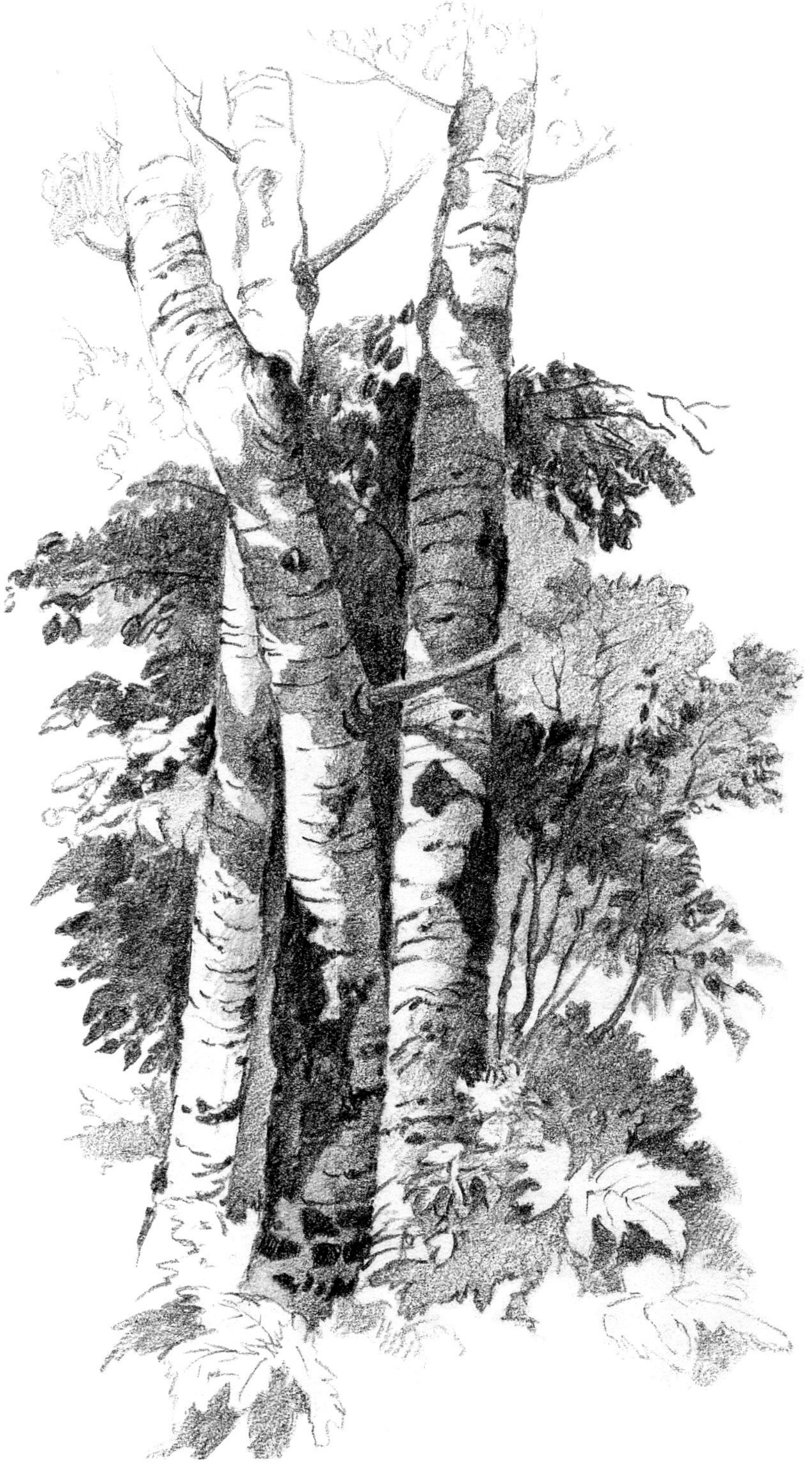

real fear that, in my dog-eared diaries and battered sketchbook, photos and paintings, I am creating a requiem. What predominates, I hope, is a reverie of rhythm and harmony, colour and contrast of the wild places. "As you sit on the hillside," writes Stephen Graham in *The Gentle Art of Tramping*, "or lie prone under the trees of the forest, or sprawl wet-legged on the shingly beach of a mountain stream, the great door that does not look like a door opens."

The mountains gave me life, and in moments of fearsome violence, very nearly took it. In those early days, you didn't mention your passion on a job resumé—employers would think you were at worst crazy, at best unemployable, which, as it turns out, was about right. Eventually, in a new paradigm, climbing became mainstream cool. In that ethos, successful climbers would become motivational speakers and adventure tours marketable. My own game was played out solely before the high, silent judges. And there was more than fair compensation for effort. In the face of such happiness, I could not ask any more.

But it all began there: in the foothills alongside the river that flowed through Bragg Creek and among the spruce-skirted rock matriarchs of Banff National Park. Where the "door that does not look like a door" opened. Unknowing, I stood at a threshold, ready to step out into the clear light.

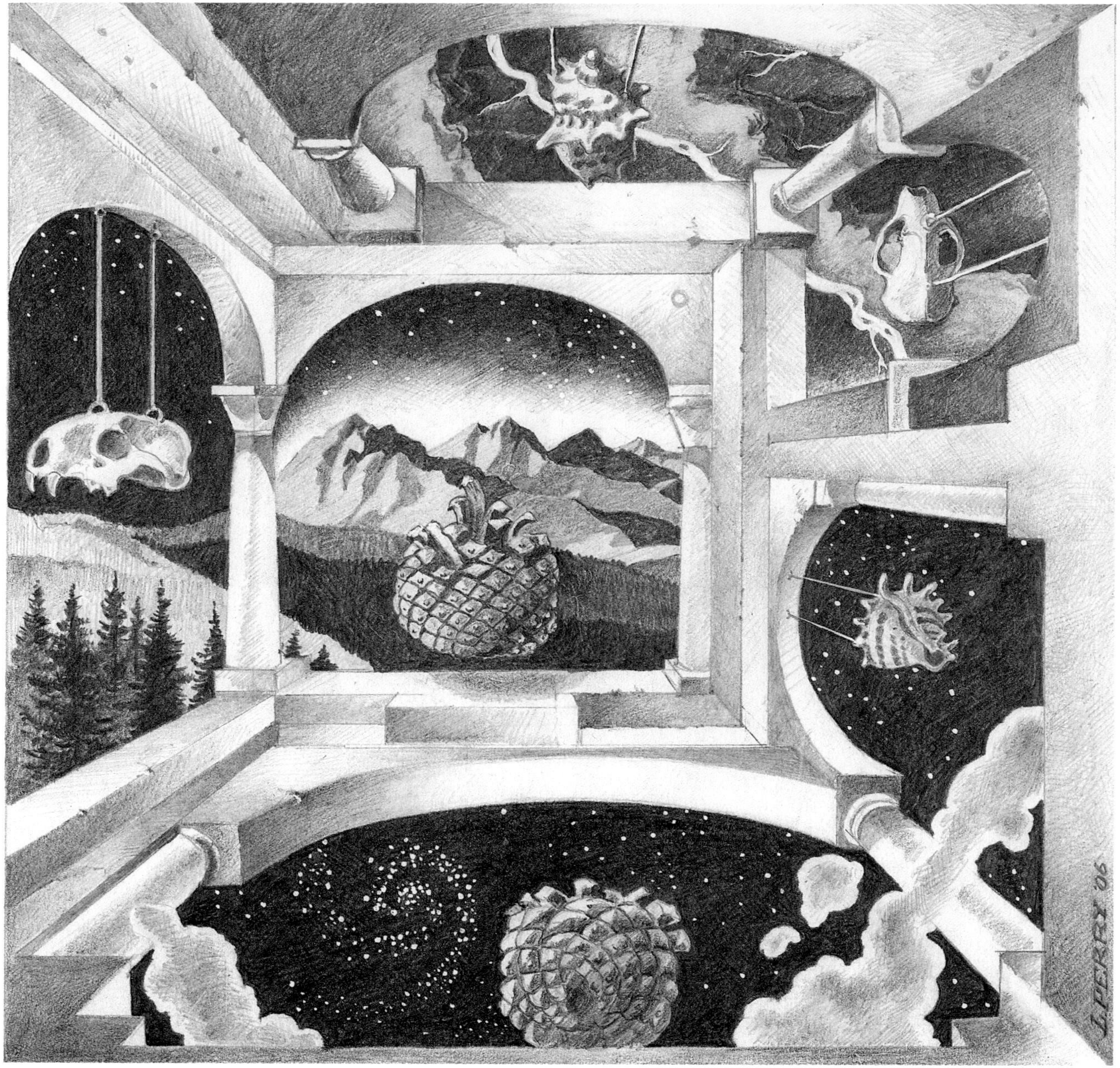

Pine cones and
spiral galaxies,
an Escher-inspired
view of the
alpine cosmos.

A Perfect Cone

THE LODGEPOLE PINE, an evergreen conifer, grows extensively on the mountains' lower slopes. Using the handy Test (see "Grasp, Hug, Nip, Sniff"), check out the needles (leaves). They're quite long, as far as conifers go, about as long as your thumb. Easily identified, these are the only pines in the Rockies whose needles grow in clusters of two. The trees propagate themselves by seed cone.

During a walk through a mature, mixed forest near the town of Canmore (about the middle of the limestone triangle), I pick up one of the hundreds of lodgepole pine cones that lie among the rotting leaves and snow. The hard scales are not randomly placed as I would have expected, but are arranged in a series of clear, ascending spirals around the centre axis toward the tip. Looking down from the top end, I rotate the cone. The spiral whorl is even more clearly revealed. In mathematical terms, this is called a "dynamic spiral." Think of seashells.

In their book, *Tree*, David Suzuki and Wayne Grady note "this spiral pattern is repeated in many things in nature that grow by an increase in basal circumference as well as in overall length: the shells of most mollusks, the twisted tusks of narwhals and elephants, the overlapping pattern of petals around the center of a rose. It is also apparent in spiral galaxies throughout the solar system and in the double-helix coils of DNA bound up in human haploid cells. In a conifer, the spiral is also evident in the structure of the cone."

I ask myself, how do trees know to do that and why do they do that? How do they do it a million times over and produce a perfect cone every time? The experts have theories, but no one really knows for sure. I feel as though I've discovered a tiny peephole into the dark room of universal understanding.

Were an image of the cone to be computer-generated in 3-D, it would appear jarringly repetitive, mechanical. Yet, in the real cone I hold in my hand, each scale is slightly different from its neighbour; likewise each seed, presents an aesthetically pleasing irregularity within order, a built-in idiosyncratic compensation for perfection. Each cone, and each tree, is just a little different, but still functions beautifully—a lot like human beings. That is the God factor, as far as I am concerned, and at the core of life itself.

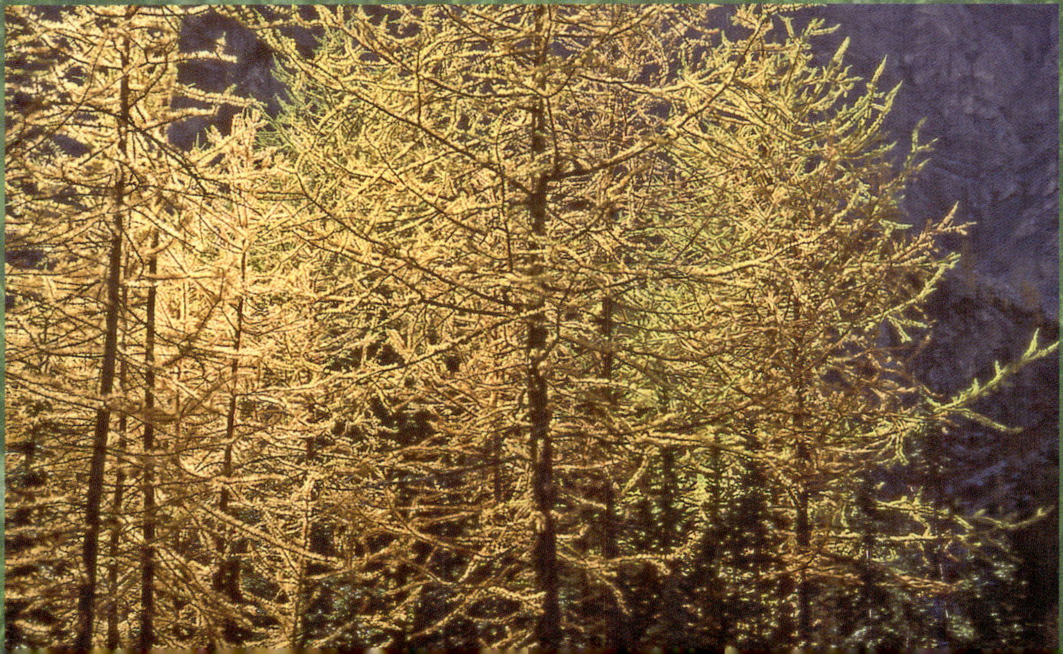

On a family hike above Running Rain Lake in the Rockies' front ranges, we emerge from the darkness of the mountains' shadow to find larch trees burnished gold by a low sun.

Seed of Generations

LUNCH DONE, LET'S GET COMFY and talk about ... sex. Tree sex. In about May, the spruce trees develop their male cones and produce vast quantities of pollen (you might say, the equivalent of semen), which they then release to the wind. I have watched clouds of bright, lime-coloured pollen blowing in across treetops, over ridges, falling on the grass, in rings around puddles, in little green drifts along the trail. It coats your hands and flies up your nose—excessive-seeming to us, but it gets the job done. The successful union of the male cone-manufactured pollen and the female cone's "egg" creates a fertile seed. The female cone, slowly opened over time, or quickly "sprung" in a fire, then disperses a new generation to the wind. Eighty years from now, will my grandchildren sit beneath this progeny, contemplating life? Who will rest under the Douglas fir 600 years hence, or walk through the aspen grove after 11,000 more orbits of the sun?

Do Lunch

MIDDAY. TIME FOR LUNCH. Sitting down beneath your average spruce tree, you pull out your water bottle (much welcome after a hot hike), your sandwich, orange, the coveted chocolate bar. Quietly, at your back, the tree is doing much the same. After just one minute, water from the ground will have travelled up the tree a distance of about the width of your finger, around 1.5 cm. Up above, the needles on their branches are photosynthesizing like crazy, converting the high-noon sunlight to vital sugars. By the time you dust the spruce needles off your pants and get ready to continue your hike, say, after an hour, a typical 10-metre-high tree will have moved the equivalent of 7 or 8 of your bottles of water from ground to its high branches. At the same time, it will have stored away about 11 chocolate bars' worth of sugar. Bon appétit! You have just "done lunch" with a tree.

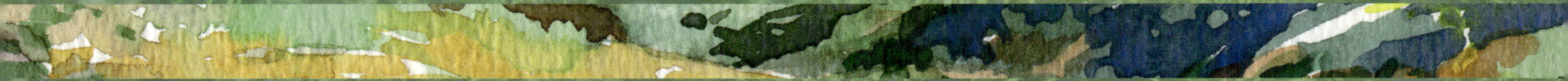

Old Lady Engelmann

HUG AN ENGELMANN SPRUCE, another common tree in the triangle. Note the bark, much rougher than the aspen. Should an average-sized woman, seized with affection for trees, wrap her arms around the trunk finger tip to finger tip, she would be embracing a tree about as old as her grandmother, around 75 to 80 years. She might find, as did my son Laurence and I near Moraine Lake during a period of heavy rain, that the bark smells surprisingly like maple syrup. **Grasp** a spruce branch—ouch! Now, snuggle up and take a **Nip** of a needle. In fact, bite it in half. You will see that, in cross-section, the needle is diamond-shaped. Yet do the **Grasp** test on a fir tree and the branch will bend softly to your touch, because of the flat form of its needles.

In September, a week before
the aspens shake their gold,
sun's equinoctial orb and deep frost
turn the pale and wanly
green needles an instant gold,
a gold in blue enrobed,
flung for a day; and in a day they're drab.

JON WHYTE
— FROM "LARIX LYALLII,"
MIND OVER MOUNTAINS

Yellow-orange larch needles against an azure sky: on the artist's pallet, a "complimentary" colour scheme lends the greatest strength to both hues.

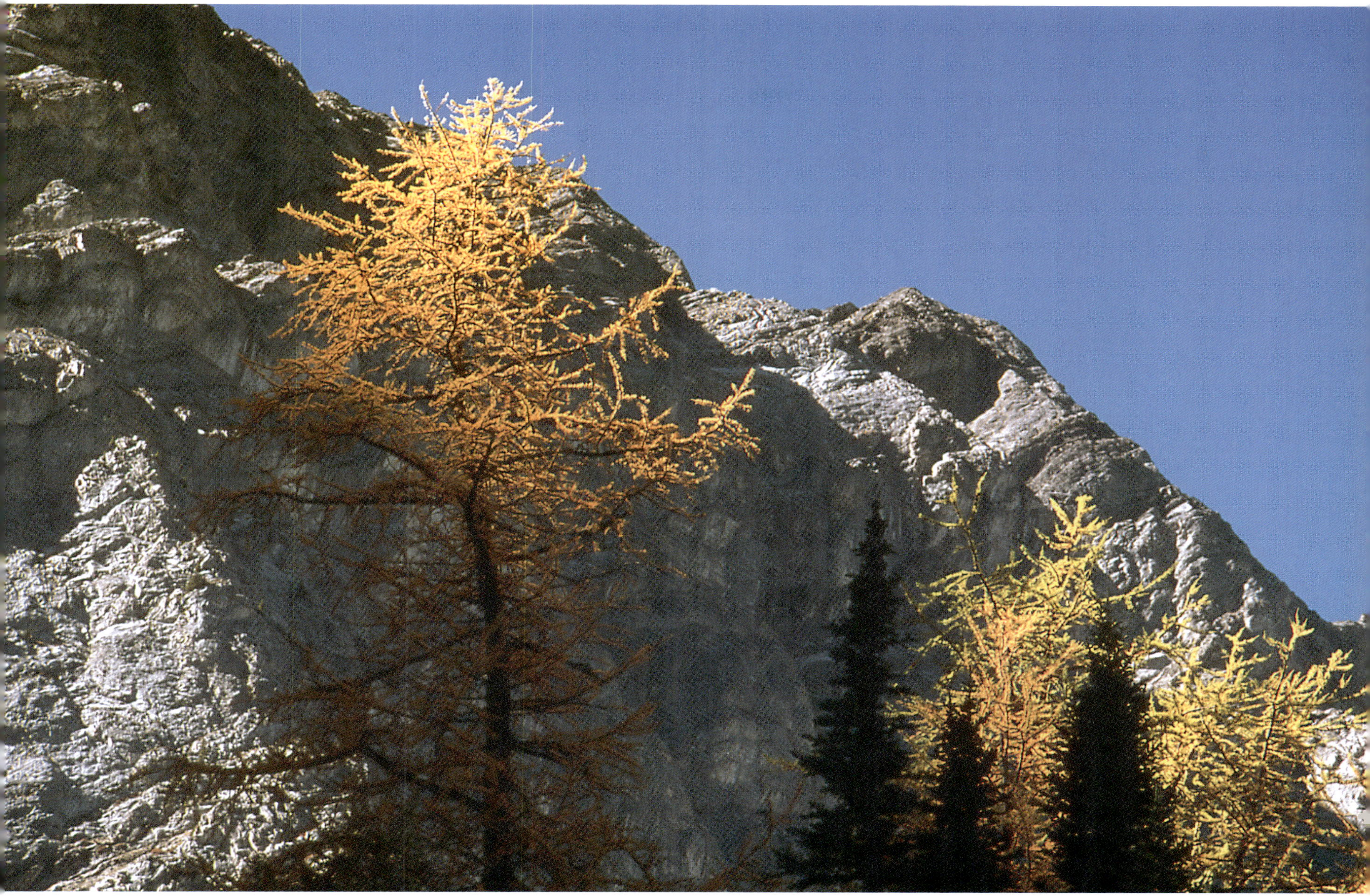

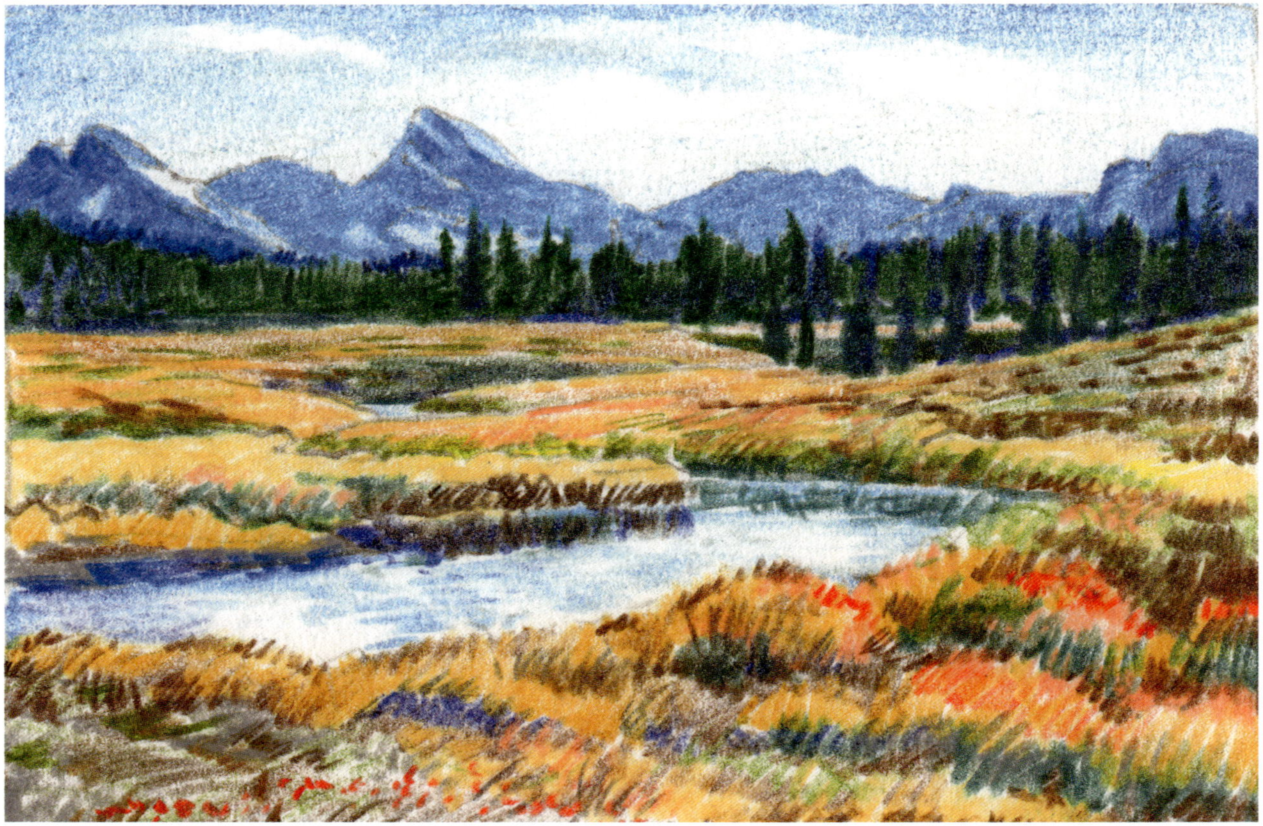

The limestone triangle

CHAPTER 2

Unless everything in a man's memory of childhood is misleading, there is a time somewhere between the ages of five and twelve which corresponds to the phase ethologists have isolated in the development of birds, when an impression lasting only a few seconds may be imprinted on the young bird for life. . . . Expose a child to a particular environment at this susceptible time and he will perceive in the shapes of that environment till he dies.

WALLACE STEGNER — *WOLF WILLOW*

Every now and then I have a dream or, to be precise, a recollection of a dream. The setting is a small, dun-coloured hill village sprawled like a weary traveller astride Ethiopia's north-south road, reeling under an equatorial sun. On the concrete veranda of an empty chalk-white house, I am lying, feverish, on a rickety acacia-wood bed. Except for the occasional flick of lizards on the wall, there is no sound. My temperature is 104. For four long days, I have been lapsing in and out of malaria-induced delirium, wandering endlessly through an Escher landscape of enigma and illusion. Slowly, I turn my too-large head. Through sucking, scouring heat waves, I watch dust devils dance across an aching yellow plain.

Into this chaos creeps a vision, a dream. Blue-grey mountains, early fall. The air is cool, the sun warm on my face. Snow trims the slate ledges above a soft alpine meadow. High on a ridge, light suffuses the golden larches, turning them crystalline. A breeze carries the fragrance of willow, aspen leaves and pine.

A bubbling, lapping sound causes me to look down. Clear water streams over limestone pebbles and dark moss. Irresistibly drawn, I watch my own boots step, step, step toward its sweet refuge. I kneel

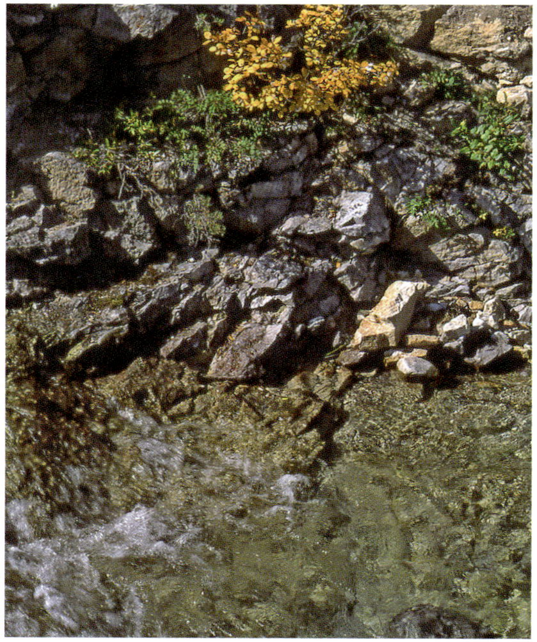

On a bicycle trip up the Little Elbow and Big Elbow rivers in the front ranges, I came across this little creek, whose waters took on almost sacred significance.

down, cup the cold, transparent liquid in my palms. And drink from my secret garden—on and on and on.

THIS GARDEN EXISTS. Imagine holding a very large pie server. Insert the tip just under the prairie and lift out a giant wedge stretching clear to the mountains. That triangular chunk is the country of my imagination, my story. The rough, upturned edge, the pie's crust, represents southern Alberta's Rocky Mountains; the wedge sloping to the tip is foothills and prairie, whose "filling" of soil and rock has formed me too. The triangular shape of our pie slice corresponds to the area a Calgary climber, living at the triangle's vertex, can reach on a Friday evening after work in a battered Toyota, carried west on the Trans Canada Highway and a liberation dream.

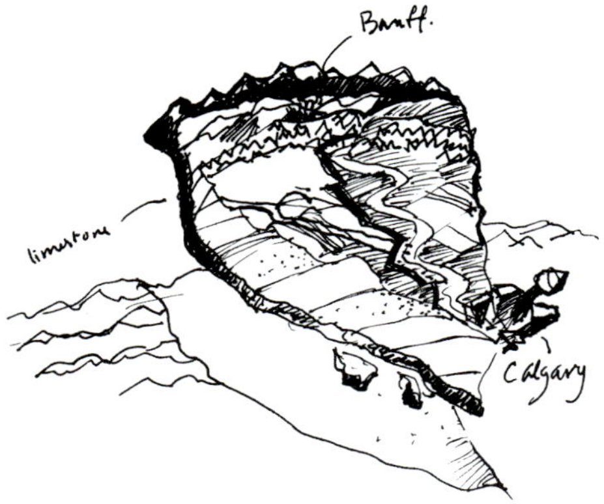

The best way to really get a feel for this place would be to put on a backpack and walk the length of the wedge, east to west, along the Bow River that divides the pie slice from vertex to crust—an eight-day trip, more or less. Not a long time, nor huge distance really, in the great scheme of things. Yet, in that short space, one would pass through several different but connected micro-worlds. In a dazzling geographical sleight of hand, nature has contrived for each a distinct life and topography, a rich and delicate individual signature of texture and scent. More prosaically, these biomes are known as prairie, aspen parkland, foothills, montane, subalpine and, finally, alpine.

At the lowest, eastern tip, the sharp end of the great wedge, your boots, wet with dew, would push through tawny, short-grass prairie. This disc of flat land would spread away to the far horizon, under Stegner's "bell-jar sky." As you move west, here and there cows graze, oil pump-jacks nod their metal heads. At intervals the gangly, square-shouldered towers of a high voltage power line stride off like the wizard Gandalf across the wide world.

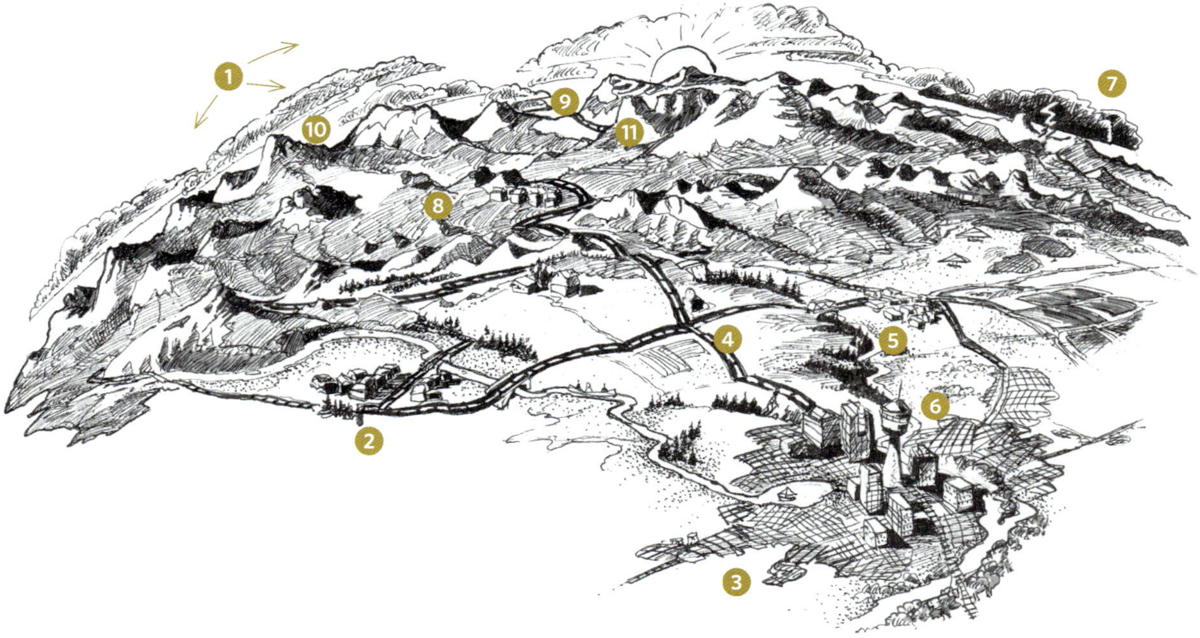

1. Rocky Mountains
2. Bragg Creek, first home in Alberta
3. Calgary, the big city
4. Trans Canada Highway, liberation road
5. Bow River, divides the triangle roughly in two
6. Place where I first kissed a girl
7. Mount Edith Cavell, a classic climb and Mount Brussels and lightening storm
8. Banff and nearby Canmore
9 To Rogers Pass and great skiing
10. Bear attack in valley
11. Castle Mountain — Father's Day climb

As you continue, the earth slopes imperceptibly upwards, cut through here and there by shallow valleys with their rivers and creeks. Notice the contrast between these valleys' north- and south-facing sides. The south-facing slopes, receiving the full travel of the sun, are dry. Thick "prairie wool" and fescue grasses grow here. The ravines are filled with wild rose, silver berry, scattered groves of trembling aspen. Here is where, in the spring, the first mauve and cream crocuses appear. Where I first kissed a girl and made the breathless, trembling discoveries that followed.

The north-facing slopes, shaded and consequently wetter, are abristle with white spruce forest, the natural home of white-tailed deer. And boy scouts. We concealed ourselves here, engaged in wild, running battles or slinking between shadows, mock-ambushing our friends. Our wide selection of ordnance included, as weapon of choice, a powerful sling-shot made with a thick, Y-shaped piece of willow and double surgical tube. A versatile piece of equipment, it could be used for lobbing rotten crab apples— effective for demoralizing the enemy in the early stages of a siege. If the campaign was at a draw and more persuasive armament required, a hard copper pellet fired at full pull had the muzzle velocity of a Roman catapult, extracting howls of pain and, usually, immediate capitulation.

After two days of steady tramping, your route becomes more difficult. The mountain backbone has begun to poke through to the earth's surface in ragged shale outcrops and, later, limestone foothills. In the warm sun, on a bend in the trail, grasshoppers click, and amber-winged butterflies sip from tiny flowers. The air is filled with the scent of close-standing lodgepole pine, so named for its use by First Nations people as the long supports of their graceful teepees. Turning around to face east, where you came from, you see a steady rise in the land. Sloping down and away is a wide wedge of prairie, checkered black, green and yellow with fields and farms.

Within two more days' hike, you have become just a tiny intruder. Your shouts echo among the canyons, vaults and towers of the Rocky Mountains.

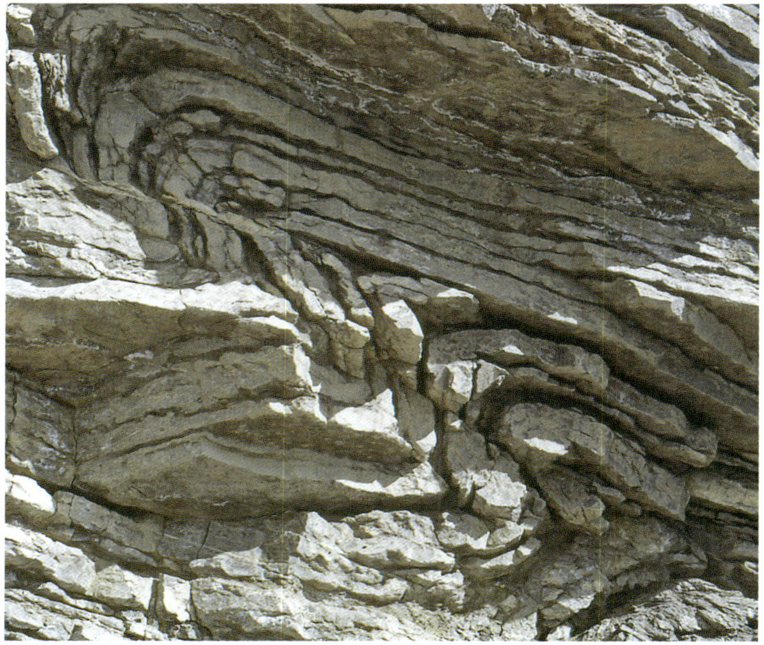

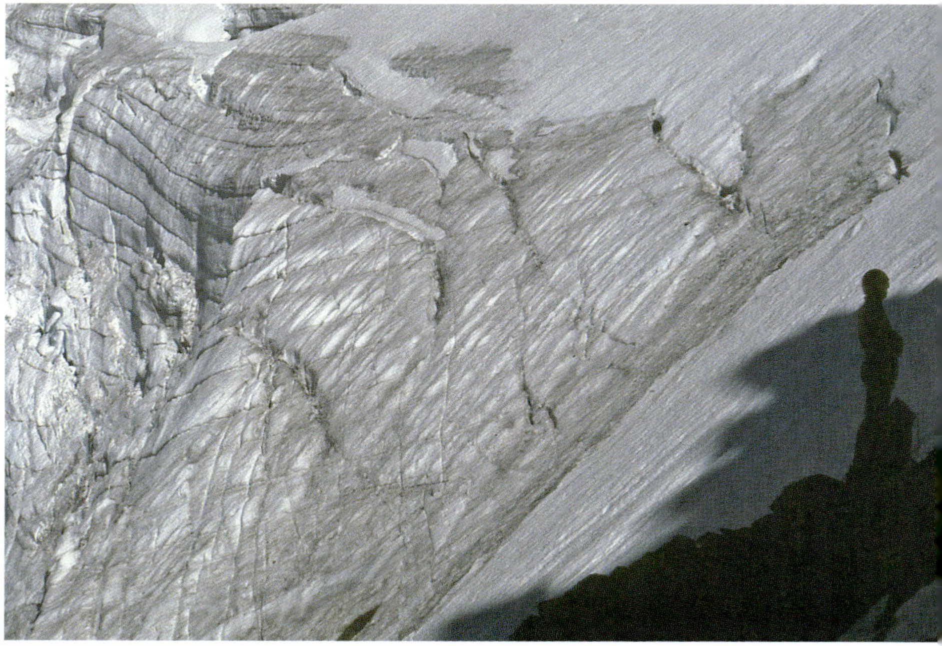

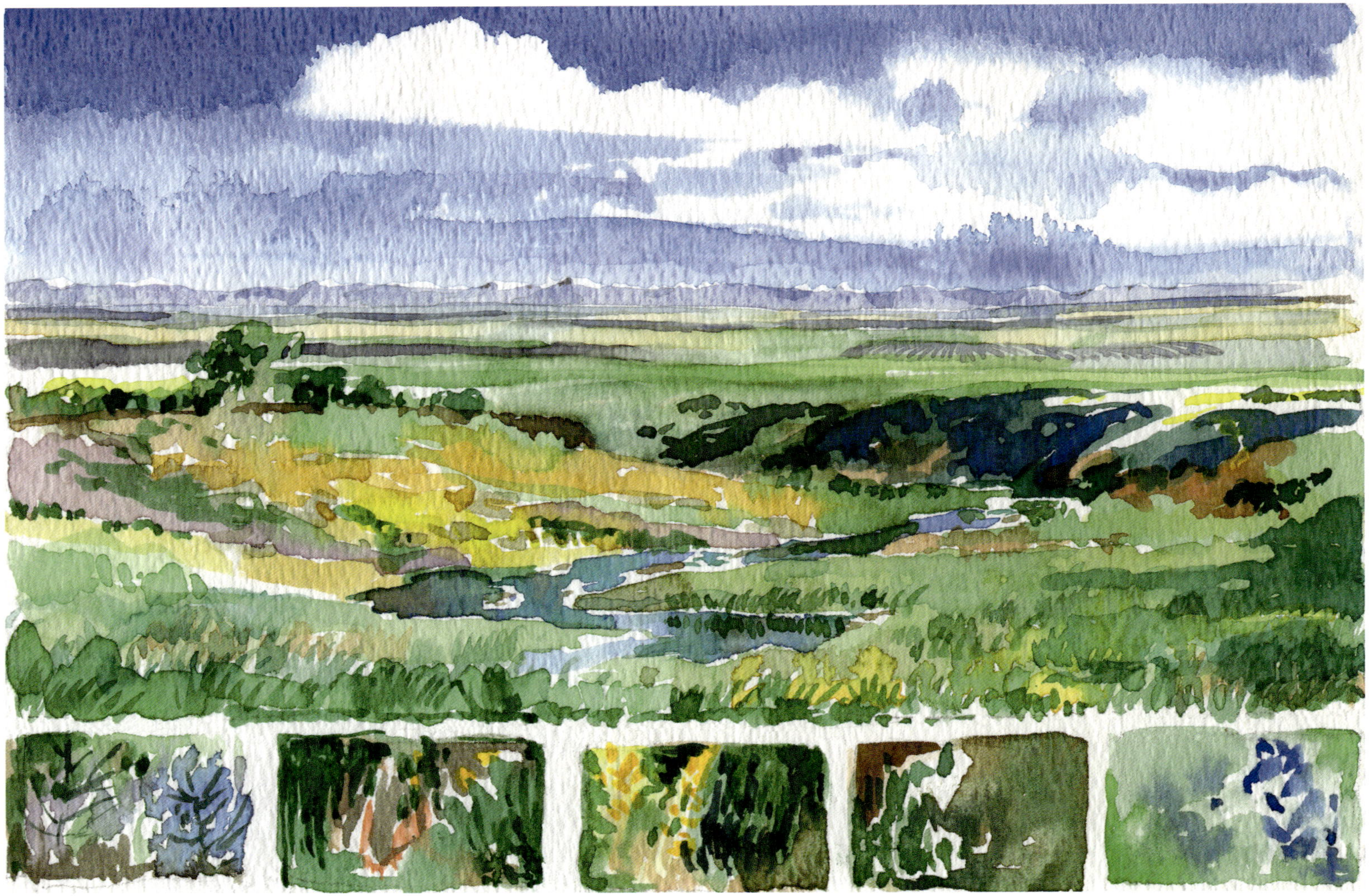

PICTURE NORTH AMERICA from a vantage point high above the earth. You would see that the Canadian Rocky Mountains are one northern segment of a long chain of alps and crags. From the searing heat and yucca cactus of Mexico's Sierra Madre, the mountains stretch up through the cool pine forests of the U.S. and southern Canada and into the Yukon to finally slip away under the black spruce bogs and tundra of the far north. Part of a vast system of compression ridges that interlace the face of the planet, the mountain range is the product of unimaginably large forces grinding away over eons to push up, fold and cut solid bedrock like a slab of warm toffee.

The mountains have been called the continent's water towers, and they are. From heady heights, their deep green glaciers and bright white snow packs pour creeks and rivers, among them the wild Athabasca, powerful North Saskatchewan and, at the western edge of the triangle, the fast-running Bow. These restless cataracts twist and turn, tumble and drop through precipitous amphitheatres, past knobby larches and lean fir to fan out over a great plain, steadily dropping, falling down, ultimately to

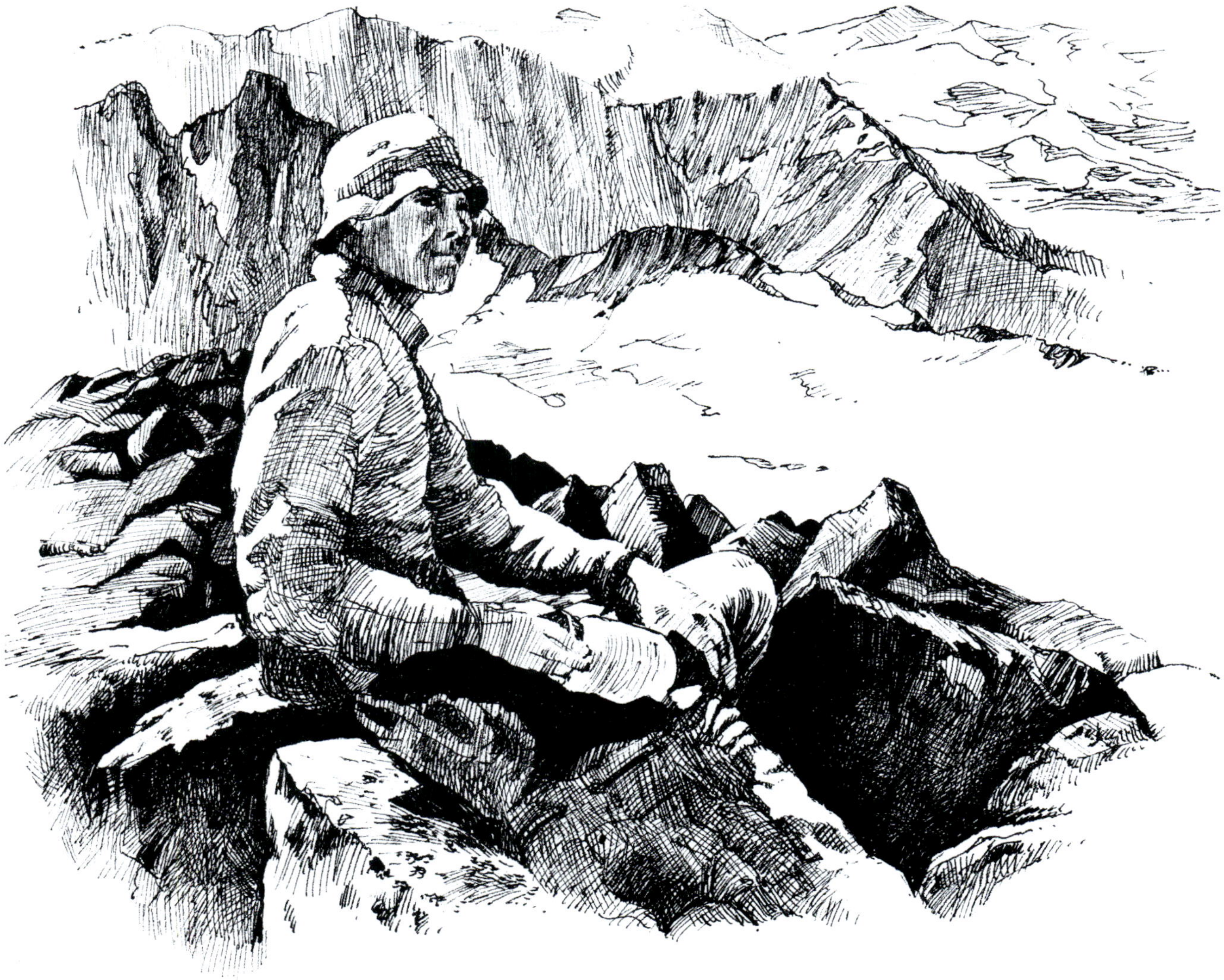

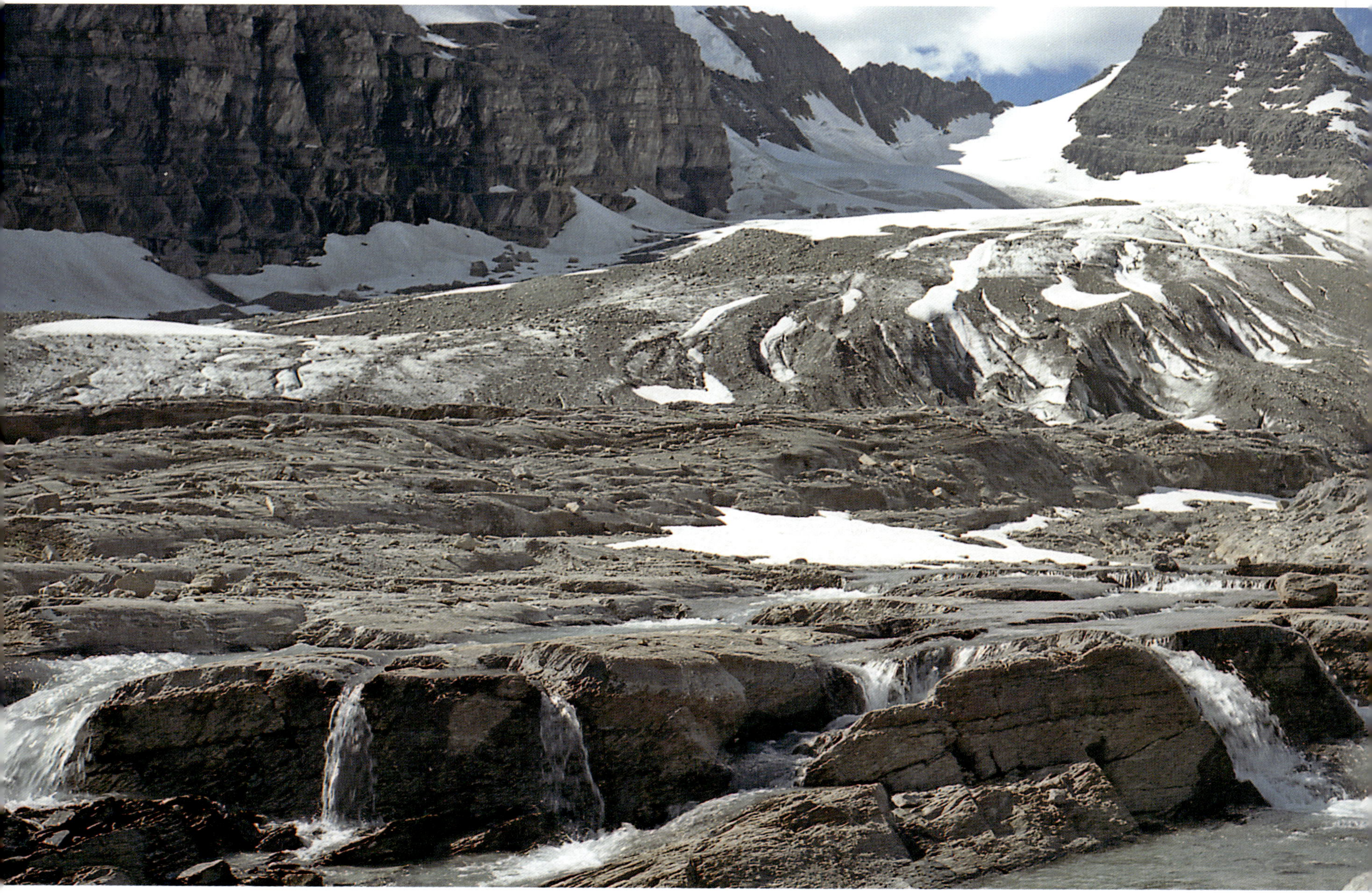

join the blue-green ice floes of the Arctic Ocean and Hudson Bay.

Coincidentally, and it could have happened pretty much anywhere along these great ridges, just north of the Canada/U.S. border, at a latitude of 51 degrees, two quiet events in human history conspired to preserve the slice of pie so vital to me and many others. The first was the creation of three precious national parks, Yoho, Kootenay and Banff. With their mandate to conserve the land in its natural state, the parks protect rugged mountain country that remains largely pristine to this day. The second event was the birth of a frontier settlement, now a city, an hour's drive to the east. At the confluence of the Bow and Elbow rivers booms wealthy, self-propelled, oil-fired, user-friendly, computer-driven, corporate-paced, unrepentant, hockey-proud Calgary. Home. A million souls, give or take. And woven into that flamboyant fabric,

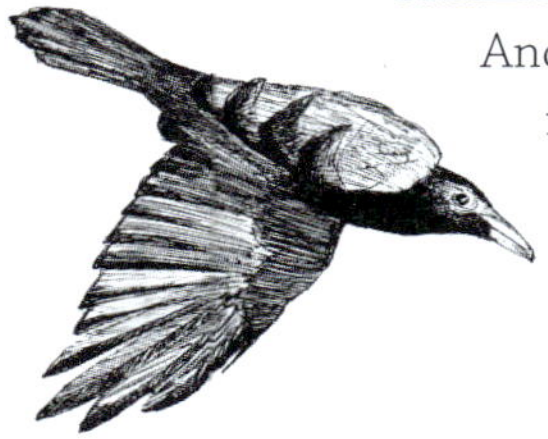

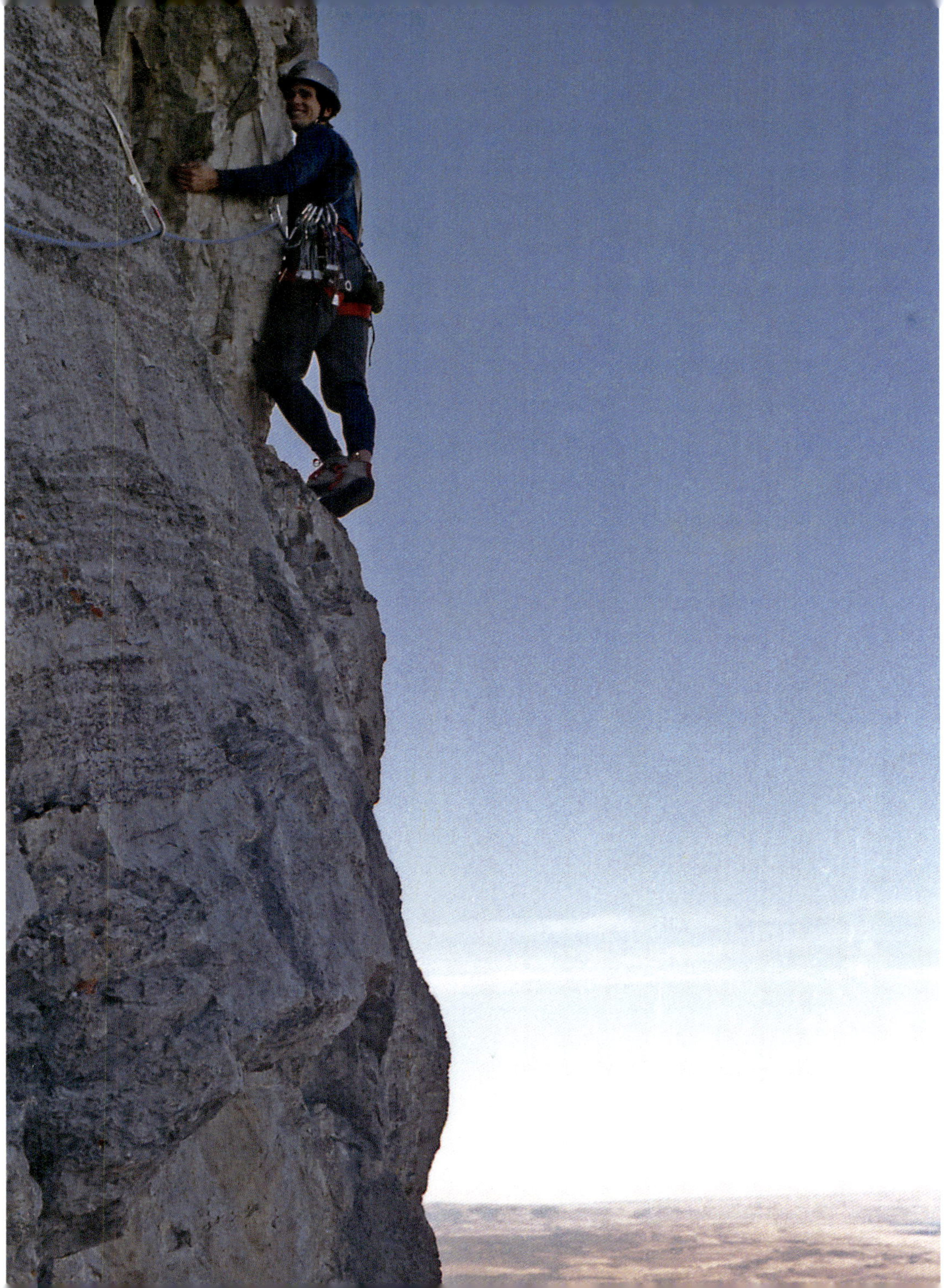

For many years in my youth, I spent weekend after weekend exploring various routes on the accessible and popular Mount Yamnuska, a short drive west of Calgary, known simply as Yam.

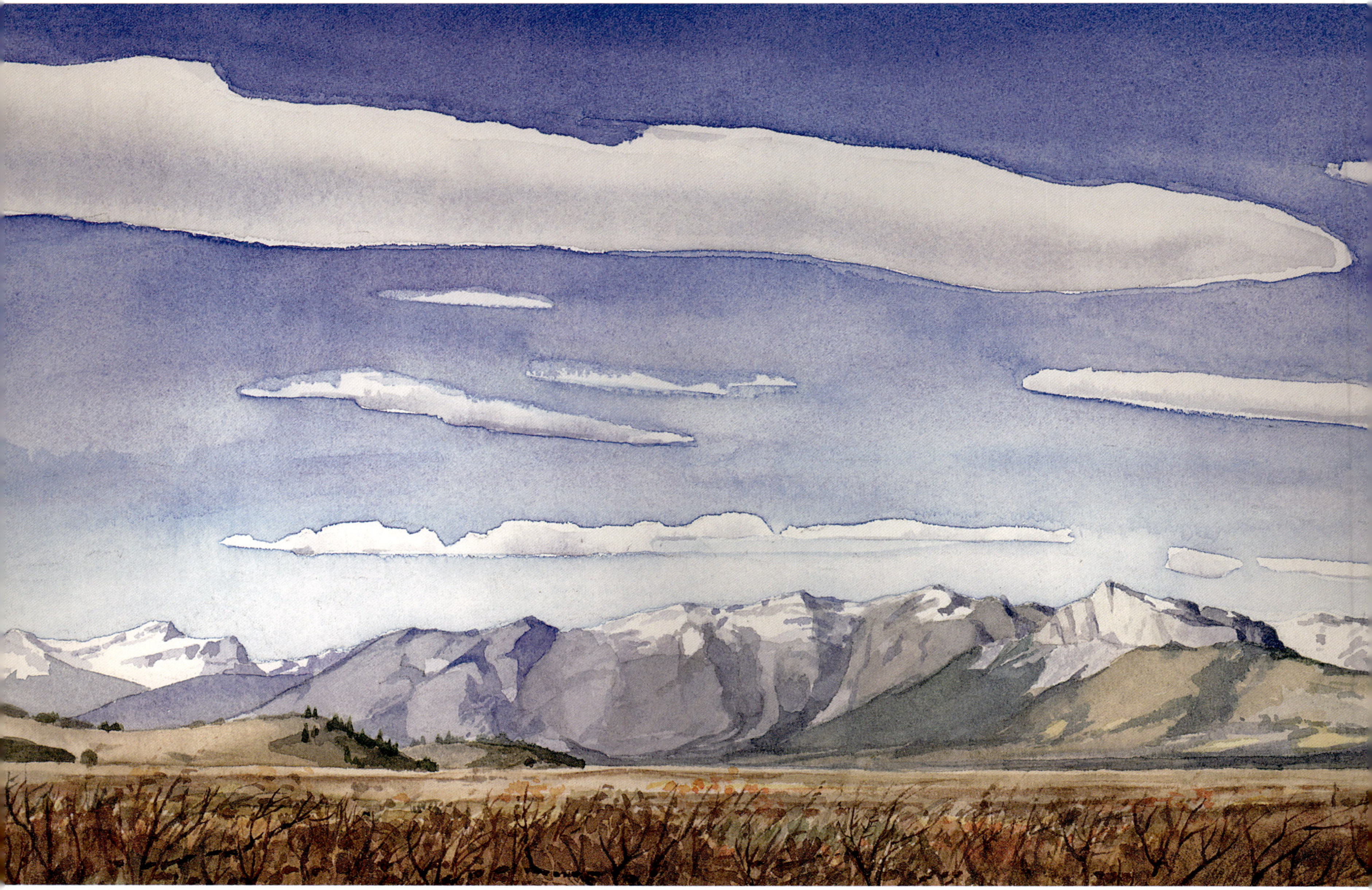

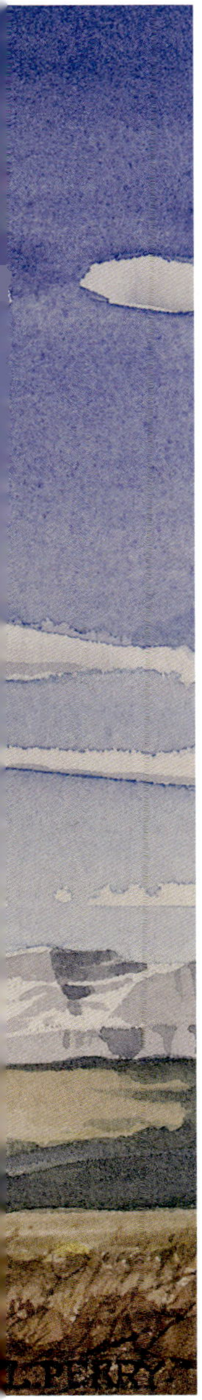

a subculture of mountaineers. Calgary. Where a climber can find a job to pay the bills, a climbing buddy to hold the other end of the rope, a place to bed down between climbs and, occasionally, get laid.

Linking mountains and city, from time to time the warm wind called Chinook huffs in from the west, barreling up and over the tops of the mountains, tumbling down across the foothills and racing out across the prairies to raise hell at the local ski hill in Calgary. It strips the soil from alpine slopes and peppers the stunted spruce with fragments of brown shale. (Some trees in the high passes simply can't grow bark or branches on their windward side.) Swirling, it blows shingles off the ranch house roofs, tears snapping tarpaulins free from hay bales, jams plastic bags in the snow fences, ransacks lumber piles and leaves the ponies on Morley Flats braced tail to wind. Along the banks of the Bow, thick clumps of willow are set shifting, shimmering silver, then green again.

Unlike the professional guides and small resident population of mountain madmen in alpine towns, most climbers of the limestone triangle are, like me, flatlanders. Urbanites. Five days of the week they're mountain voyeurs, all craned necks and longing glances from office and car windows. The other two days: freedom's paradise. Sometimes I wonder whether the alpine fauna in "high traffic" areas—overweight marmots, skittish pikas, bored sheep—ever cotton on to this bizarre schedule that follows neither season nor sunlight.

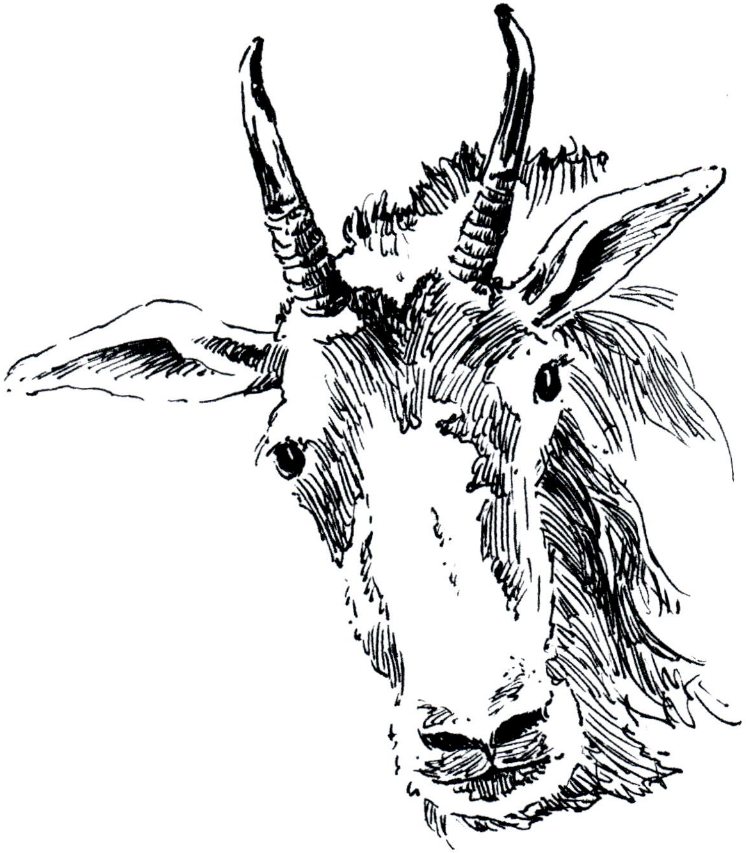

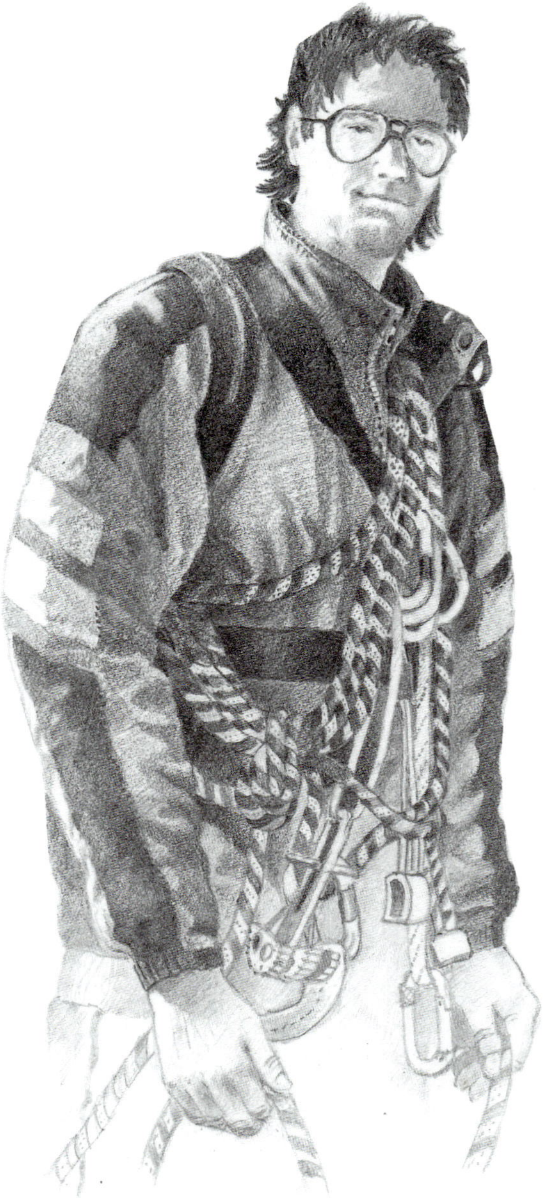

AT THIS ROUGHEST, HIGHEST PART OF THE PIE CRUST, soaring ochre, grey and yellow limestone faces have replaced the low ridges. These towers fly, buttress and wall, up to the clouds. A stunning change.

This is the mountaineer's world—a brilliant and desperate vertical choreography of sharp crampon and steel ice axe high above the valley floor. Falling rock whines and buzzes past long run-outs of bright yellow rope, plummeting into the hazy void where ravens ride the updrafts and the clank of alloy hardware vies with shouted commands.

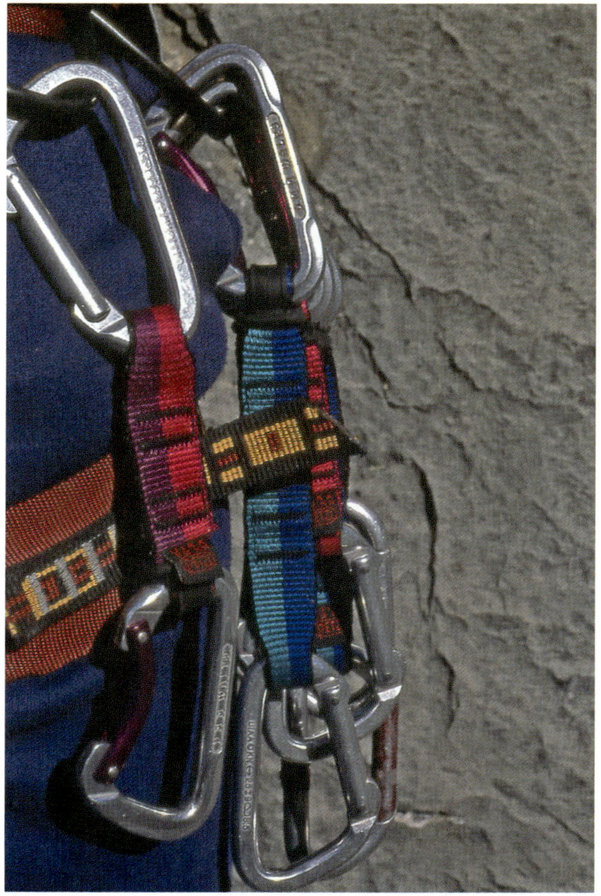

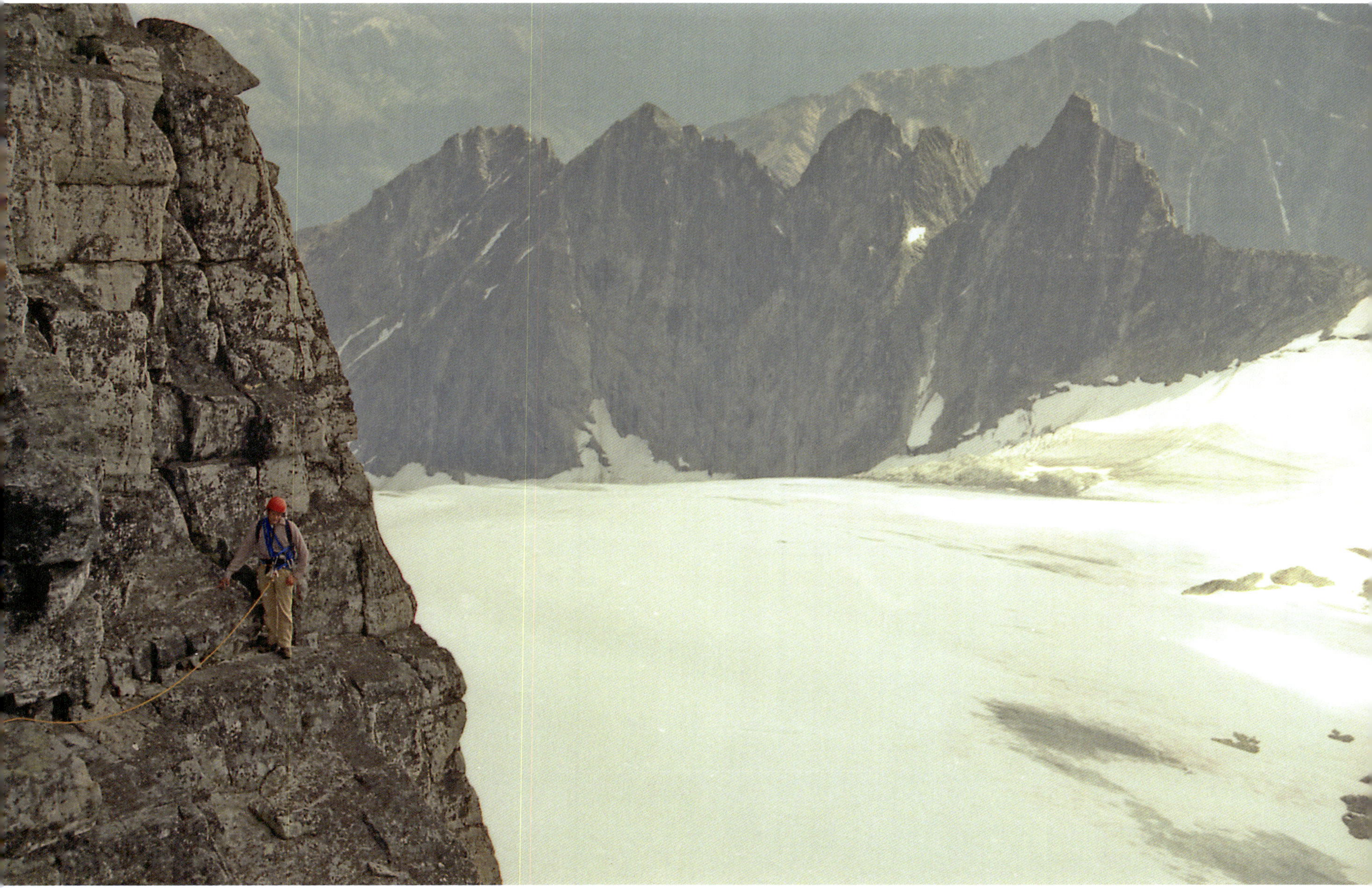

On a ridge below the summit of Mount Hector near Lake Louise, Bob Saunders looks out over the valley.

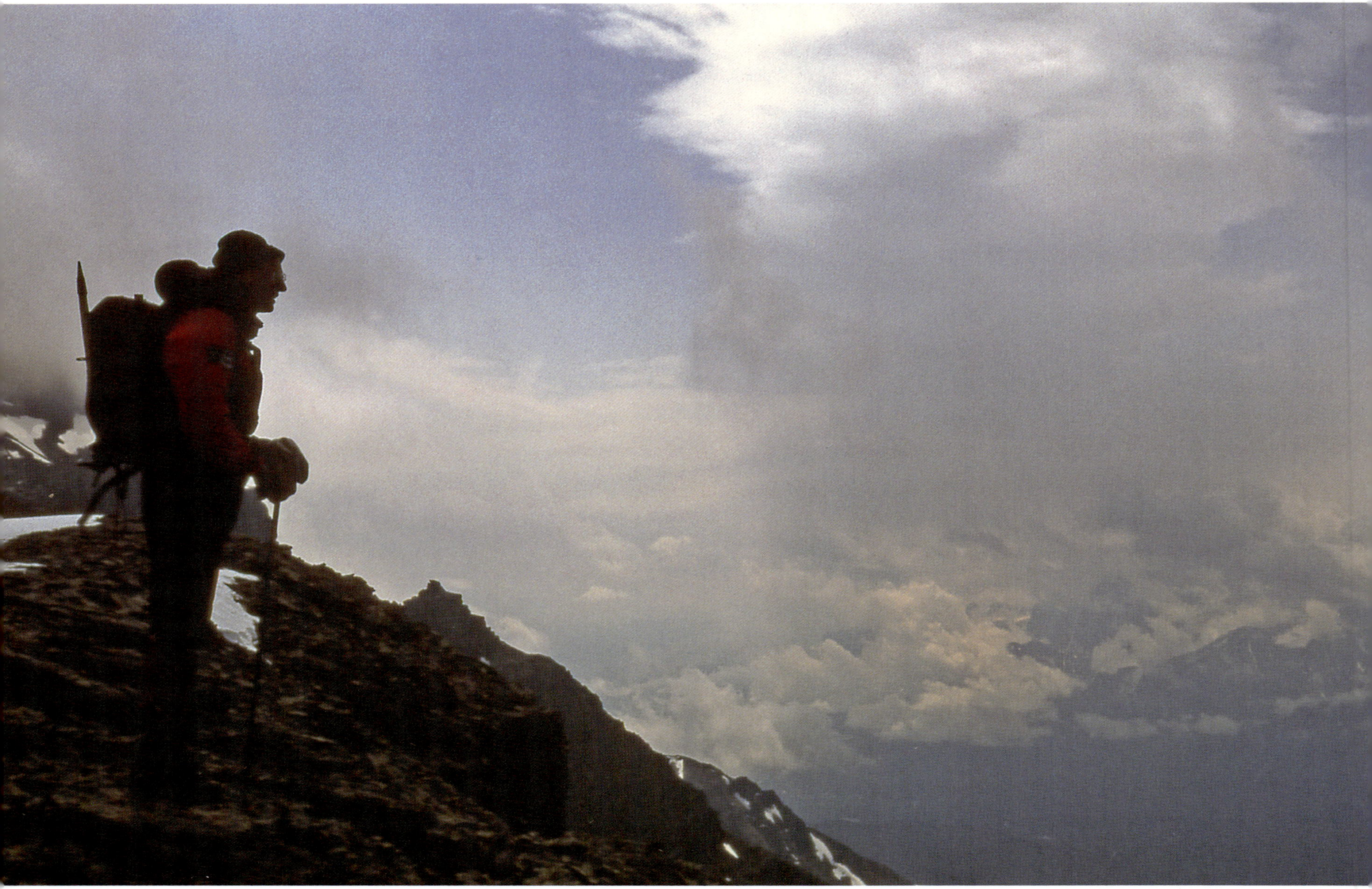

A fine kind of madness

CHAPTER 3

Beyond the neatness of any rationale for life lies its untranslatable glory, the elemental courage of wanting to live. Climbing is serious because it is like life for us who do it, not like a sport; perhaps we betray it by trying to explain our reasons.

DAVID ROBERTS — *THE MOUNTAIN OF MY FEAR*

My father, an astute observer of the human condition, had a joke about mountaineering. "Why," he would ask with a sly grin, "are climbers roped together?" Then he'd pause for dramatic effect. "So the smart ones won't go home! Haw, haw, haw!"

He had a point. Behind the humour lurked an apparent truth. Fresh in the public mind were some frightening mountaineering sagas—Joe Simpson's heart stopping *Touching the Void*; the macabre colour photos of Mallory's freeze-dried corpse; disaster in the "death zone" on Everest graphically described in Jon Krakauer's *Into Thin Air*. A mountaineering documentary televised around this time featured footage of bodies, flattened and misshapen as winter road kill, tethered together at the ankles, slung and slowly spinning below a fast-descending alpine rescue helicopter. Public exposition had by now made a persuasive argument that repeated exposure to cold, exhaustion and the prospect of death could not be considered "fun." In fact, mountaineering might be seen as absolute madness. Why wouldn't the smart ones go home?

Mountains are climbed for different reasons—challenge, adventure, risk and reward. Bragging rights, ego. For the love of the doing, pure joy, aesthetic experience. Escape and renewal. Absolute freedom. For me climbing was all of these at different times and in different measure. What endured, however, was the transformative lightness of spirit, the stripping away of limits on reaching a summit. At such times, I felt winged, as though at any moment I could take flight. To paraphrase Thomas De Quincey in his *Confessions of An Opium Eater* (1822), if this were madness, it seemed a very fine kind.

MY CLIMBING LIFE BEGAN in a stark corridor of a young University of Calgary. A fine arts student, I "majored" in painting. My minor was drawing. One eyebrow still stung where stitches closed a recent wound acquired in a bar fight. I stood squinting at a bulletin board plastered with a disorderly collage of notices competing for my glance. A simple handbill caught my attention: "Rock Climbing School. No Previous Experience Required. Chief Guide, Charlie Locke." A brief description followed, along with a contact number.

Arrogant, destitute, a cauldron of angst and anger, I had at that point abandoned the values acquired in the natural world of my childhood. All

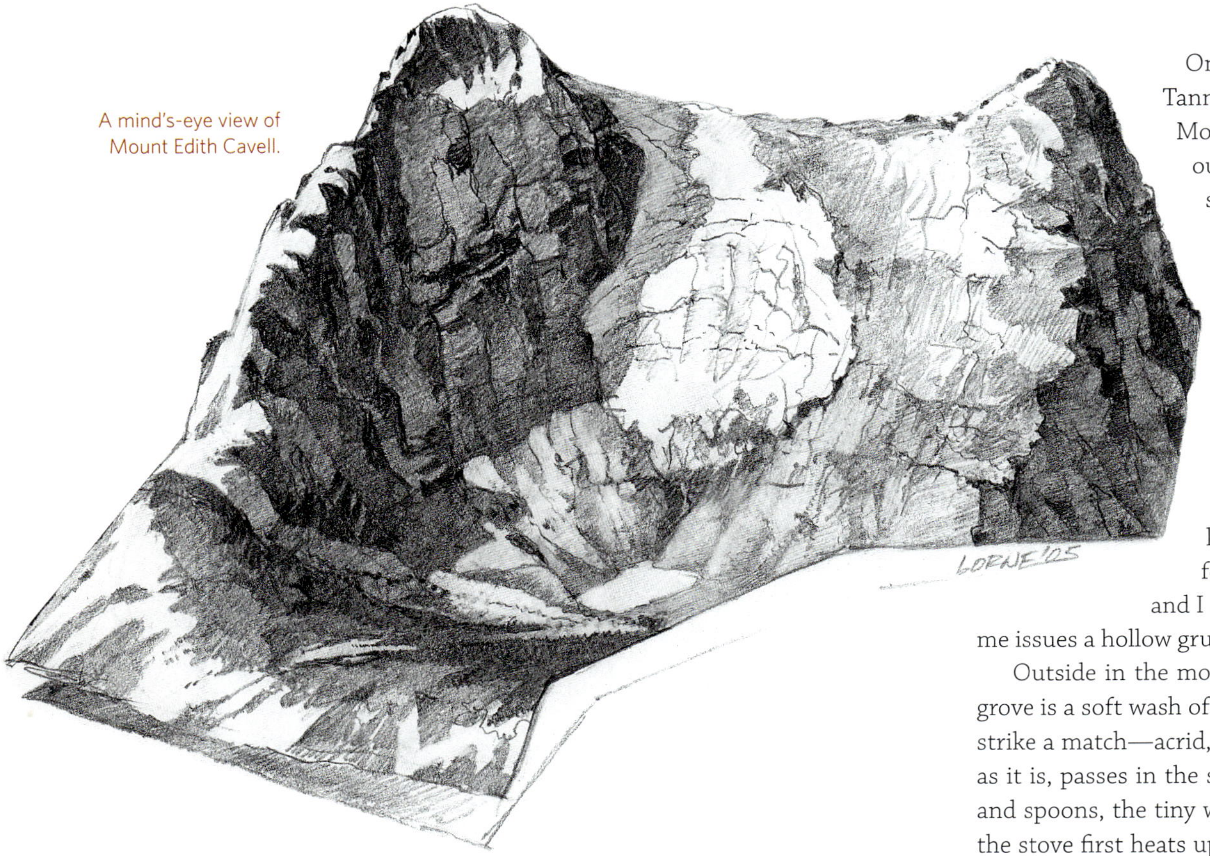

A mind's-eye view of Mount Edith Cavell.

those wonders of creek wading, slingshot whittling, tree climbing and wild games in the bush had been abandoned in favour of the darker side of hippie culture, then in full flower. Tune in, turn on, drop out—I'd bought it all. A confused contradiction of innocence and over-confidence, I was adrift, chasing an elusive high in an intensely urban, imported culture heavily influenced by foreign artists, writers and Hollywood actors.

THIRTY-SEVEN YEARS LATER, I'm still at it, still looking for the pusher, still looking for the highs. But for the former I need look no farther than my mirror; the latter only demands a habit of high peaks.

On a cool August morning, climbing partner Jim Tanner and I have set our sights on the east ridge of Mount Edith Cavell. In the predawn darkness of our tiny tent, my watch alarm is urgently beeping somewhere under a sordid black mulch of damp socks, dirty running shoes—the accumulated detritus of tent life. My right hip, on which the warranty has long since run out, is sore from sleeping on a thin foam pad. My eyes remain fixedly closed. Independent of my inert body, my fingers run a quick grid search, encountering wallet (lost until now), cold metal frame glasses, dog-eared paperback, used Kleenex, a dry shoal of mosquito husks, finally my watch, now mercilessly strangled silent. It is 3:30 a.m. My mouth feels like a sack of dirty pennies. It's time to get up, and I say so into the void. The amorphous shape beside me issues a hollow grunt. Our climb has begun.

Outside in the morning stillness, the river beyond the dark spruce grove is a soft wash of sound. By feel, I pump the stove's pressure valve, strike a match—acrid, sulphur—touch it to the burner. Breakfast, such as it is, passes in the semi-darkness accompanied by the clink of mugs and spoons, the tiny whine of an occasional mosquito, the tink-tink as the stove first heats up with its blue jetstream, then cools. Gas vapours mingle with the sweet aroma of hot chocolate. Mumbled communiqués. Metallic rattle of climbing hardware—click of alloy carabiners, solid thunk of wired nuts—being stowed in packs. Jim takes the blue climbing rope; I take the hardware and slings.

I have not taken on a climb of this size for some time. "What ifs" begin their devil's play in my mind. A sour ache, which I recognize as plain fear, lodges in my gut. Will I even be able to hold the food down? The sorry truth is I will visit the campground washroom at least three times, sadly lacking the iron constitution that eases some through. Still, I derive some comfort from experience; it has always been this way before a climb.

By 4:15, we're loading the van to leave. Wheels crunch gravel, and we *will* the vehicle to tiptoe out of the sleeping campground. Driving through starry darkness, we begin to gain altitude. From the broad riverbed we climb up and up to the parking lot at the foot of "our" mountain. A faint light in the sky reveals the looming Cavell monolith. Here in the predawn, we emerge to the tang of alpine fir, a sensory landscape beyond which anything might wait.

Far from the world and each other at this moment, we live our own realities. As it should be. Only when each takes responsibility for his equipment and himself can we form a strong alliance. Rubber rand hard against fingers, bootlaces carefully drawn just tight enough. Car keys are hidden in moist soil under a rock. A plastic water bottle—flexible, cool—is crammed in pack, the top flap cinched, helmet and cold metal ice axe secured to the outside. A black plastic buckle is pressed closed with a click. The pack, slung on, is firm weight on my back. The few words exchanged between our two solitudes form little links across the void. As it has so many times in the past, my stomach does a flip.

For me, every preparatory step has seemed less conscious action than sense experience. In much the same way, events on the climb itself will set off detailed recollections of past climbs. Like the warm smell of a lover's body or the crash of waves on a beach, for me the sound of distant thunder, the feel of rock on fingertip has the potential to disrupt the mundane march of time, turn it back on itself. Such moments can happen quickly, and I move on, but they form the body of knowledge that is my experience, in every sense keeping me alive. And so, with every climb, along with the looking ahead, comes a looking back. At 5:30, as we take leave of the car, unseen but undoubtedly here, a younger me sets out as well.

THE TRAIL RUNS PARALLEL TO A TUMBLING, NOISY CREEK, contouring up through the huge boulders of ancient glacial moraine. The air, absolutely still, is fragrant with willow and alpine fir. In the shadows of my headlamp's beam, the trailside rocks march steadily back. The great pyramid of the Cavell massif is more felt than seen, its huge face defined by the clatter of broken rock plummeting a couple of kilometres down. Then, an explosion. A single loud report echoes across the valley. From the glacier high above, a thousand-tonne piece of ice has broken off, cascaded down. And now silence again. Venus, a bright morning star, glides above the dark silhouette of the trees. Back towards the dark valley, Jim's LED headlamp is a tiny blue satellite space-jogging along a black ridge.

Up on the moraine, the growing dawn more clearly defines the jagged boulders. Out of the jumbled landscape of my earlier disconnection, mind, body and spirit begin to reunite. Some kind of rough trail lies further east. I work my way over and begin ascending the talus slope to the col (a high pass between peaks). Maddeningly loose, the scree causes me, with each step, to sink in and slide down nearly as far as I have stepped up. And now I see two other parties ahead of us.

We reach the pass between Mount Edith Cavell and a smaller peak to the east at seven o'clock. Centered in the col is a wall of loosely fitted stones about thigh height, encircling an area just large enough for two or three people to lie down. Known as a bivouac site, or bivy, such a shelter provides basic protection for overnighting climbers planning an early start at first light, or conversely, for desperate climbers caught in horrendous weather retreating from the summit. By necessity, these wonders of design fit perfectly into their environment, taking advantage of small flat spots (rare on a mountain), following knife-edge precipices or accommodating the round hulks of immovable boulders. With Machu Picchu-like simplicity, they convey an architectural respect uncommon in our urban world of cement truck and dynamite. In our wanderings, my climbing friends and I have inhabited many of these stone shelters. Built some, occupied others. We've seen bivouac sites perched in such precipitous places, they could have been born only out of the most desperate need. At the other extreme, I've come across three and four together, arranged and improved over time, sharing walls, accommodating each other like swallows' nests slung beneath overhangs or cells in a beehive.

Ranged below us now is a sea of snowy peaks. The dark green of the lower forest shades to pale blue in the distance where peak, ridge and cloud meet. The wind, from the west, delivers alternating patches of bright sky and cloud. Throughout the day, these clouds will rise and fall like a tide, darkening the pinnacles and sending shadows across their flanks. Just visible on the horizon, squalls of rain will come and go as the weather sweeps

Rose-coloured dawn, near Mount Edith Cavell

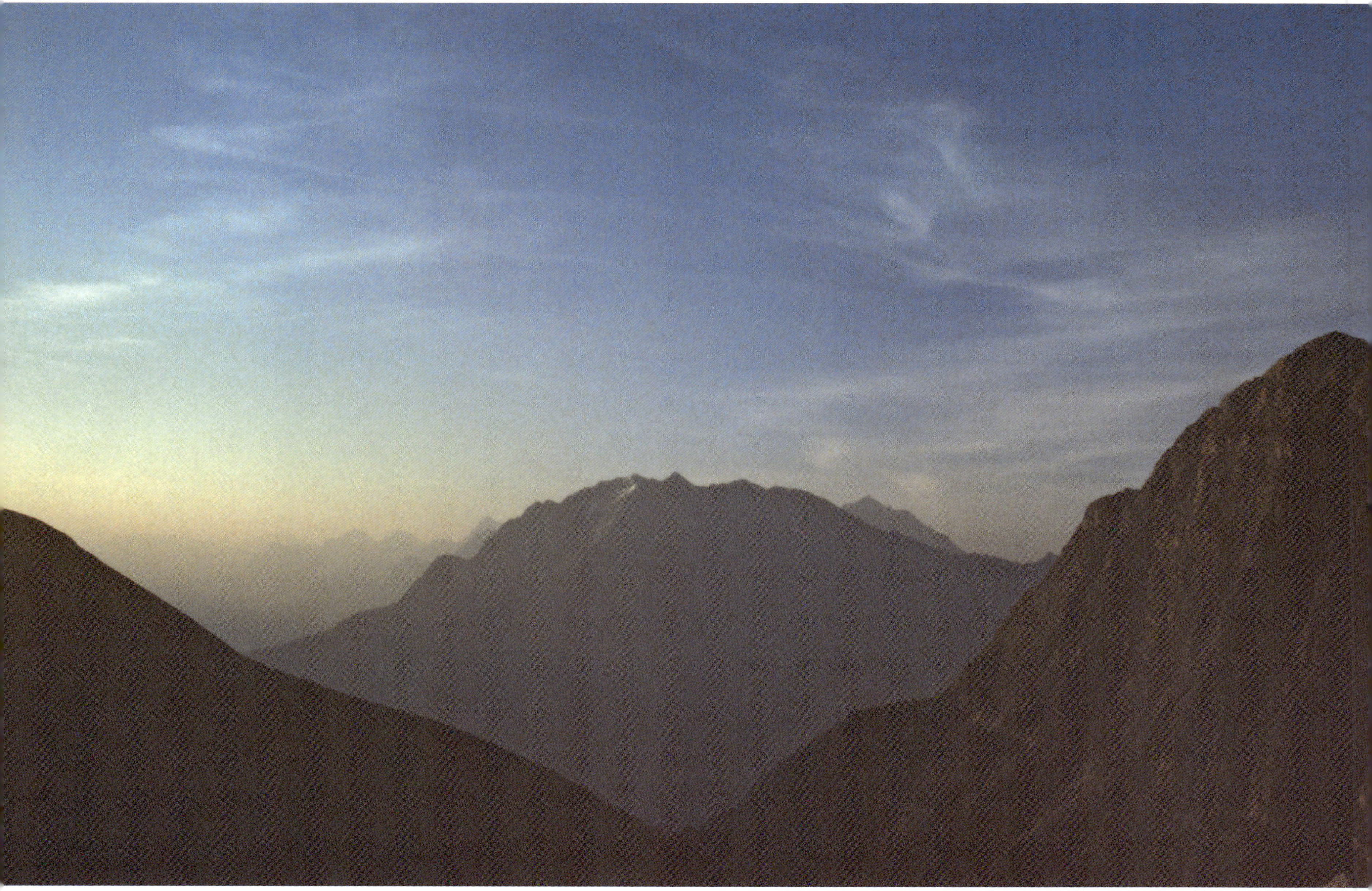

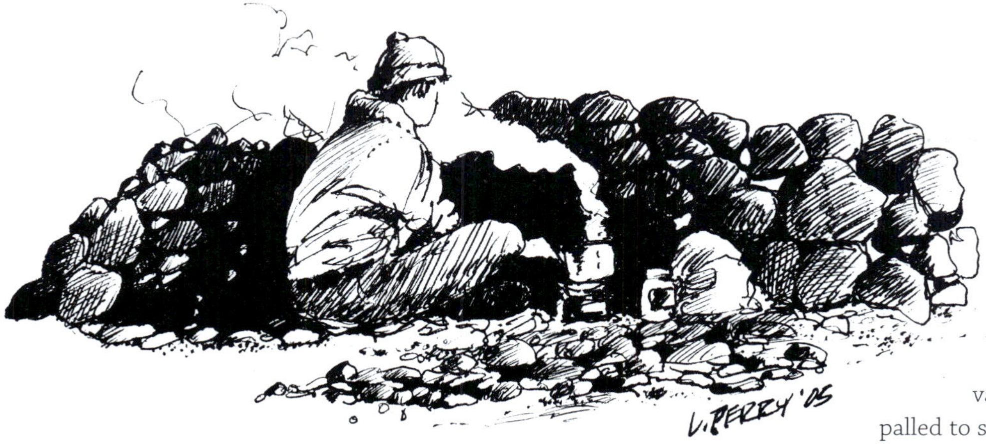

steadily eastward to the plains. Thunder will be rumbling around those distant peaks, and I recall a similar day more than 30 years ago.

ON A CLIMBING TRIP INTO THE MOUNT FRYATT AREA, a few minutes' drive south of the town of Jasper, the weather had been unstable, alternating hot sunshine, wind, rain and snow. High on a col, our great pleasure at discovering a pre-built bivy shelter was quickly replaced by apprehension. It wasn't nightfall, but to the north, the sky was darkening from horizon to zenith in a grand spectacle of towering cumulus, undergirded by a threatening plum-black belly—a vast, alluring malevolence. Jeezus, what was that? It was, in fact, what a Parks biologist later would describe as the most violent, prolonged electrical display he'd ever seen. Afternoon heat, huge masses of unstable air and moisture—a volatile mix of exactly the right conditions. The perfect storm was on its way.

That time, Jim and I were travelling light. For protection from rain and snow we carried just a tent fly, a thin sheet of nylon with attached guy lines. We secured this temporary roof in the rock walls of our tiny shelter and climbed into our sleeping bags. After all, we'd seen storms before. We were young and immortal. What the hell—it would pass.

It did not. In the dead of night, we were awakened by an aggressive wind that whistled through cracks in our rock walls, thrummed the guy lines, grasped at the fly fabric, and threw grit straight into our faces. Just over the ridge, lightning coruscated the night, thunder groaned and echoed. Closer and closer drew this Wagnerian scene until we were no longer watching a storm, we were inside it, drowning in a tumult of fear. Again and again, the Valkyries rode down in a white-hot passion of fire and sound. With each lightning strike, the entire valley instantly paled then faded to blackness. I was appalled to see Jim's face flash alternately a deathly white mask, then, in after-image, a fluorescent skull. My hands, feverishly working with equipment, were rendered in stop-action frames. Even with our eyes tightly closed in an attempt to retain some night vision, it was bright as day and a soft, bloody pink. On the wind blew a heady musk of ozone, sulphur and fear.

I struggled to control the tent fly that by now stood straight out, snapping madly in the blackness. If we didn't do something, our only protection would be ripped away. The wind lashed our faces with cold rain. My mouth was open, ears ringing; though I was working my jaw and shouting, I could hear nothing over the roar. Like storm-tossed sailors reefing a sail, Jim and I struggled at either end of the precious nylon sheet. Finally captured and subdued, it became our best friend, and we wrapped ourselves in it, partly to fend off the storm, partly to keep it from the jaws of the wind.

Caught like imprudent ground squirrels away from their burrows by an enormous predator, we had nowhere to go. As we watched in disbelief, every stone along the length of the ridge lit up. First it would glow a luminescent green that would then waver and die. Explosion, report and glow. Again and again and again. The strikes steadily grew more frequent, more intense. Though he said nothing at the time, Jim, not normally given to pessimism, felt sure our death sentence had been pronounced. Which would explain what happened next. In a desperate, last-ditch effort, Jim grabbed our precious rack of metal hardware by its nylon webbing and, forsaking the relative security of bivy shelter and sleeping bag, sprinted out barefoot across the ridge. Wild-haired, clad only in undershorts, this mad comic figure slipped and slid along the broken crockery of wet shale. With each stroboscopic burst, he was caught mid-stride in black silhouette. Then he stopped, flung the rack into the void and retreated to the shelter, hunkered down amid the maelstrom, unable to move or do anything but endure.

The hours wore on, and I reached a state of acceptance, a calm born of the simple knowledge that nothing could be done. Slowly, slowly, the wind began to ease. Exhausted, shaken, mauled, we felt lucky to be alive. The roiling, vengeful juggernaut moved off south across the valley, throwing back, as its parting shot, the occasional fiery pink flash and some distant grumbling.

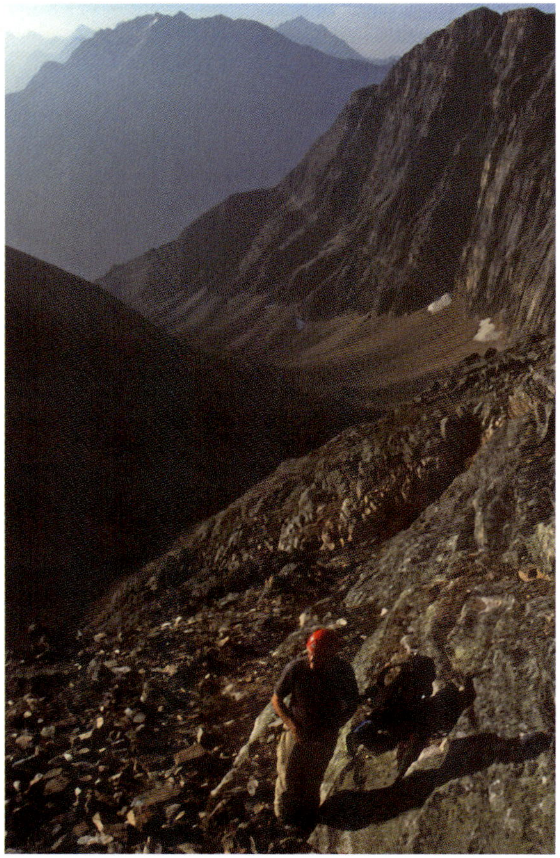

As the steeper sections of Mount Edith Cavell begin, we pause to put on helmets in case of rock fall, assess the route above us and admire this view to the east.

JIM AND I CONTINUE up the ridge of Mount Edith Cavell. By 8 a.m., the light that first graced the ramparts is slowly moving down toward us. The air is still and pleasantly warm. I take a long, wary look for signs of threatening weather, relieved to see there is nothing to concern us. Above the bivouac site and the relative safety of the col, our climbing route becomes steeper until it is lost on a rough face of narrow ledges and exposed outcrops. Revealed in the light, high above us and nearly invisible on the vast hulk of rock, tiny figures wind their way upward in apparent defiance of gravity and risk. I can tell by the speed of their appearance and disappearance among the crevices that they are unroped. I'm aghast, knowing it was here in 1986 that a climber, apparently impatient to move more quickly, unroped, lost control in the steep gully and fell to his death.

The climb is mainly comprised of two steeply sloping ridges, or arêtes, and a single long horizontal traverse. On the steepest sections Jim and I stop to climb singly, belaying each other with the rope. On the more horizontal sections we move simultaneously. Along the arêtes we are accompanied consistently by vistas to the horizon and giddy prospects down vast faces on both sides. To the south, the peaks are a dark blue-grey against a hazy sky. Patches of mist rise up their faces and dissipate in the morning light.

Now and then the narrow ridge is cracked apart and I am obliged to stride across the abyss. Then I get a spectacular glimpse straight down to the pea-green lake and trails that lie at the distant foot of this north wall. A few cars, tiny moving dots, start to arrive in the parking lot. The trails that lead day hikers around the lake are tan-coloured threads, like ant trails in sand. We are far too high to see the actual people who wander singly or as affable, noisy family clusters, casually indifferent to the sublime gulf between us.

I look ahead or at the toes of my climbing boots, step by step by step the whole way. I must keep a pace and level of consciousness appropriate

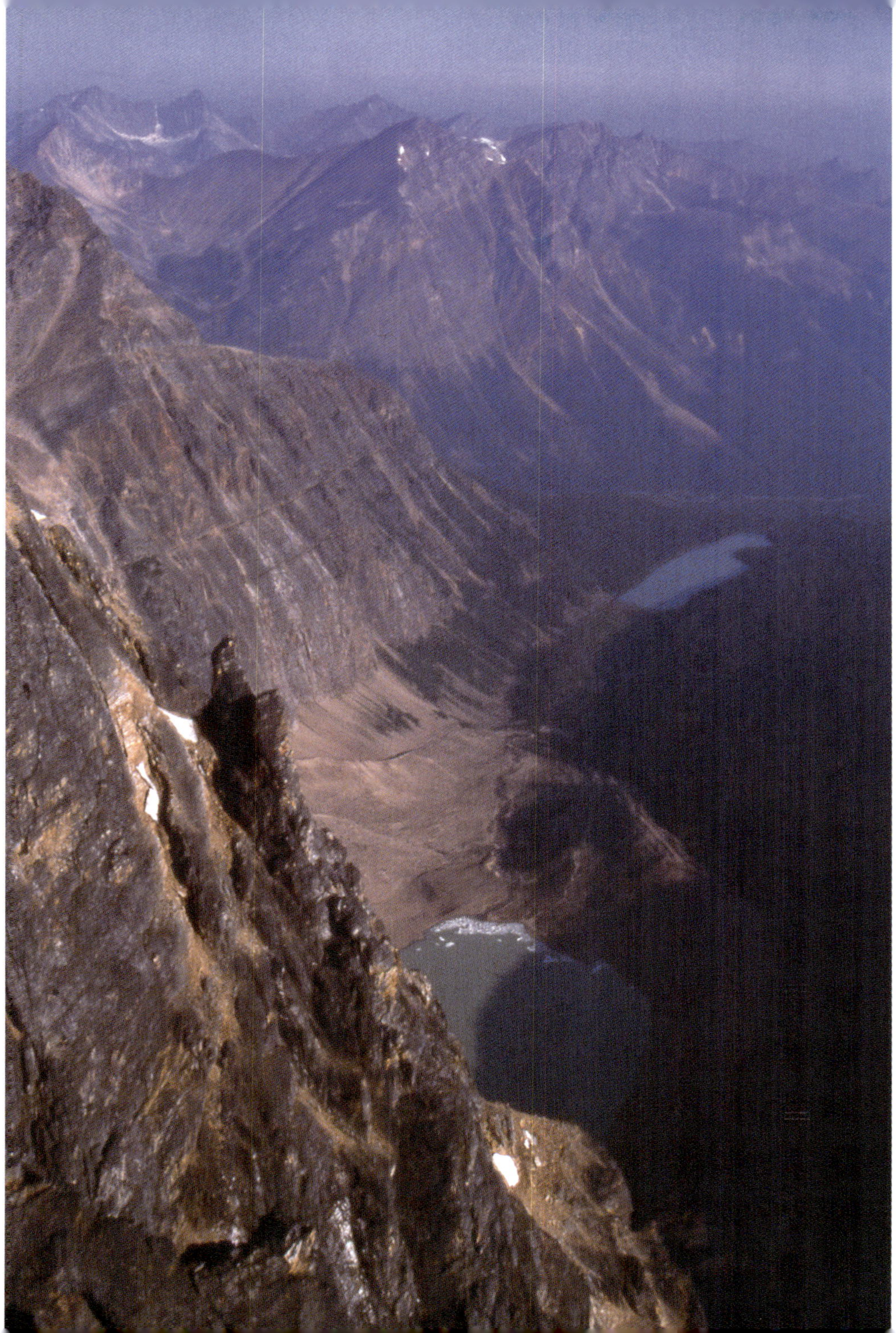

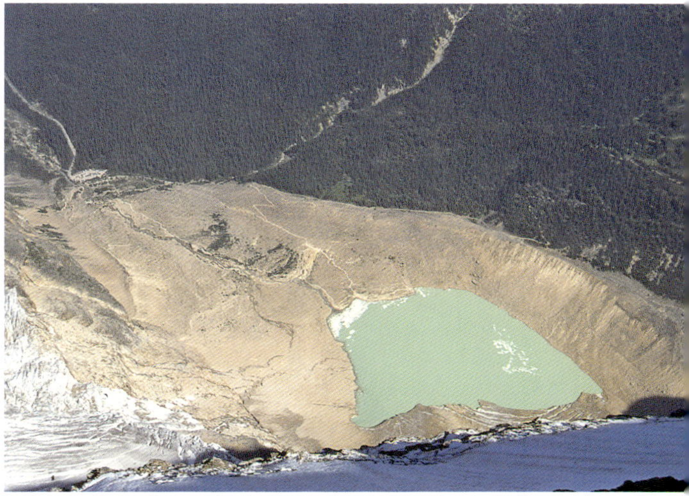

A careful look down the steepest face of Cavell reveals parking lot, hiking trails and a pea-green lake fed by the glacier high above.

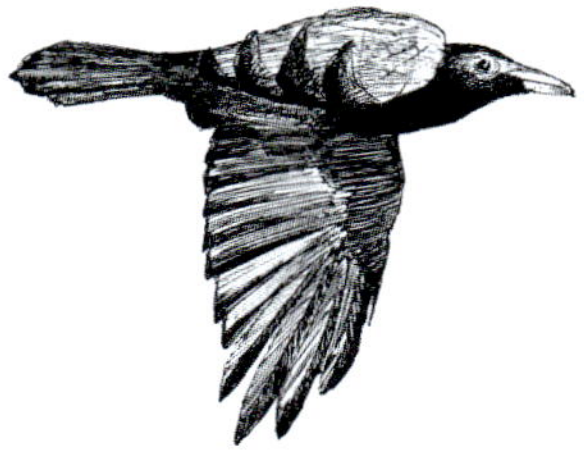

I never cease to be amazed by how high our own two feet can take us. After just a couple of hours of climbing, the valley floor is already far below. The north face of Mount Edith Cavell is in the foreground.

to maintaining good judgment, as any one step, inaccurately placed, could spell my end. Like Jim, I carry not one, but two water bottles. One I constantly refill at rivulets that trickle from melting patches of snow. The other I keep in reserve for higher up. Experience being the unrivalled teacher, I've learned my lesson well: dehydration is as deadly as cold.

I WAS 25, FULL OF CONFIDENCE. And energy? There seemed to be a limitless supply. Deep down, I think I was determined to find out where those limits were. Our enthusiastic group of neophyte climbers had nearly reached the top of Mount Yamnuska. Less than an hour's drive from Calgary, its sheer face was a favourite challenge for weekend climbers from the city. Close to reaching our goal, the four of us were shocked to discover that the rock on the remaining part of the climb was completely covered in a thick coat of verglas—a smooth, hard ice, simply impossible to climb. This changed everything. After a brief, intense discussion, we decided our only remaining option was to try the black wall to our left—a much more difficult route, especially in the cold and dark of a November night. Having not expected to be climbing at nightfall, we carried no headlamp, no flashlight, not even a match. We wore no helmets, and our equipment, by today's standards, was primitive.

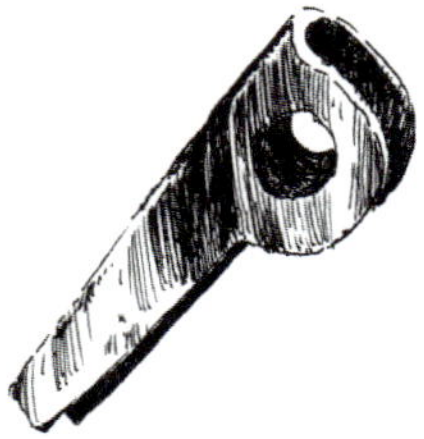

I was leading, blindly manufacturing my own slow progress entirely by feel. In the darkness I unwittingly placed the piton—a metal pin about the length of a construction spike—that secured my rope into a crack filled with loose rock and ice. My weight pulled it out. A quick slip, and I was plummeting downwards. Light exploded as, headfirst, I struck a ledge. Then silence. My body folded double, then toppled again out from the face, backwards and down.

When I regained consciousness, I was dangling upside down on the bowstring-taut rope, dripping blood into my patched down jacket. In my inverted state, I looked straight into the startled gaze of the lead on the second rope team coming up. High above me, at the business end of the rope on which my life currently depended, was Ron Robinson. Very fortunately for me, Ron was a man possessed of great calm. This Zen-like

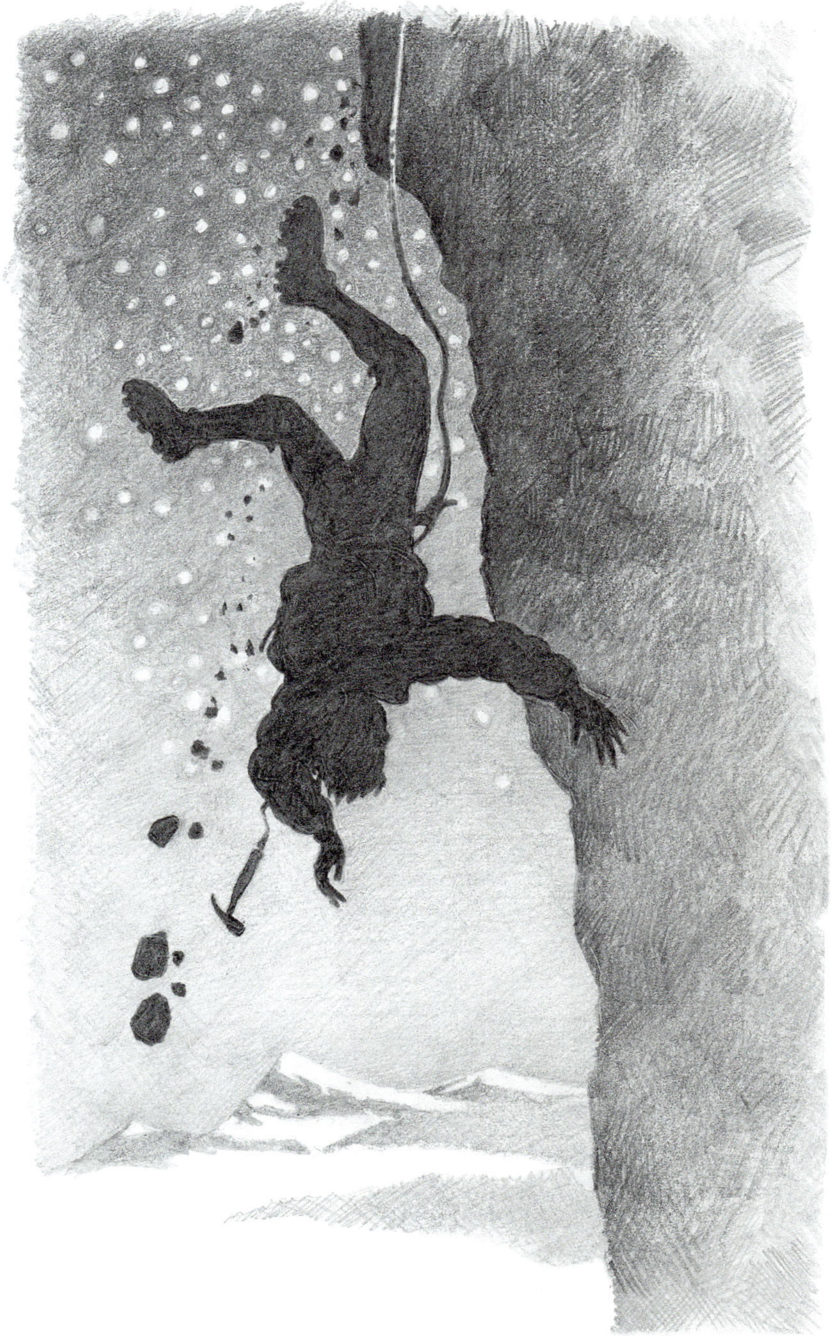

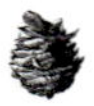

demeanor had proven particularly useful while my falling body was ripping him clean out from where he'd sat braced and slamming him right-side first against the rock face.

The single piton to which Ron had attached himself, thereby preventing the two of us from cartwheeling down into darkness, was bent hard over and wrenched flat against the rock. This piece of hardware, which Ron had found hammered into a shallow crack by a previous climbing party, was made of a low-quality alloy, hardly designed to withstand the extreme forces to which it had just been subjected. Rather, it was meant to take the weight of a single climber in controlled descent. In other words, what was known as a "shit peg."

There we hung in the night above the crusted snow patches and sharp talus far below. I swallowed hard to ease the constriction in my throat and fought to right myself. Using my toes to gain a little purchase on the smooth outcrops, I pulled on the rope. But my cold hands were beyond command. Dehydrated and tired, I had definitely found my limit. With each attempt to pull myself upwards, my fingers cramped shut. On the power of adrenaline alone, I was forced to reach up, let my fingers spasm closed on the rope, pull, then bite them open with my teeth, one at a time, repeating the process until I slumped, completely exhausted, beside Ron's dark form. Ron's only comment was that the impact, though not painful, had jogged his memory. In his packsack were some crampons, a set of metal spikes that can be affixed to climbing boots. These should penetrate the ice so we could complete the route. It was our only hope.

In the eerie half-light, we were just tiny figures, hushed voices and dark shadows among the cracks, clinging to an immense vertical wall. When darkness fell, we were obliged to wait in extreme discomfort on our ledge until the moon came up. We had over-estimated our strength and under-estimated the effect of harsh winter conditions. I was dazed and shaken. Having been divested by gravity of my glasses, wool mitts and toque, I could do nothing but stare though a drab blur and wait for whatever was to befall us. Meanwhile, with cold-stiffened fingers, Ron fumbled with the crampons, strapping them on. Cautiously, he turned and stood up. Driving the points that now protruded beyond his boot-tips into the ice-slick rock, he punched bit by bit up the few short metres to the mountaintop.

He belayed each of us up on the rope, where we emerged, one by one, on a frozen grey-blue and silver landscape. It was absolutely still, not a breath of wind on the top of the world. Joyful, we hooted and hollered as the moon cast a million diamonds in the snow and the northern constellations danced their stately minuet across the sky. Then we strode off down the gentler backside of the mountain into the sombre forest below.

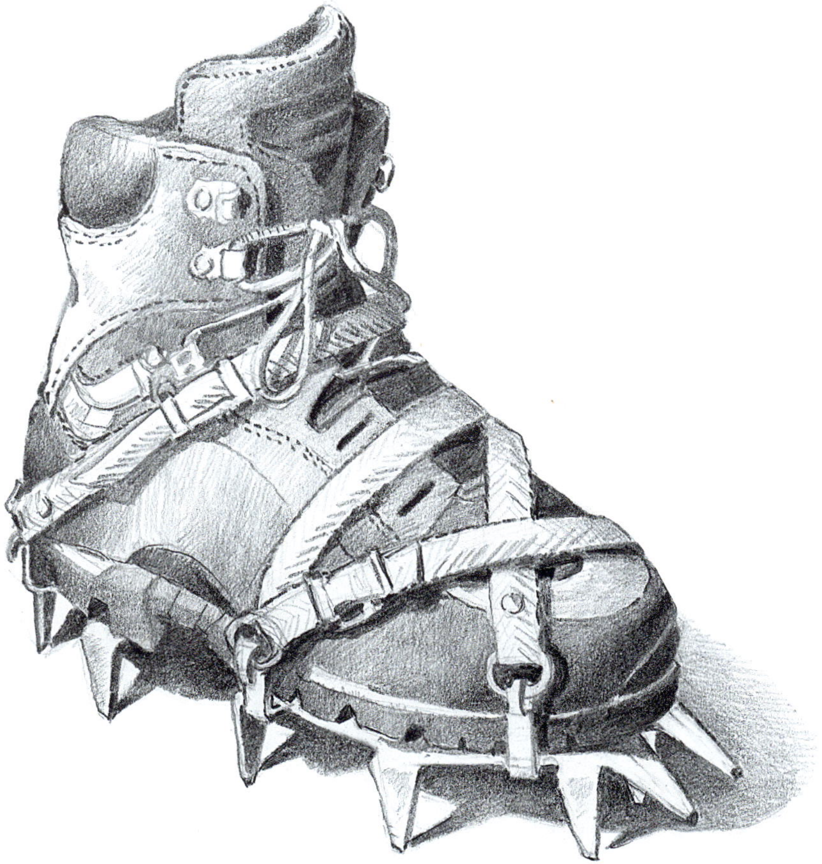

WE HAVE REACHED THE MOST DIFFICULT SECTION of the Cavell ridge—a short steep section that forms the second of two steps. It is now 10:45 a.m. and the sun is bright. I've been drinking water continually and sucking on the latest performance-enhancing syrup—piña colada-flavoured—packaged in a handy pouch. From the list of sophisticated ingredients and flashy hype, one could infer that, in about 20 minutes, he'd be a world-class athlete, but my simple hope is to avoid the cramps and stupefying fatigue I've experienced in the past. At the foot of this crux pitch, we pause to get out the rack of hardware.

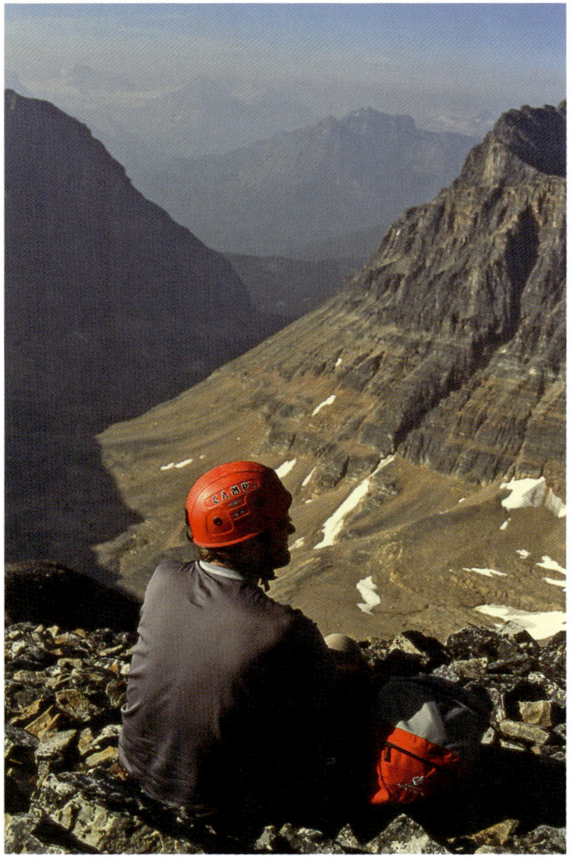

From time to time we break to drink and eat, while admiring the view west to the Verdant Creek valley.

Jim uncoils the blue rope; we tie in, check the figure eight knot and harness buckles. My stomach, meanwhile, is busy tying itself up. My heart pounds, and my chest rises and falls against the bright nylon webbing slung over my neck and under my right arm. This steeper pitch follows a crack system that angles out over the horrendous north face. It was near here that Ekhardt Grassman and his partner cart-wheeled down into the abyss, falling halfway to the valley floor. They were found by the rescue party, lifeless but still bound together and hanging from their tangled ropes. "Jesus Christ Almighty," I whisper to myself, "why do I get myself into these things?" My own rope, barely as thick as my little finger seems desperately inadequate. Should it fail during a fall, I'll suffer the same fate.

But of course this is what it's all about, it's why I've come: for the moment of truth—and of doubt. The game becomes beautifully simple. I must put aside my fears and replace them with coordinated action. Like the high-wire walker alone above the crowd, I must behave as though there were no danger at all. Turn fear into focus. I reach up, find the holds, place the edge of the boot sole in virtually invisible fissures and pull up. Over and over again. Sometimes there is absolutely nothing below me. I am spread-eagled, legs bridging empty space, my weight supported solely by the friction of my boots pressing either side of a vertical crack. I hear the too-fast cadence of my breathing and will it to slow down.

My attention wanders a moment. Foolish of me. I find I have, in mid-step, pulled myself up against a rock bulge that is forcing me off balance. Maddeningly, the weight of the pack and my body is trying to pull me off the mountain. Panic rises. I push it back, brace with one hand, reach deep inside a crack and make a fist. This jams in the fissure, and I pull up. My feet find purchase, and I move on.

Gradually, my worries of falling are replaced by a reverie of movement, handhold to handhold, until I'm no longer conscious of individual steps but rather of a general upward advance. I work my way up over graceful cracks and fissures, angling right, left, then rounding the sharp ridge to travel up the opposite side, where I gain a glorious view down a new valley. Below me, on a ledge, Jim is a miniature figure paying out rope and craning anxiously upwards now and again to follow my progress.

Squinting against the sun, I tilt my head back to seek a route and my helmet bumps against the flap of my backpack. At my left hip clanks

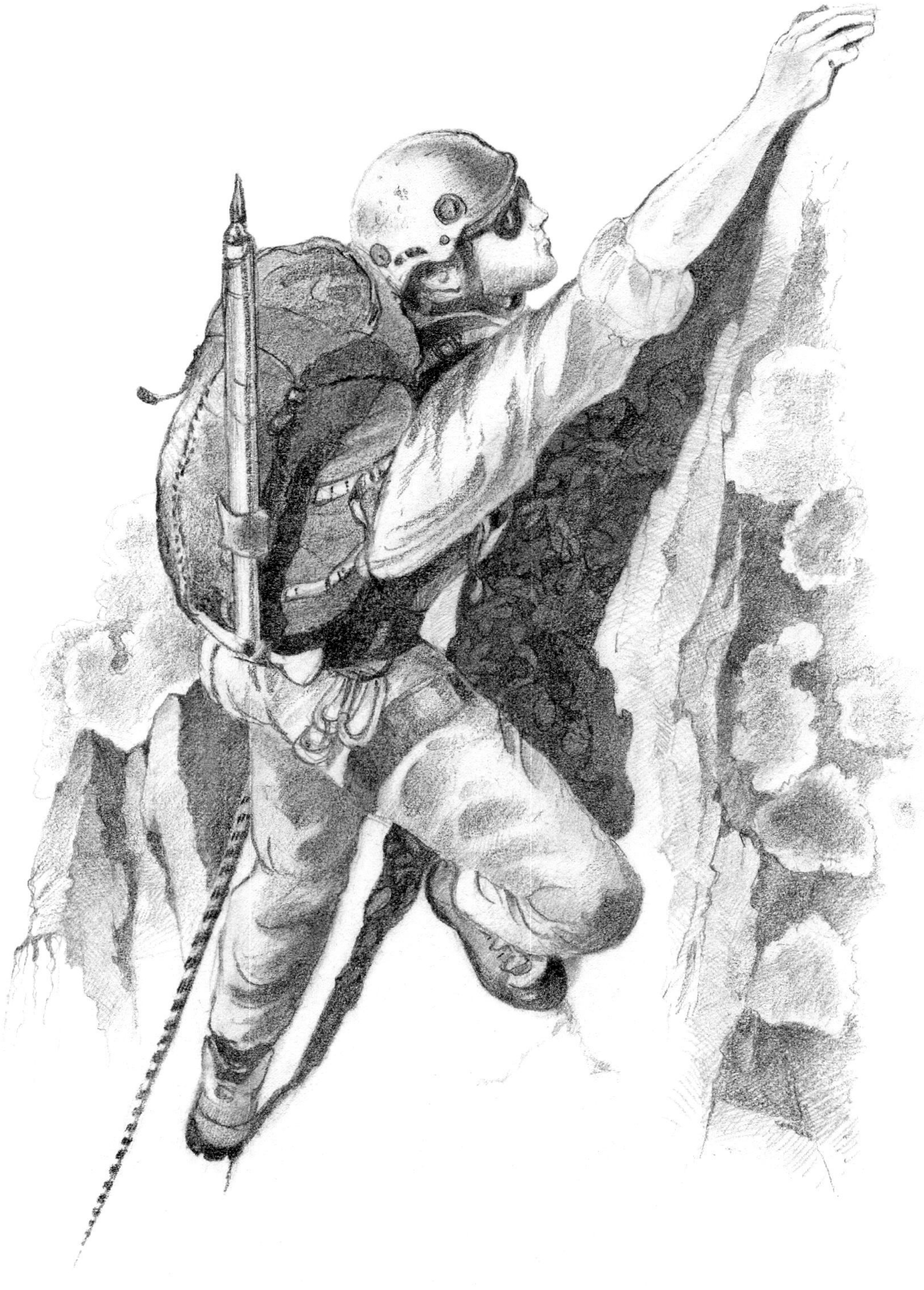

the hardware rack, carefully prepared so I can reach any one of the many pieces of protection, unclip it and secure the rope—all without looking down. This rock is not the typical limestone to which I am accustomed, but quartzite, a very hard rock that splits along clean cracks. In contrast to the rough grey runnels on limestone, it is smooth to the touch and glistening with crystals—tiny, nested mirrors of coral pink, warm tan, rich purple. Water stains and black lichen define its undulations and corners. Without stairways, handrails, steps or platforms, minus signs to guide or nets to catch me—to this intimate relationship with the rock, I bring only myself. Entirely alone, I've penetrated a thin membrane to emerge in a parallel universe. Far removed from the frenzy of 21st-century life, I've become fluent in the vocabulary of movement, irrevocably responsible for my course through time and space.

The rope is now run out to its full length, about the height of a ten-storey building, and its zigzagging path across the rock makes the friction significant. With each step, I must pull against that resistance, balancing on holds no thicker than a dime. The heavy pack carrying Nikon, crampons, ice axe, full water bottle, spare clothing, lunch, climbing

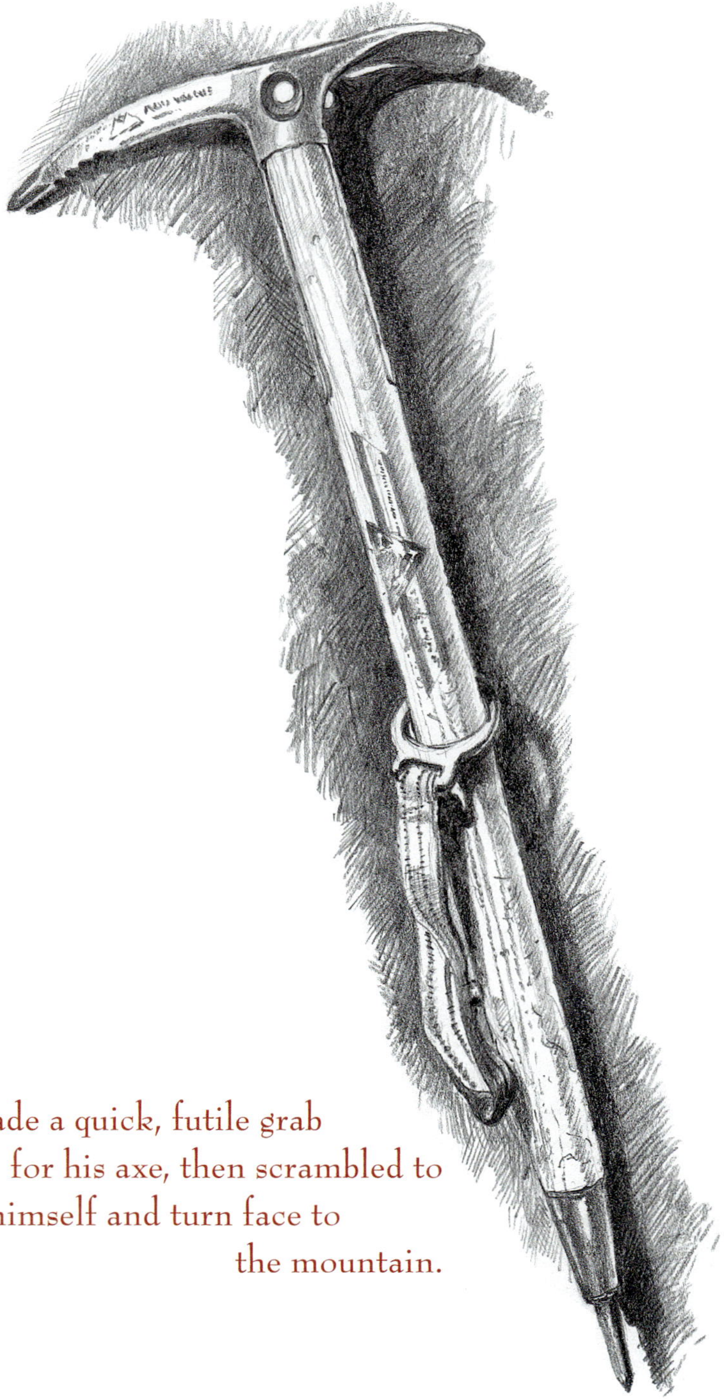

He made a quick, futile grab for his axe, then scrambled to right himself and turn face to the mountain.

hardware, jackets and other items pulls hard on my shoulders. It's exhausting work, and when I reach the top of the pitch I'm breathing hard. Finding a small secure ledge, I put in protection, clip in and put Jim on belay. Climbing second, his rope coming from above and drawn in with every step, he can travel faster with impunity. Still, we strive to remain focussed, knowing even the slightest loss of concentration may have serious consequences. Mountaineering is a beguiling but jealous mistress, demanding one's complete attention at every turn. A straying mind, a momentary loss of focus, an action influenced by impatience, arrogance or fatigue—any of these lapses can prove at best painful, at worst, fatal.

IT WAS ONLY MY THIRD BIG CLIMB after completing snow and ice school—boot camp for high-altitude mountaineers. With my partner, Brent, a tough but affable Kiwi, I was descending Mount Assiniboine after successfully summiting that spectacularly beautiful peak. Elated and in a celebratory mood, we both were also near exhaustion as we traversed a last steep snow slope that swept down to a gaping precipice. Brent was ahead and moving quickly, his ice axe, like mine, stowed away in loops on his pack. Now we unroped—the quicker but more risky mode of travel. But in our rush to descend, we failed to retrieve our axes, the principal means, other than the rope, by which a climber can arrest a fall on steep snow. This was a fundamental error, one of the climber's cardinal sins. The Alpine Club of Canada, an authoritative voice on alpine matters, warns on its website, "It is possible to self-arrest on snow, but it is important to have an ice axe at the ready, to be very familiar with self-arrest techniques and to act immediately."

The snow, now softened by afternoon heat, suddenly slipped out from under Brent. Instantly, he was accelerating toward oblivion. He made a quick, futile grab for his axe, then scrambled to right himself and turn face to the mountain. In panic, he dug in hands and feet, which now became ploughshares flinging fluffy rooster-tails as he shot away toward the brink. There was precious little distance to stop. I could see him trying to find ways to dig in deeper, grab on with everything he had. The edge was drawing nearer. It was over so quickly, I had no time to react and was, in any case, powerless to help.

Though I could not have seen from where I stood transfixed, the snow levelled out just a little before the ledge. What I saw later persuaded me a bungee-jumper couldn't have called it closer. Having managed to slow himself just enough to overcome gravity's pull, Brent had slid to a gentle, timely halt, spread-eagled in those big baggy trousers, face down, looking a bit like a circus clown. Pant legs shoved above his knees and crammed with snow, his gangly legs and big feet stuck out over the abyss.

He rose a chastened man, and in businesslike fashion, though taking a little more time than seemed absolutely necessary, he brushed away the snow and resettled the pack on his back. He had been thinking something over, and with a meaning-filled glance up at me, tacitly admitted the oversight. Exceedingly carefully, hubris firmly in check, he made his way off the snow and over to the rock ledges step by step, to continue the descent.

The same website reports a similar incident on that mountain as follows: "He tried to self-arrest but failed, although he was still trying when he slid down a snow gully past [his partner] and fell 2,000 feet. His helmet...was smashed and torn from his head and was found near his body. He had severe head and other injuries and no doubt died during the fall. His ice axe and crampons were not found."

IT'S 10:25 A.M. ON THE CAVELL RIDGE. Jim and I are travelling carefully roped up. On narrow parts of the ridge, I can neither take too big a step, which might pull Jim off balance, nor slow too much, which could result in a dangerously snagged rope. Occasionally there is a vertigo-inducing glimpse down the horrific maw of the north face. The summit is now visible, and, contrary to yesterday's misgivings, yes, even attainable. I'm breathing hard and stop to regroup. Pulling in an arm's length of rope, I plant my feet so as not to teeter. Reaching out, I grab rock and try to get a sense of where to go from here.

Except for one short break, we've climbed steadily since dawn. By one o'clock, the ridge angle eases and suddenly there is nothing above us. We are on top. It is a glorious place, level enough to permit comfortable seating. The wind that just skims the peaks is cold and we are obliged to keep on our jackets and fleece. Still, in all directions, the weather looks fine; no need for hurry. Before sitting down for lunch, though, we cross the summit and, exceedingly wary, peer down the descent route. What will it bring? Steep rock? Snow and ice? Craning our necks, we see, to our great relief, the twists and turns of a viable route disappearing then reappearing on buttresses, through gullies and along red shale ridges. Looks straightforward enough.

This is the moment we've climbed toward. Our view embraces all 360 degrees. Wide, green valleys are laced with the silver threads of creeks and rivulets. The main mountain range, on which we stand, forms a great, unbroken arc from northwest to southeast. To my left as I face east, beyond the horizon, lies the Yukon and high arctic; to my right, across the earth's wide curve will be Mexico. The dark, turreted towers of Oldhorn and Throne mountains, Thunderbolt Peak, and in the distance, the cobalt-blue walls of The Ramparts rise straight out of *Lord of the Rings*. Just above us, little clouds cast cotton-puff shadows that drift slowly east. Jim and I are completely absorbed by the simple clarity of our difficult accomplishment. We've completed, for the moment, the task we'd set ourselves, and maybe that's the real source of our satisfaction. Without other agenda or needs, our single role here at the apex of the world is to revel in the grandness before us. I take off my helmet. The wind cools the sweat on my hair, the sun warms my face. I'm weightless.

Just after two, we begin the descent, abandoning the summit to sun and raven, and very nearly a collection of candy wrappers I'd temporarily shoved under a rock during lunch. Wrappers finally retrieved, we descend a long ridge to steeper outcrops, which in turn drop to a long talus slope. Mindful of Brent's near-fatal slide those years ago, we eye our intended route with suspicion until we are satisfied "it goes." Only now do we doff the rope and put away our axes.

Boots grind and scrape, broken shale clatters and flies. Rock powder smokes around our feet as we jump, slide and scramble down the talus. Rocks scoot out ahead and come rattling down behind. Jim and I travel closely together to reduce the chance of any large, loosened boulder picking up enough speed to do us serious damage. One minute, we're dancing heavy-footed, still in control, through deep rubble. The next, we're running to catch up to our own momentum as we drop over a sudden bench.

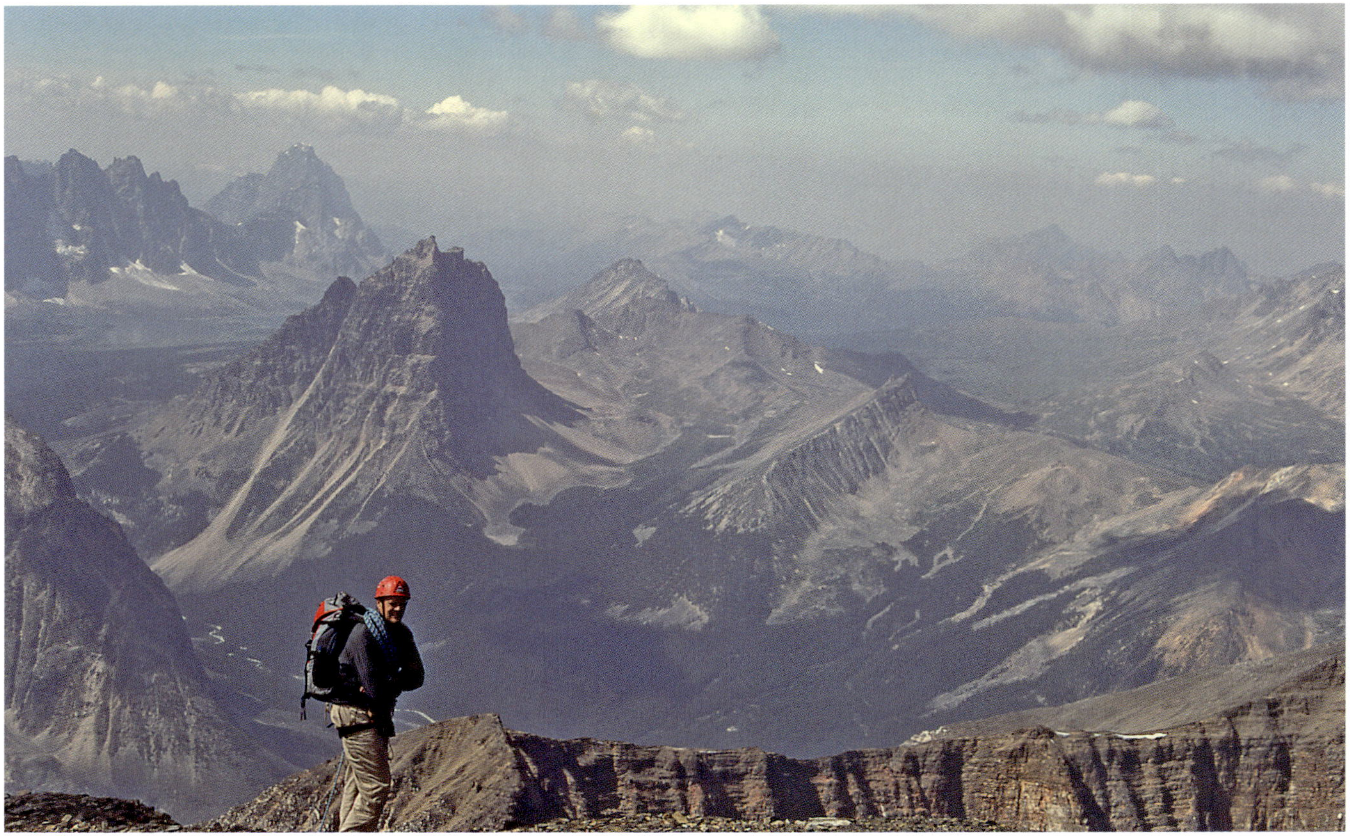

To the west, wild alluring peaks—Old Horn Mountain, the Ramparts—appearing straight out of *Lord of the Rings.*

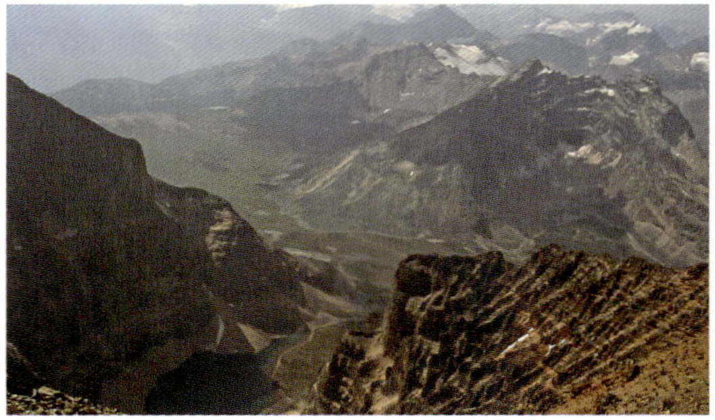

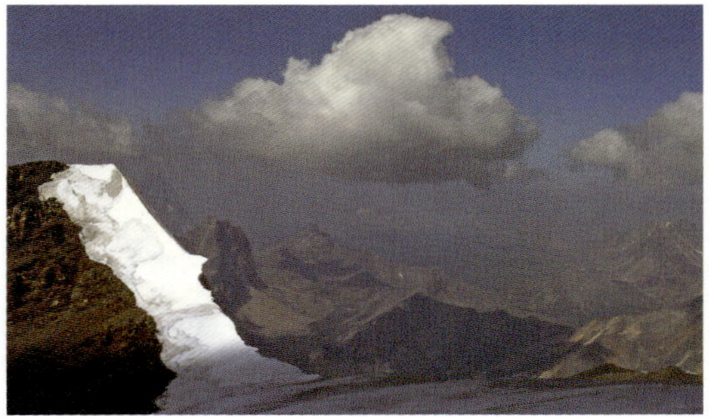

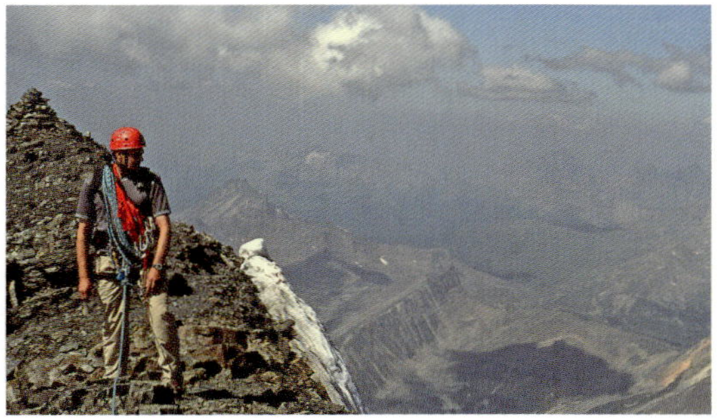

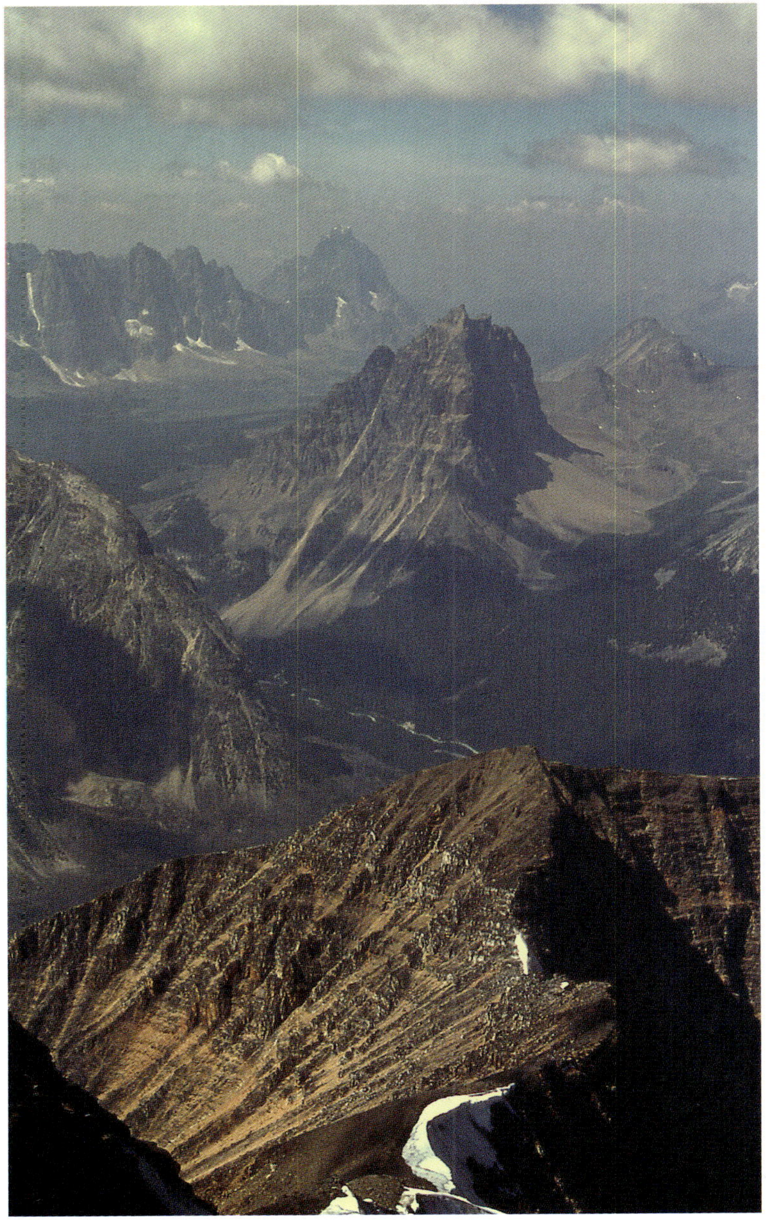

The descent from Cavell's summit is the climber's dream. No rappells or steep snow slopes—instead, we traverse the line of snow patches, then turn abruptly left to follow long talus slopes down into the valley.

Or we're slithering wildly over flagstone slides on which even our deeply treaded rubber soles find little purchase.

Even in our haste we can see that the trail mysteriously vanishes just above some high cliffs. At this point on the descent a less fortunate climber simply came too close to the edge, slipped over and fell to his death, only a few paces from a perfectly safe slope. We pause, unsure, spend some careful moments hunting back and forth like dogs on a lost scent, retrace our route. Finally, we pick our way around a corner over narrow mossy ledges and continue down.

By mid-afternoon, we are in the mountain's west bowl, which has become a solar oven. In the concave rock amphitheatre, fully exposed to the sun, my face and arms are baking. My feet are hot and sore where they have been endlessly, relentlessly hammered into stiff, narrow-toed climbing boots. (One side of my foot, in fact, will be numb for months.) Part way down the scree, we take a break. A stream trickles from the rubble, splashing bright ribbons over the darkened rock. The spray from the waterfall creates a tiny effervescent world. Droplets appear on my arms, cooling my overheated body. The water is clear and delicious, and I gulp a couple of litres.

We are down in the meadows by five. No more cliffs to climb, no more scree to descend. Jim is out ahead, thinking his own thoughts, a lone brightly clad figure on the vast, green wild. Singing softly to myself, I follow a clay-white trail along a creek. The water seems especially beautiful, the alpine flowers stunning. From time to time, I wrench myself out of my reverie, keeping a wary eye out for large mammals of the four-legged, big-clawed, furry kind.

Toward evening the sky clears and the wind dies. Calm prevails. The setting sun throws hazy shafts of light over our heads. Clouds darken,

A grand time of day: the climb over, the evening pensive, we simply stride along in happy silence. Lost in his own thoughts, Jim walks on ahead.

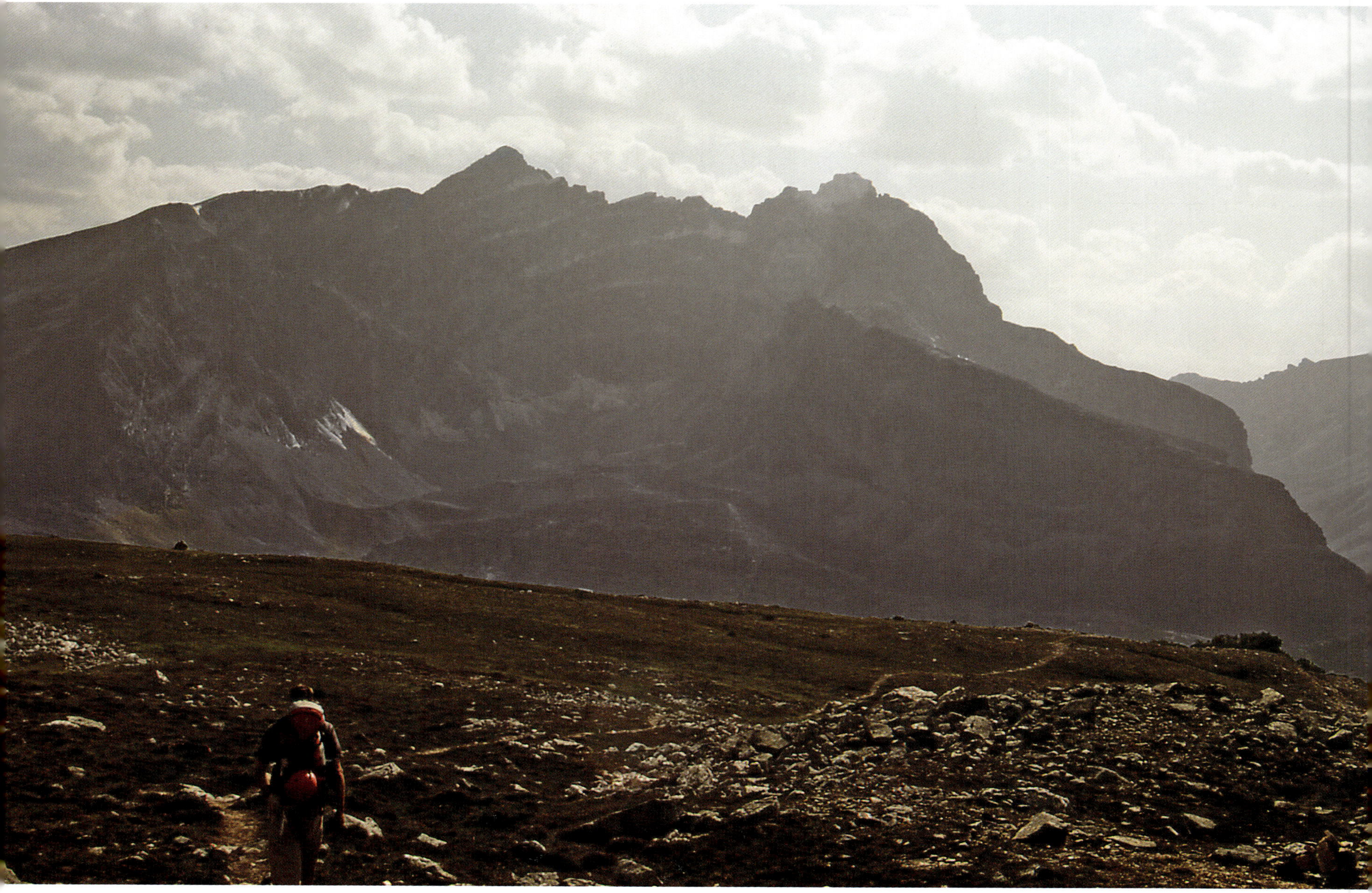

blues deepen. The full eastern horizon, north to south, glows a soft rose. The climb itself is over but it will still be several hours before we rest. Having descended on the west side, we're now obliged to walk around the mountain to reach our starting point on the east.

The last few weary minutes along the road, I hitch a ride with an ageing but sprightly pair of tourists, Irish, from Dublin. The white-haired man turns to me. "Where have *yew* been?"

I point up at the distant summit of Edith Cavell. "Up there."

They both look skyward through the windshield. "B'jaysus, up there? Sure, yer fit!" Another peek. "Or daft...or both!"

"Yeah." My smile is huge. "But a fine kind of madness."

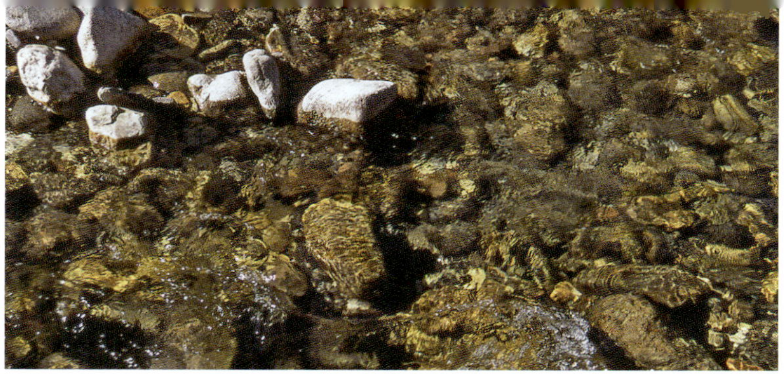

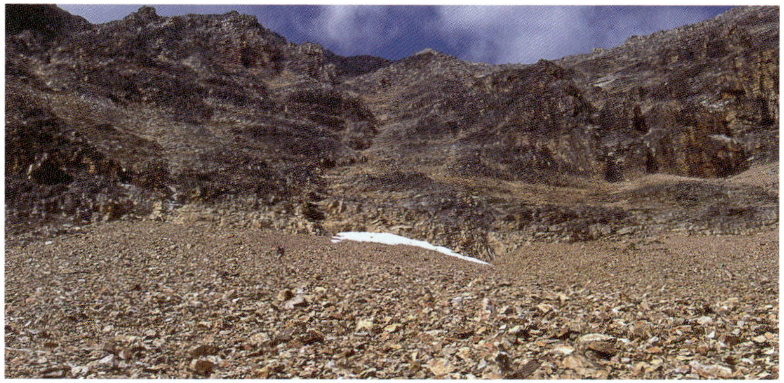

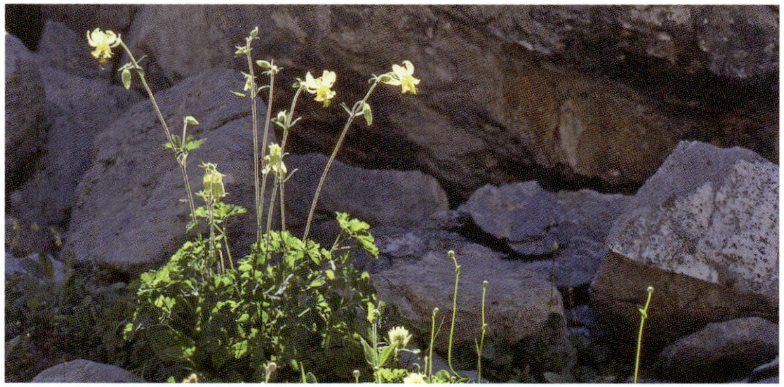

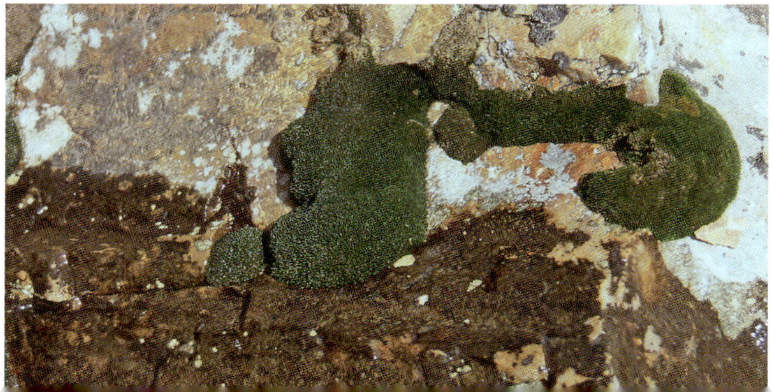

Warm weather has reduced the size of the snow patches, and thus the flow of the stream. Water trickles over reddish quartzite, feeding a deep green sponge of moss.

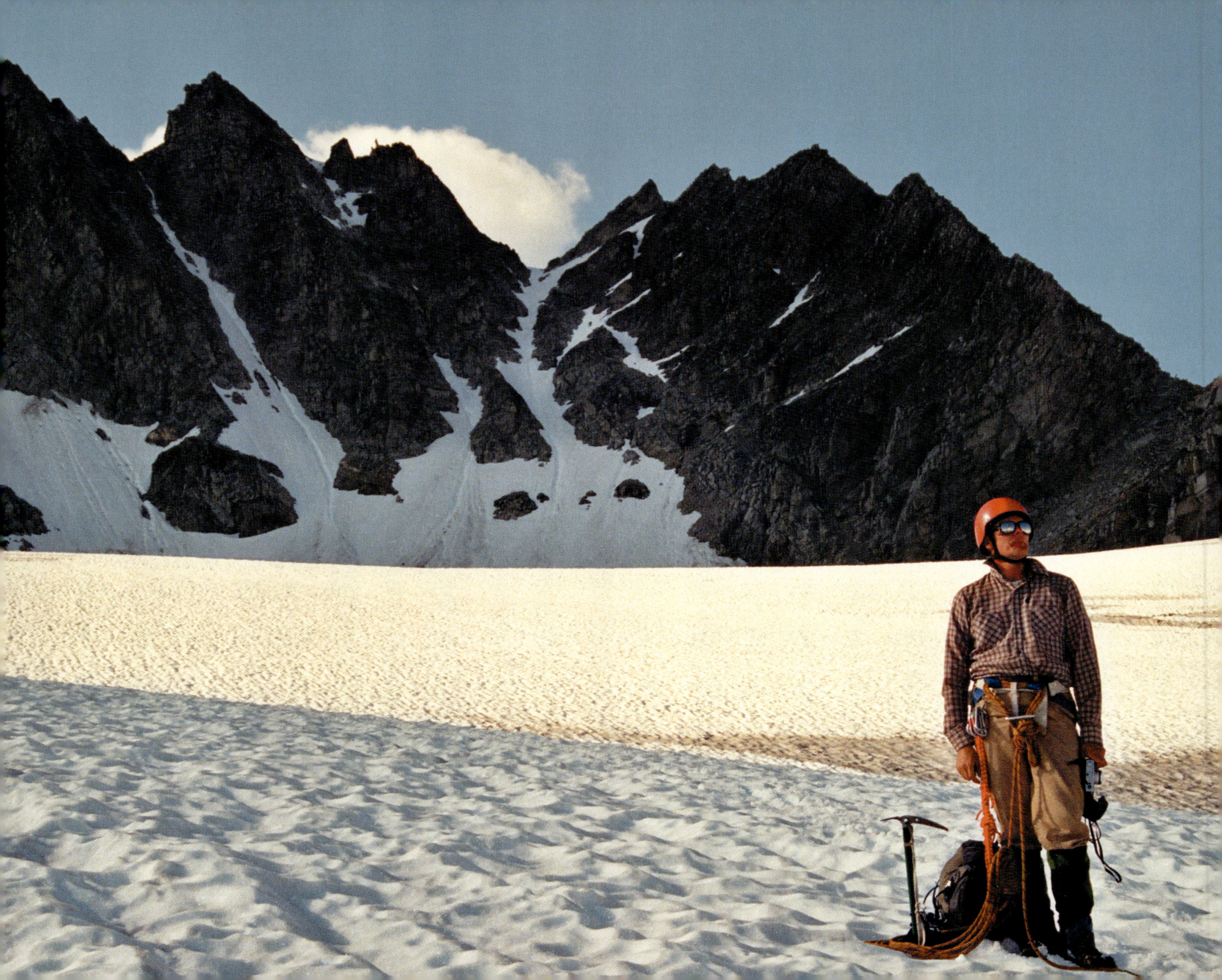

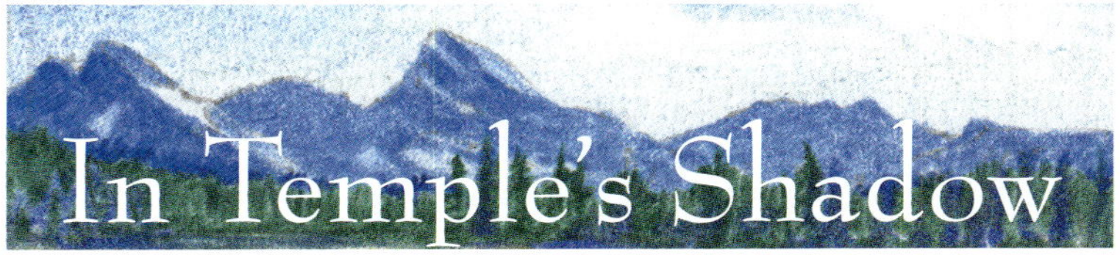

In Temple's Shadow

NEXT TIME YOU'RE IN LAKE LOUISE, stop in the Samson Mall parking lot. Stand among the Winnebagos, New-Age flower children, ravens squabbling over discarded French fries. Face south and look up—way up. That monster rock wall capped by a glacier is the north face of Mount Temple. If you had a very big telescope that could shrink time as well as distance, you might see a pair of tiny figures slowly making their way up that vertical world. That would be Ron Robinson and I, 37 years ago, ascending one of the few "mile high" faces within easy reach of the highway.

Similar in objective hazard to Switzerland's infamous Eiger, in 1971 that particular route on Mount Temple had been climbed only five or six times. Although today's vastly improved equipment and training techniques have reduced the perceived challenge, at the time it was considered a very serious undertaking. The climb would require a full two days, the intervening night being spent, unfortunately, in an exposed bivouac somewhere high on its dark walls.

For reasons neither of us could recall, Ron and I had decided this was our logical next challenge. Our intended route was first climbed by Charlie Locke, my early mentor, and Brian Greenwood. Brilliantly talented and utterly determined, they were our climbing heroes, and, as one might expect, the route they put up was a "son of a bitch." On the lower half of the giant face, which is climbed unroped to save time, a single slip could be fatal. In August of 1986, a descending climber had proven so when he slid on a steep upper snow slope, rocketed out of control and died of massive head injuries from impact on the rock below.

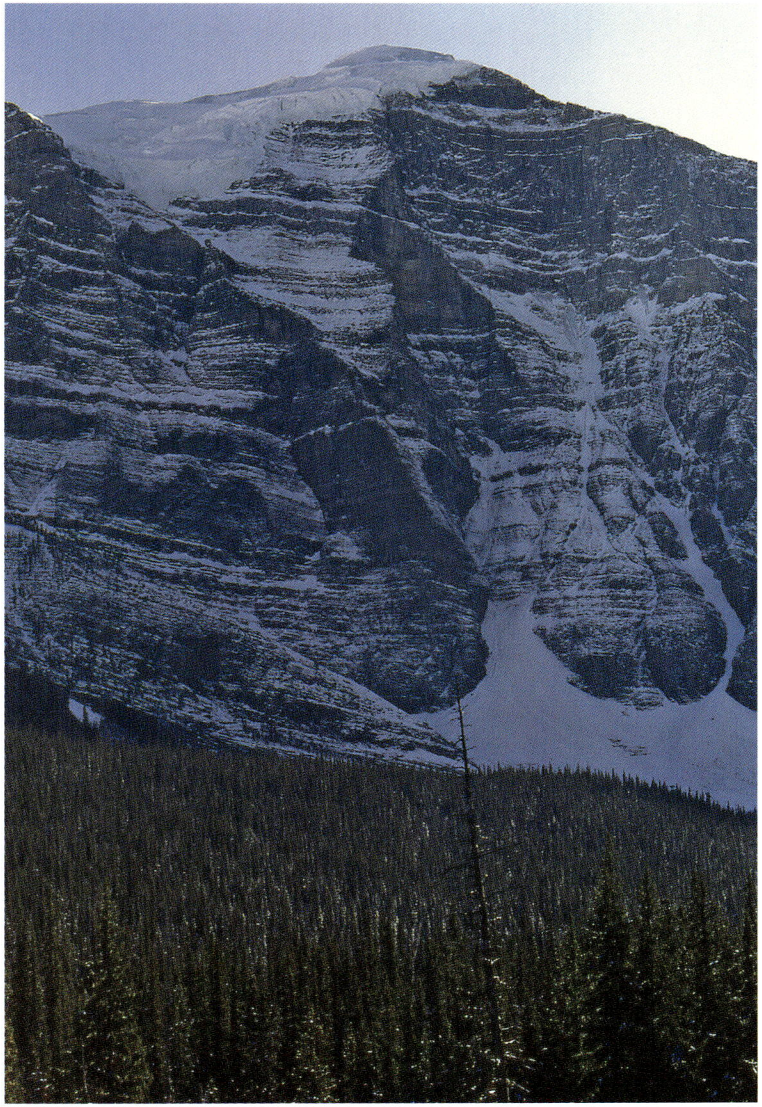

Our route follows the long snow gulleys up the centre of Mount Temple's north face, then angles off to finish just right of the summit. At this point the face is about a kilometre high, the equivalent of about six 80-storey buildings stacked one upon the other.

Literally cheek
by jowl on
a sloping
ledge, every
movement
edged us
toward the
precipice.

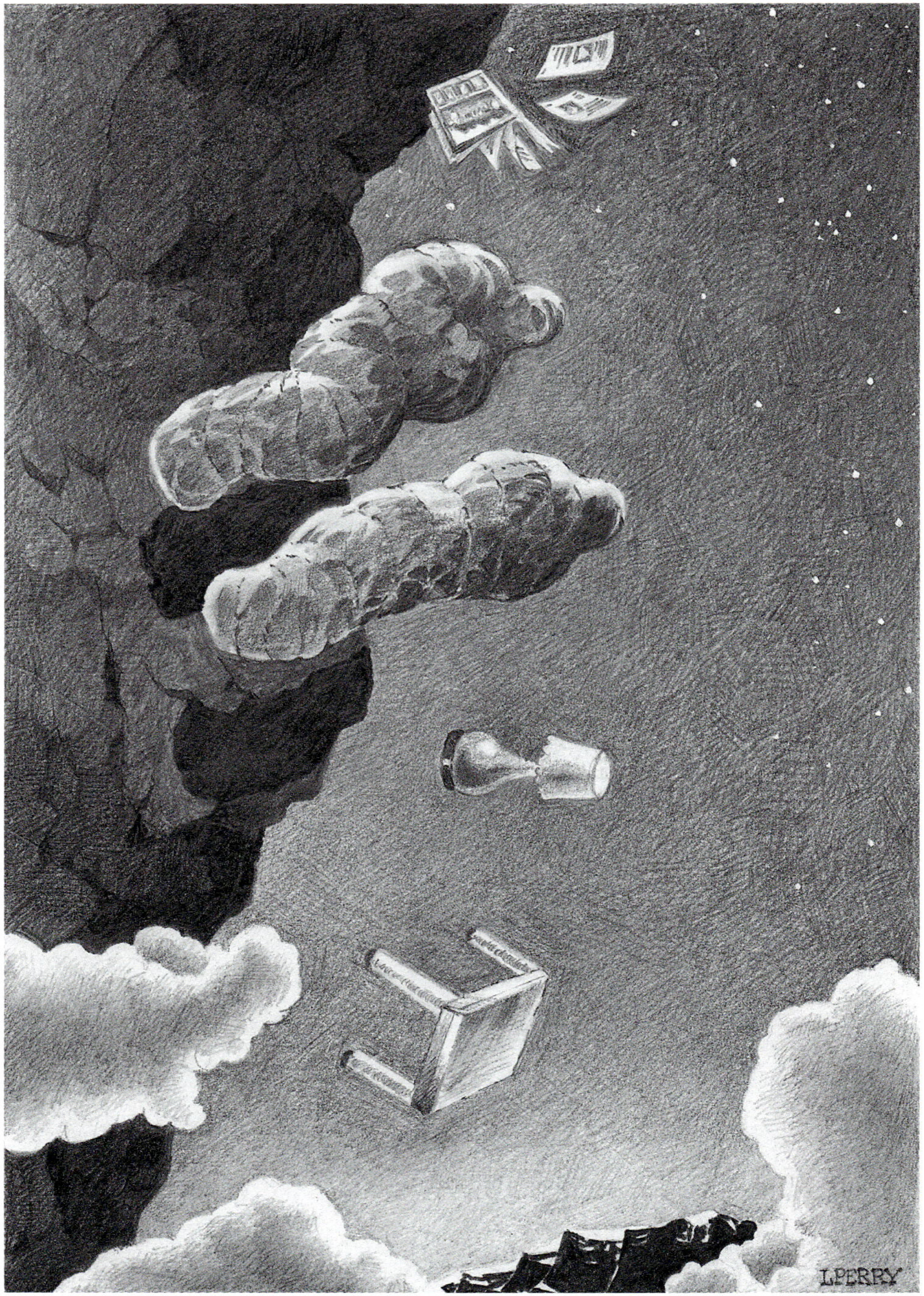

A mountain's orientation to the sun lends each side or "face" a vastly different character. The south-facing slopes are relatively warm and dry —my kind of place. The north-facing ramparts, always in shadow, are dark and cold. Consequently, as the weather warms and melts the ice, the lower part of the route we were to climb is exposed day and night to a lethal bombardment of rock and chunks of ice. The upper half is characterized by good solid climbing interrupted by dangerous loose ledges and "flakes," where it is often next to impossible to affix protective equipment. As Sean Dougherty, the plainspoken author of *Selected Alpine Climbs* suggests, real protection here is "illusory."

The night before the climb the atmosphere was tense in Ron's tiny apartment living room where we sat cross-legged on the floor sorting our hardware. A varied selection of battered pitons, nylon webbing and scratched nuts lay scattered across the rug. Technically, we were ready, but when the moment to commit finally came, Ron admitted wondering if we hadn't simply taken leave of our senses.

Were we mad? By the end of the first day, it seemed a reasonable assumption. Not only had I very nearly fallen off the mountain, which would have killed us both, but we realized we had forgotten one of the water-bottles—a serious lapse. In addition, a falling rock had severed a nerve in my wrist, I'd bitten through and nearly swallowed a temporary dental crown to expose a broken tooth *and* I'd managed to drop a critical piece of our already-meagre rack of gear. Even at the halfway point, we were so far from the valley floor, it could have been an aerial photograph. I was shocked to find the smoothed limestone pitted with white scars caused by ricocheting rocks, remembering a photograph I'd seen of an outcrop similarly pockmarked—by bullets, in the American Civil War.

The setting sun abandoned us high on the wall. Clipped in to safety lines, Ron and I were trying to find a little rest in our tiny overnight bivouac (one of the desperate ones). Literally cheek by jowl on a sloping ledge, every movement edged us toward the precipice. The right side of my face rested comfortably against Ron's pillow-like down jacket. My left, on turning over, was creased by the rocky edge of a nightmarish void. Should I awaken disoriented, it would be wise to remember there was no night table with shaded lamp, no book turned face down just beyond reach in the blackness. Rather, a trap door at my bedside sat silently drawn open.

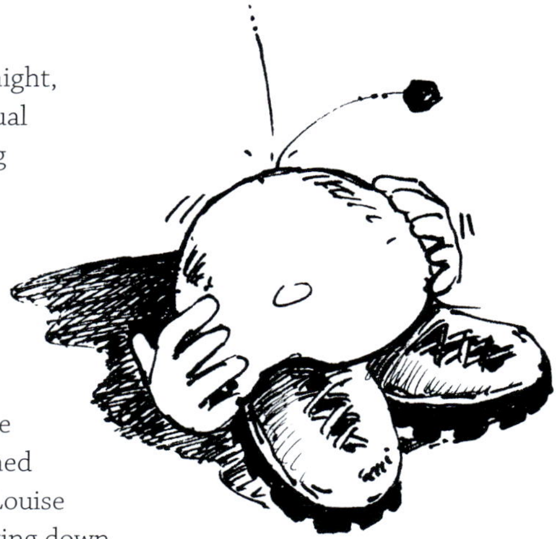

Throughout the interminable night, we were serenaded by the continual high-pitched buzz of rocks zinging down. I imagined a bizarre cartoon image: my entire body—head, arms and legs—jammed into my climbing helmet, heavy-soled boots protruding like flapping Daffy Duck feet. (I guess I figured my toes could be sacrificed to spare the rest.) In the cold and wet and darkness, we watched the twinkling lights of the Lake Louise townsite float far beneath—like peering down from a midnight flight. That kind of separation. As the nightlife got underway below, activity increased: lights going on here, cars parking over there. We even imagined we heard music starting up. Hours later, still awake, we watched in helpless envy as, one by one, cars slowly moved off and the scattered lights were doused. Partygoers pairing up, no doubt, to spend the rest of the long night together in warm, dry beds.

At last dawn arrived; the fine weather it brought warmed our joints just enough to resume the climb. On the last few pitches the technical challenges abated, and we "topped out" in fine style. As I pulled over the final ledge, I could see the entire climb between my legs, right down to the valley creek—bright thread on a green mat.

The descent, however, found us exhausted, dehydrated, totally spent. (Recall the forgotten water bottle.) We threw ourselves, utterly careless, into Ron's Volkswagen. It was driving home that we saw it, both of us: an entire grove of spruce trees hiked up its green skirts and skedaddled across the road. Momentary pause. Exchanged glances first, then raised eyebrows, confirming we indeed had seen what we'd seen.

Ron pulled over and slumped forward, instantly asleep on the wheel. Next to him in the passenger seat, I probed the broken stump of tooth with my tongue. As my head tipped back into unconsciousness, I vowed to never again climb the north face of anything. And I never did.

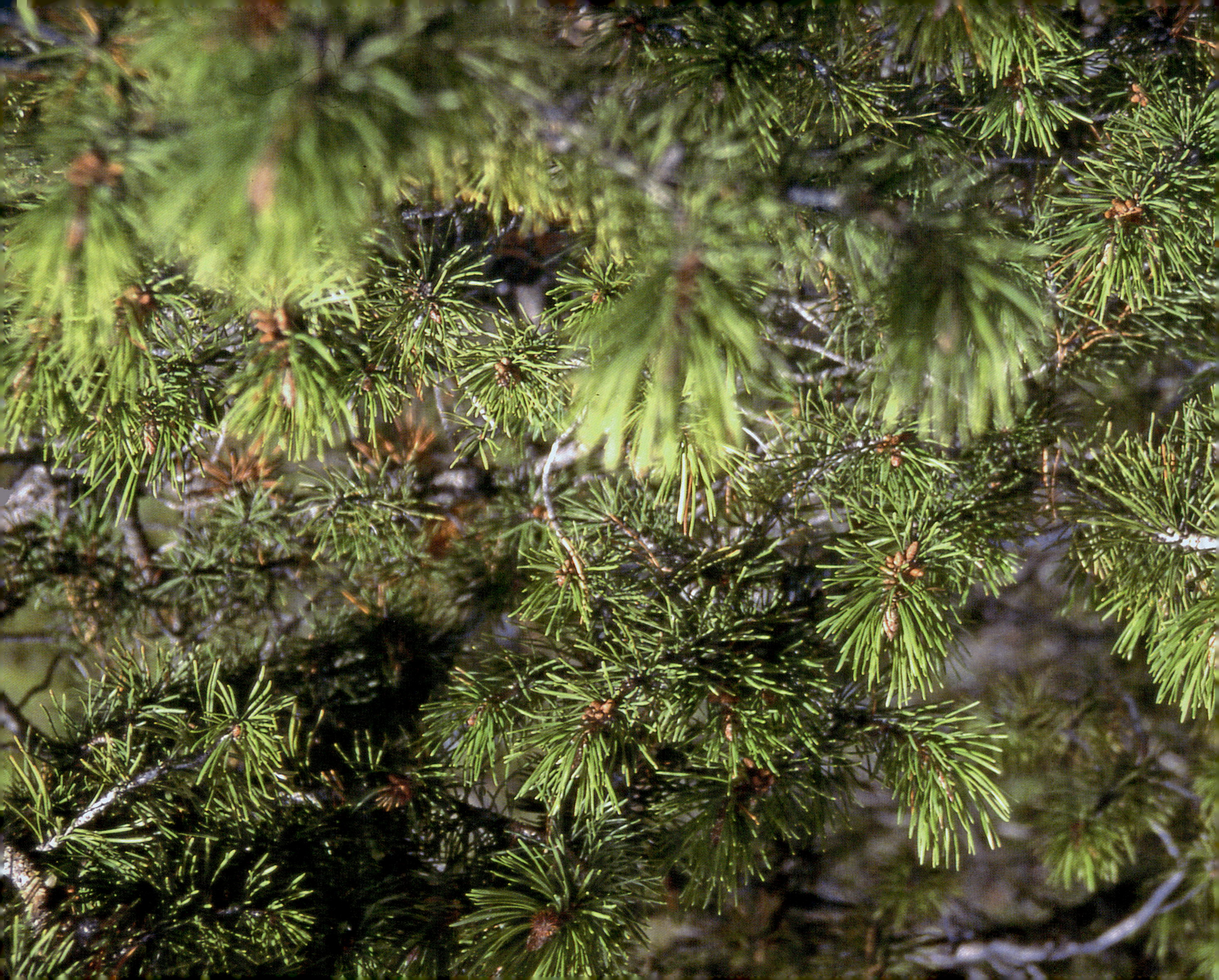

“Real good” stories

CHAPTER 4

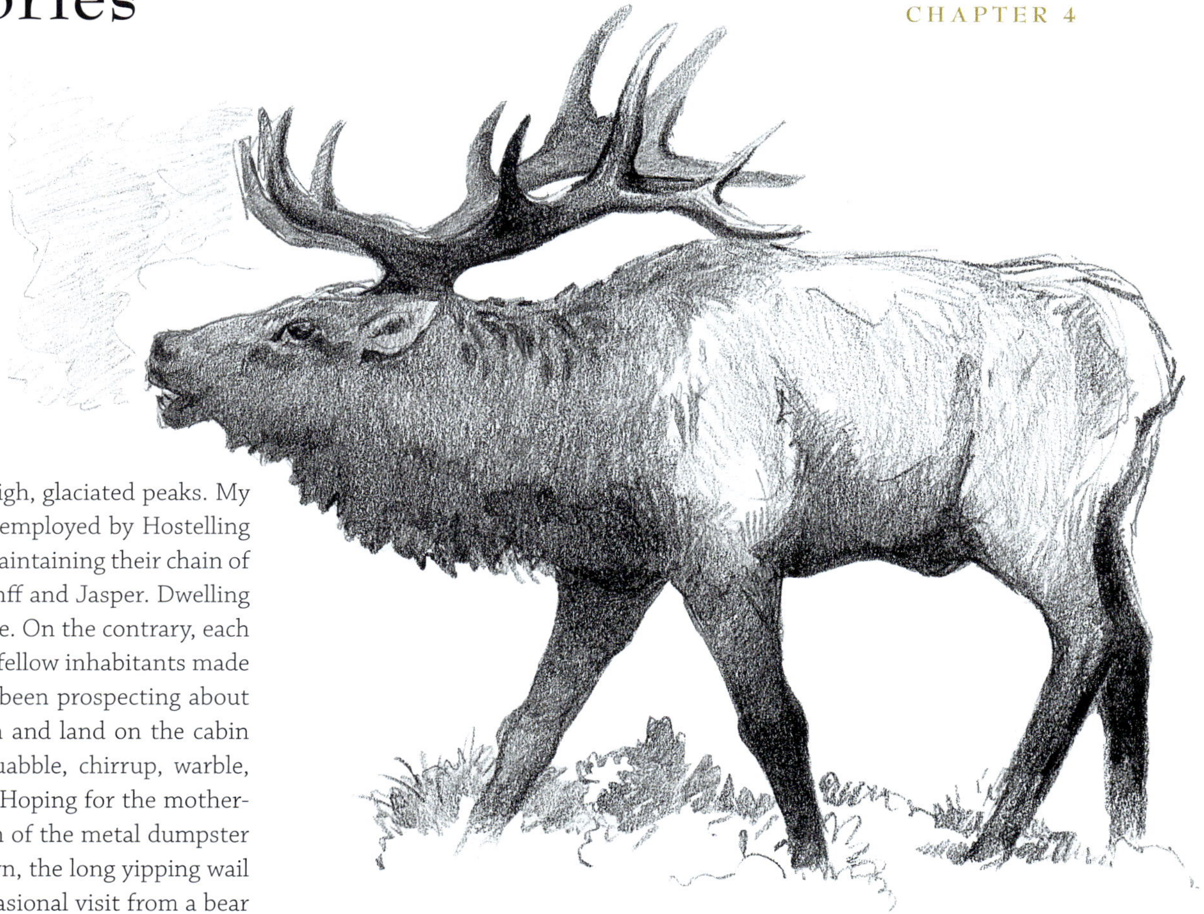

I had a cabin in the woods, at the foot of high, glaciated peaks. My refuge for a number of years when I was employed by Hostelling International, the cabin was my base for maintaining their chain of hostels situated along the highway between Banff and Jasper. Dwelling in the woods, however, did not mean I was alone. On the contrary, each morning, as I stepped out into the clearing, my fellow inhabitants made their presence known. Whiskey-jacks that had been prospecting about the Jack pines’ lower branches would swoop in and land on the cabin roof. From this vantage point they would squabble, chirrup, warble, chirp, preen, hop, scratch, watch for predators. Hoping for the mother-lode, crows noisily picked and jimmied the latch of the metal dumpster out by the highway. In the quiet just before dawn, the long yipping wail of coyotes echoed in the meadow. I had the occasional visit from a bear in the night, and one morning in fall I awoke to find an elk stag standing perfectly still, right outside my door. I could smell his big animal smell and see his sides and chest heave with each long, falling yodel. In the spring, pairs of squirrels intent on mating, enthusiastically inscribed double helixes up and down the tree trunks in spite of predatory martens passing that way.

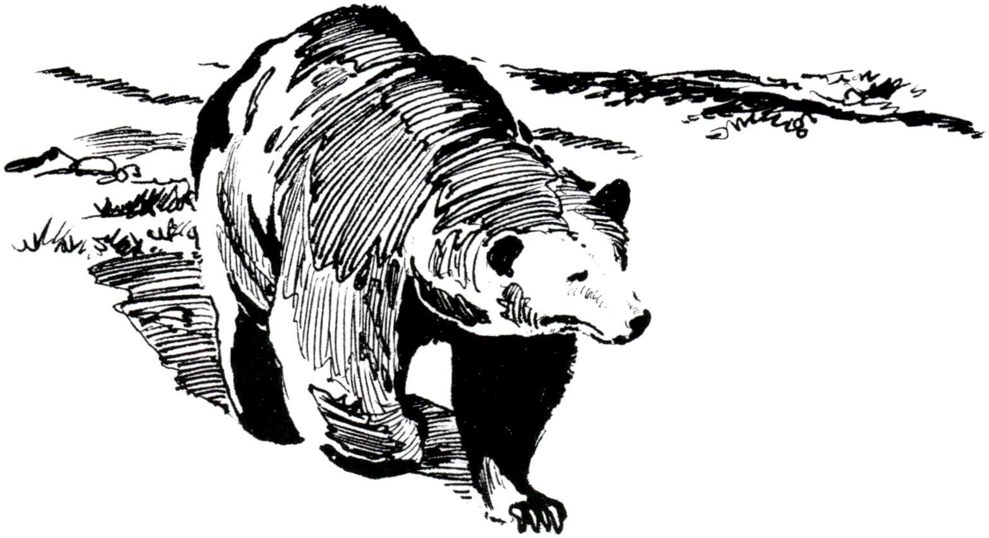

My cabin is gone now—nothing left but a few bits of wood where the foundation lay. The trail to the creek is overgrown. What persist are memories: the richness of fauna I found there, the individuality of the animals' characters and, of course, the stories.

Coyote Watch

MY DAY OFF, AND I WALK OUT FROM MY CABIN simply to see what I can see. I turn into the forest, toward a low ridge along the margin of a swampland. Replete with dwarf birch and long grass, the area attracts a smattering of the local coyotes.

Higher and drier, the ridge alternately bares an ancient backbone of lichen-covered rock and withdraws into secluded forest glades made soft by the annual accumulation of sweet and tangy pine needles. As needles fall and dry out, they build a thicker and thicker pile—red-brown on dark soil—beneath the deep green of kinnikinnik and Labrador tea. A perfect hideout.

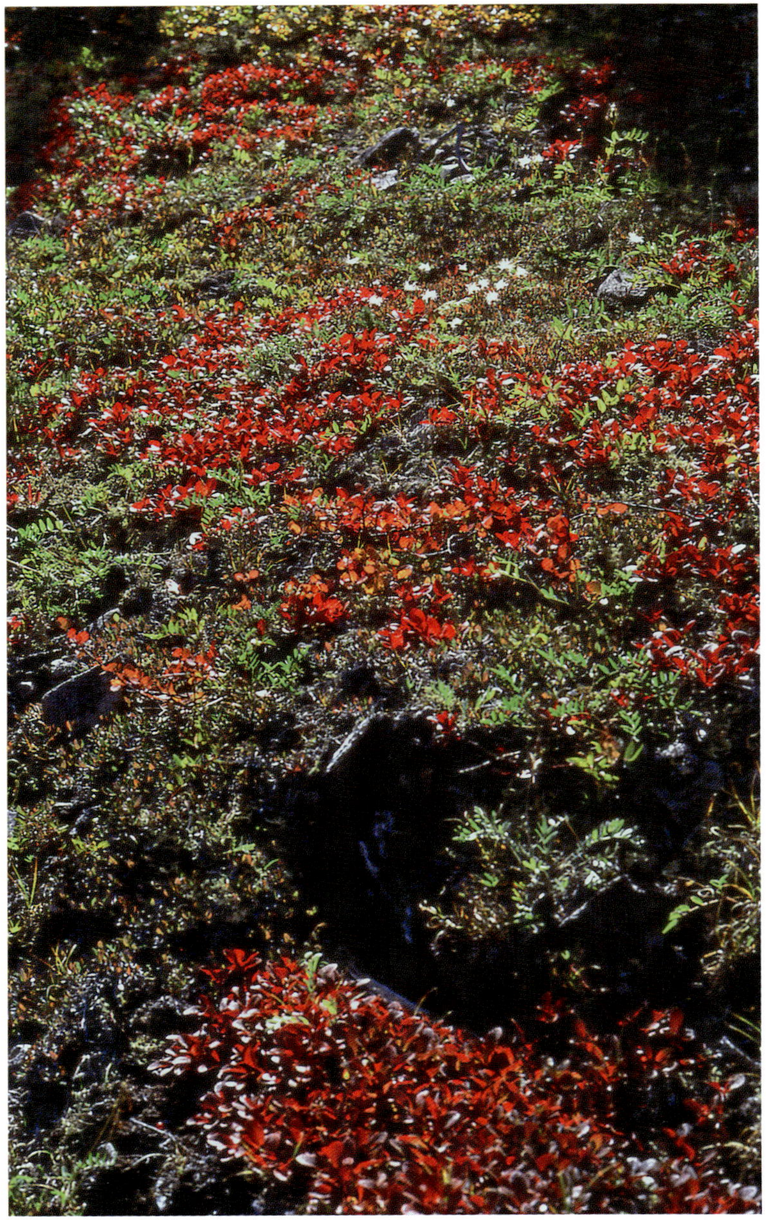

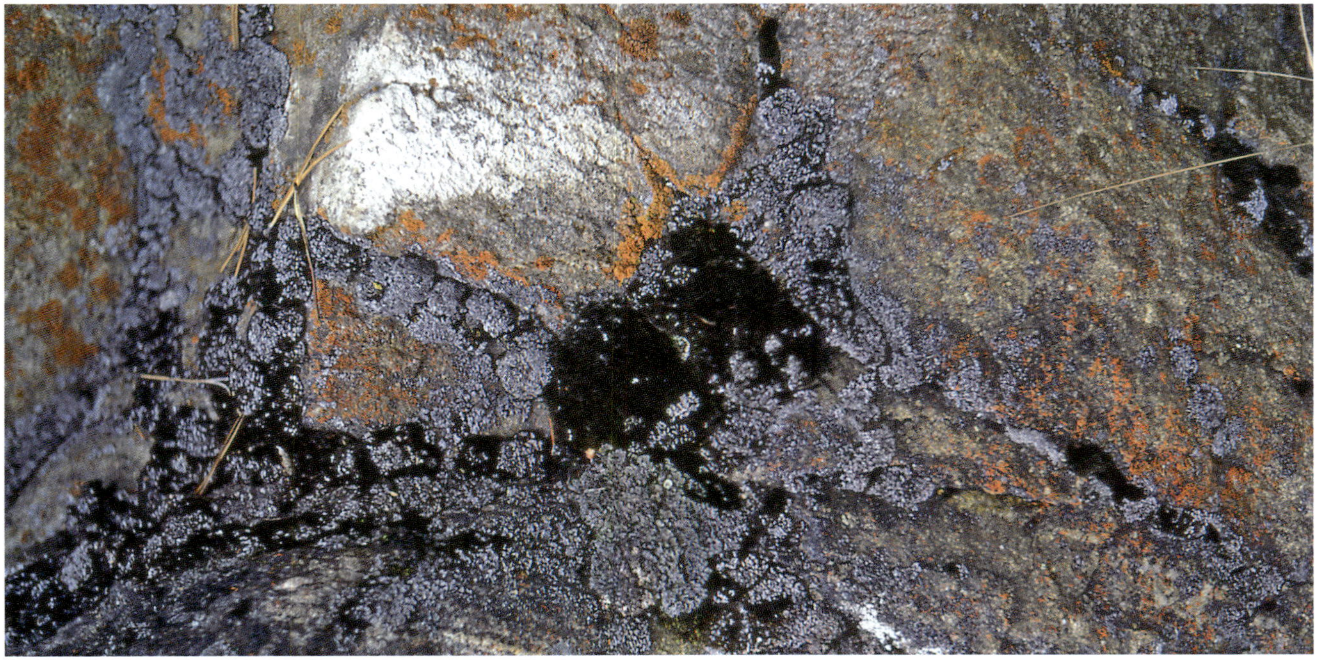

... the ridge alternately
bares an ancient
backbone of
lichen-covered
rock and withdraws
into secluded forest
glades made soft
by the annual
accumulation of sweet
and tangy pine needles.

Two days of steady rain have made colours richer, smells more pungent. I find old, ash-white coyote droppings with increasing frequency, and eventually some that are very fresh. Their contents include bone chips and hair (probably a ground squirrel) and a metal bologna ring, proof of eclectic taste and an unfortunate interface with this valley's dominant species.

I begin to move more slowly, first crouching and moving parallel to the big rock ridges and finally on hands and knees, stealing up behind an outcrop. My excitement is growing. I've never been so close to a coyote in an unguarded moment. With a small patch of dwarf birch for cover, I raise my head bit by bit. Just the other side of the rock, I can see a coyote sleeping—a curled up ball of rich, tan fur that rises and falls steadily with each breath. Precise ears and thick hair frame an intelligent face. Like carefully applied mascara, dark markings define the tightly shut eyes. The sensitive black nose is cradled in crossed paws.

I am so excited, I want to squirm like a kid, jump up and down and shout out my find. But I wait and watch. So far, I haven't been found out. My legs grow numb. Two long hours pass. Looks like a female, I think, as, on three separate occasions, she changes position, rising, stretching then settling again. To my astonishment, she is limping on an injured back leg and does not seem as alert to sound and smell as one would expect. Which might explain why I've been able to get so close. Her leg is stiff; movement appears painful. Then it hits me with a mental thwack—road accident. Damn! A quick stream of emotions passes through me: sadness, guilt, pity and then, slowly, admiration for the quiet courage which she must surely show to stay alive. Bears or an occasional wolf, given the opportunity, wouldn't hesitate to make a meal of her.

The watch continues. About 10:30 in the morning, she rises again. Stretches, first arching her back upwards, then each leg, left side then right. She is so close I'm startled when she raises her head and breaks

Two days of
steady rain
have made
colours richer,
smells more
pungent.

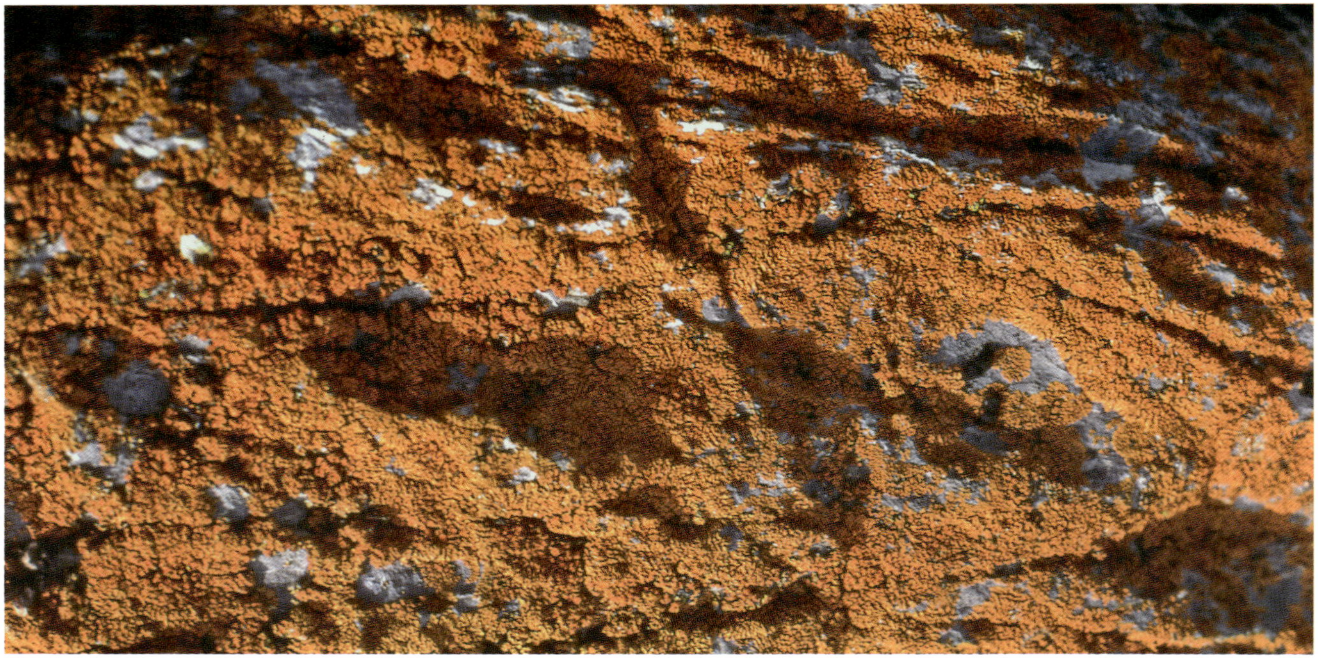

the warm, morning silence with a loud, long call. Her mate, hidden on a hill at a distance of a couple of city blocks, replies immediately. One longer howl, a few short yips. The female barks again, is answered and she replies, this time with a longer call that dies away slowly.

The Jack pine forest is thick, the terrain convoluted, and the sound bounces from hill to hill and back again. But with each of her mate's replies, her head swinging left and right, she scans the dense forest with ultra-keen ears. She settles on a location and, limping steadily, vanishes into the undergrowth to find her mate. Without her, the forest seems suddenly empty.

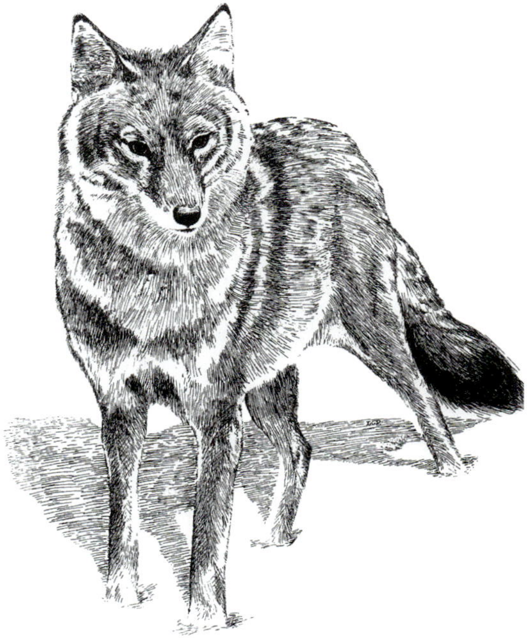

Elk Empires

IT'S GETTING LATE IN FALL. Through a cloudy haze the low sun suffuses the cabin with a pale, weak light. I peer out through an icy window. Early morning and everything is absolutely "pictures at an exhibition" still. On the meadow, ice crystals have turned the tawny grass a brilliant white. Across that plain toward me step three elk—a male with short horns and two females—the *huff-huff* of their breathing a white vapour against deep green spruce. When I open the door and step out, they stop their earnest foraging, raise heads as one, turn and run for the forest to the north. Heads held high and steady, muscles working smoothly, they pound the frozen turf with strong, black feet

Last night, the stars clear and cold overhead, I heard the *clak clak* of horns as males fought for supremacy. Quietly as I can, I walk out, but the soft crunch of my boots on the new snow crust and freeze-dried grass must give me away. I linger in deep shadow beneath the thick-boled spruce, out of reach of silver moonlight. But somehow, beyond the heat and din of combat, they know—and move their private, ancient battle elsewhere.

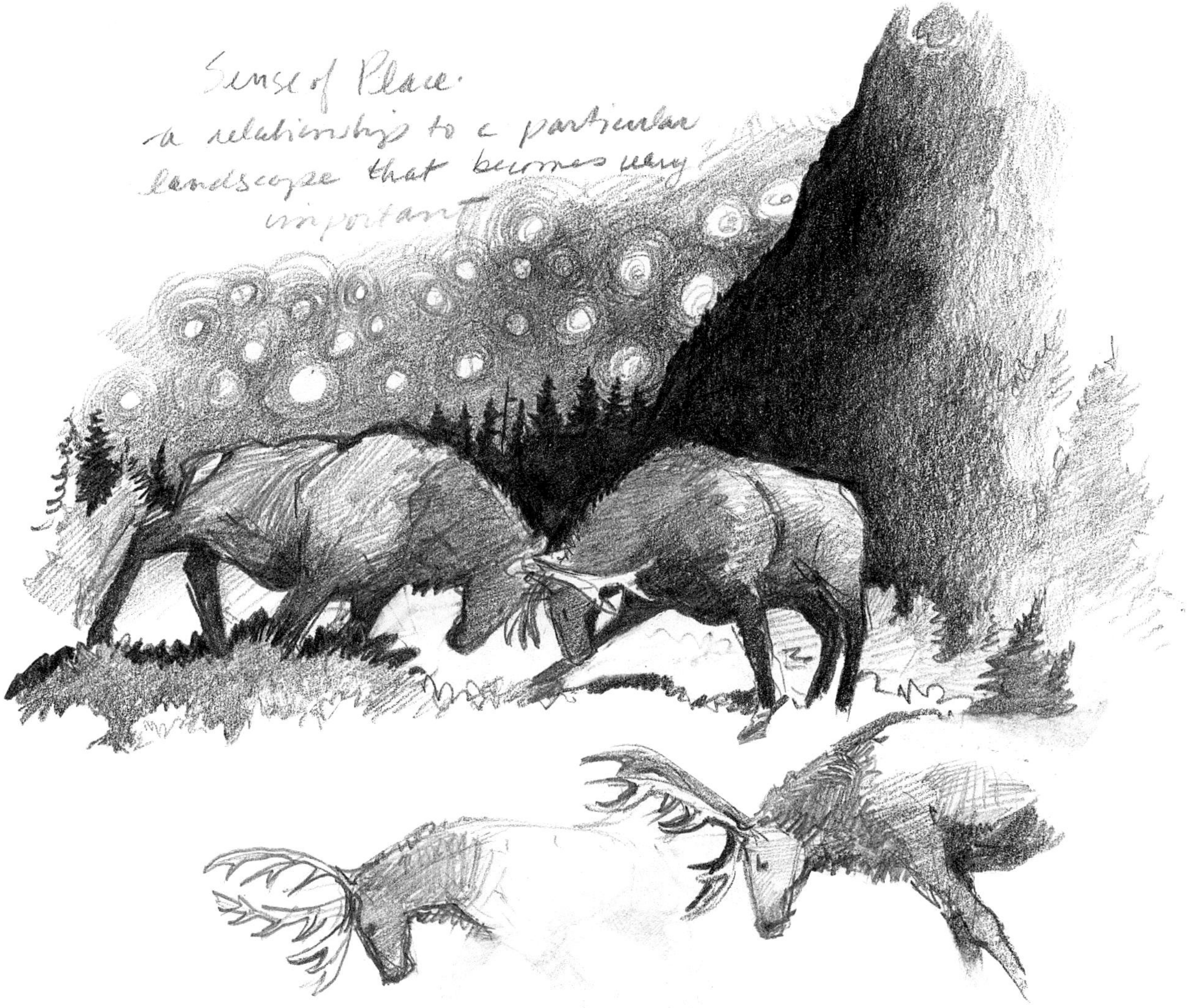

Toilet Terrorist

OUTSIDE THE CABIN, I'm examining the lid of a storage box in which I sometimes temporarily store kitchen scraps before taking them out to the dumpster. The lid has been chewed and the plywood shredded where, judging by the size of the excavation, some animal has got in. Protruding from the box's dark interior is a bit of pork bone, which I grab. Two bright, dime-sized eyes appear, and there is a simultaneous tug on the bone's other end. From the darkly furred, deceptively smallish throat of a marten comes a truly menacing growl: "Yowwwl!" I'm so surprised I nearly fall down. A short tug of war ensues. Lest I lose a chunk of hand, I let go, and the dark figure, bone firmly clamped in jaws, vanishes instantly into the shadows under the cabin's log foundation. But that's not an end. Sounds emerge: more growling, counter-growling, scuffling. Possession of the bone seems to be in further dispute.

Ben Gadd, in *Handbook of the Canadian Rockies*, reports that American martens (their correct name, but locally called pine martens), competing with each other for territory and mates, actually stand on their front legs to box with their hind feet, presumably because their teeth are so lethal they could quickly put an end to their own species. Elegant, sleek, quick and feisty, they are one of nature's quintessential killing machines. Belonging to the weasel family (same crowd as the wolverine), they are, fortunately for us, no bigger than a house cat. And, fortunately for me in my particular living circumstances (martens, like their weasel brethren, have a distinctly musky odour), the under-the-cabin differences are resolved and they eventually move elsewhere.

Other backcountry visitors have not been so fortunate. Reported first in the Banff Crag and Canyon newspaper, another story, perhaps apocryphal, concerning these fearsome furry fellows survives among the Calgary mountaineering cognoscenti.

No one knows to this day what motivated the marten, whether a predatory or territorial matter, but seeking a definitive story, I visit a friend who was actually there. The first to offer to stop the bleeding, a trained first aider and practicing physiotherapist, Johanna, I believe, can be trusted to deliver the straight goods. Her husband of many years,

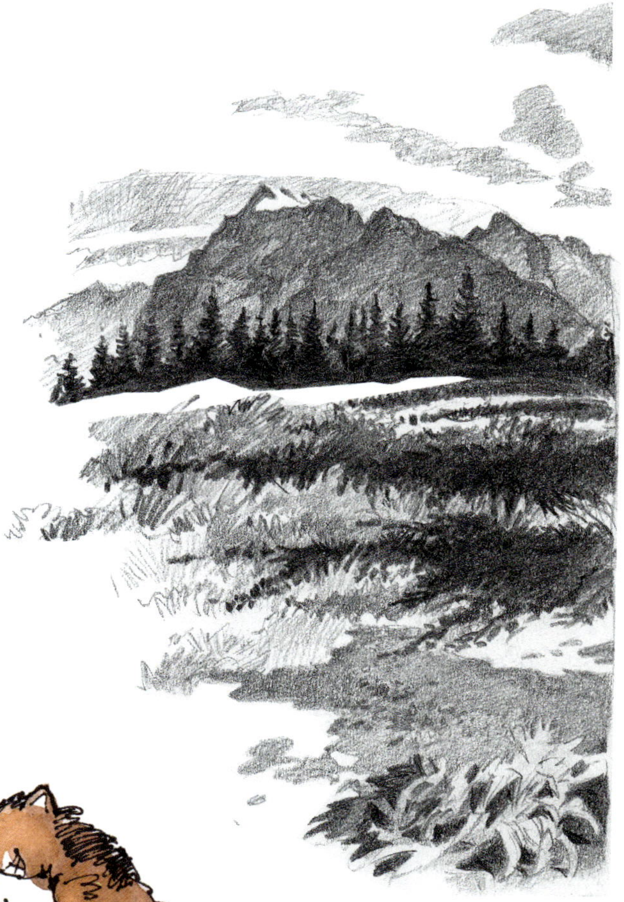

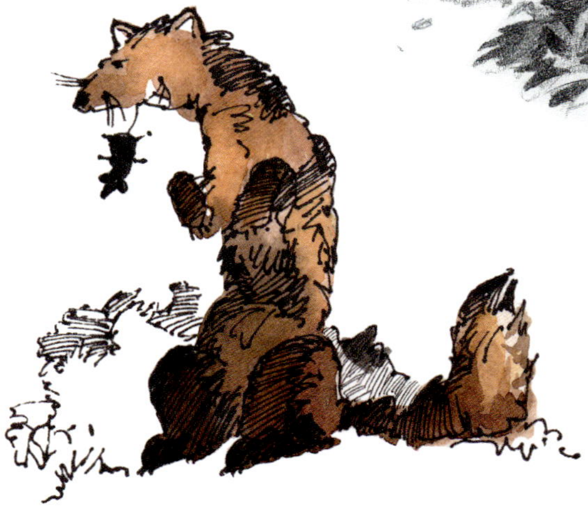

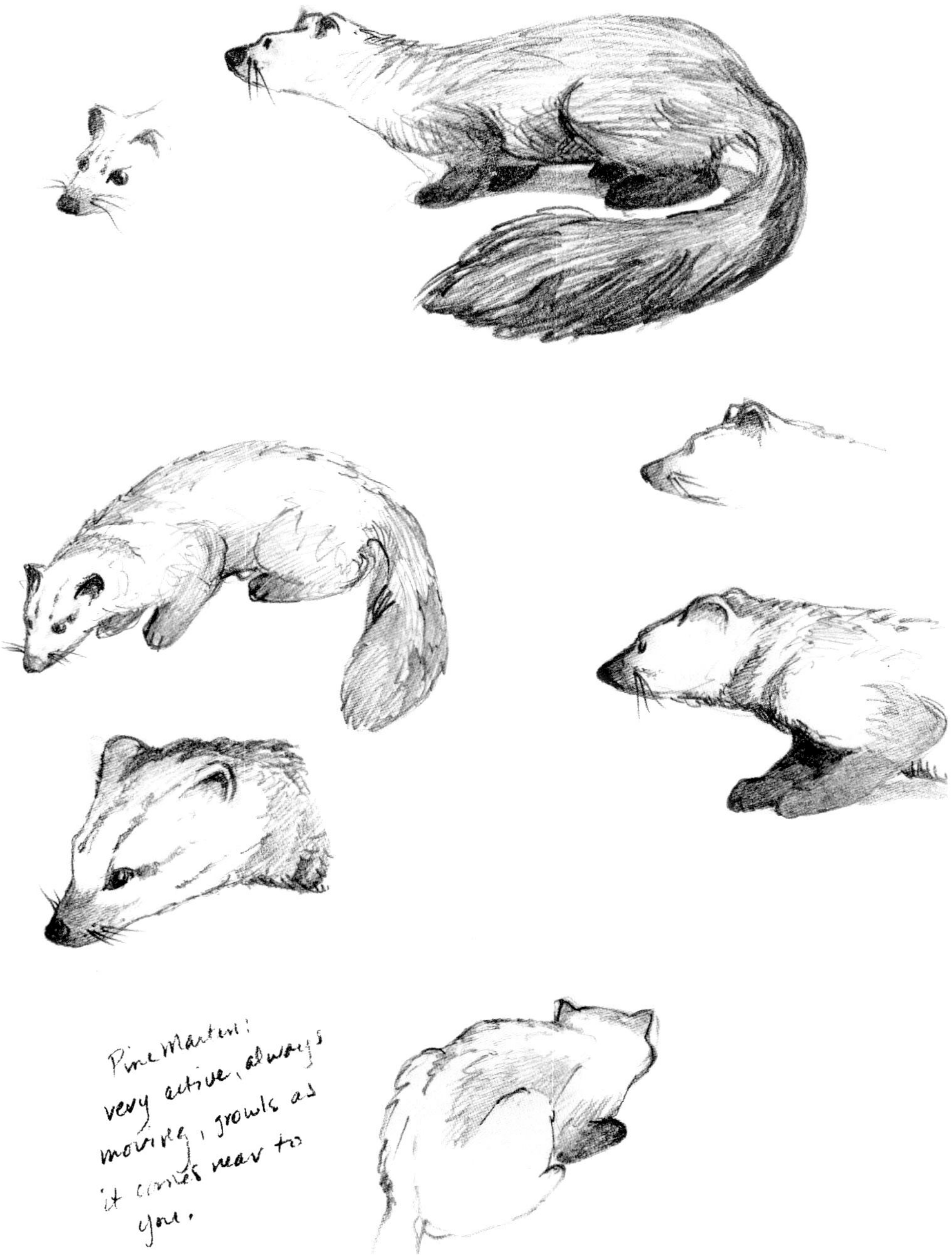

my partner on Mount Temple and the Yamnuska fiasco, Ron claims, much to Johanna's surprise, to also have been there.

In any case, it is established that this story happened in winter, sometime in the late sixties at Castle Junction International Hostel, 30 minutes' drive west of Banff and much more commodious now than it was then. One evening a rough collection of climbers and skiers sat around the table swapping mountain tales in the house parent's tiny room. Suddenly, the tranquil evening was shattered by a volley of loud shouts emanating from the outhouse.

"A man came running, shouting," says Johanna. "He threw open the screen door and burst into the room. His pants and underwear were down around his knees and there was a lot of blood. A lot! Significant amounts on his thighs. It looked like major, arterial bleeding." (She should know, she works in a hospital). "He was in complete shock and was shouting for someone to help him. He said something about being bitten, looked really frightened. We had to do something; I offered to apply direct pressure."

I ask how they knew the tourist hadn't just hooked his willy on a nail on the underside of the seat, reminding them of the sometimes sorry state of repair of those old toilets.

"I guess he could have stepped on his dong with crampons too, for that matter," Ron drily suggests. "It was pretty obvious what had happened."

"From the marten's perspective, then," I continue, trying to get at the meat of the matter, "here he is, inside a shit house, under the toilet seat, in the winter, in the dark..."

Ron takes up the thread. "The guy sat down. His dangler was all there, maybe he even pushed it down a bit, and... *bang*. Maybe the marten thought it was a piñata."

More likely, I think, is that martens eat a lot of rodents, including mice. Perhaps the resemblance made the tender morsel irresistible.

Back at the scene of the crime, upon Johanna's offer of compression, the victim only backed away, apparently more horrified by the perceived indignity of the offer than the possibility of bleeding to death. A towel was found and quickly passed, and the victim applied the necessary treatment himself. Meanwhile, the marten, now somewhere out in the night, had achieved super villain status. As first aid commenced, anxious glances were cast out the cabin windows to see if the tiny threat were about to return. Picture the scene: this normally phlegmatic collection of sturdy mountaineers aghast and reduced to abject fear by an oversized weasel.

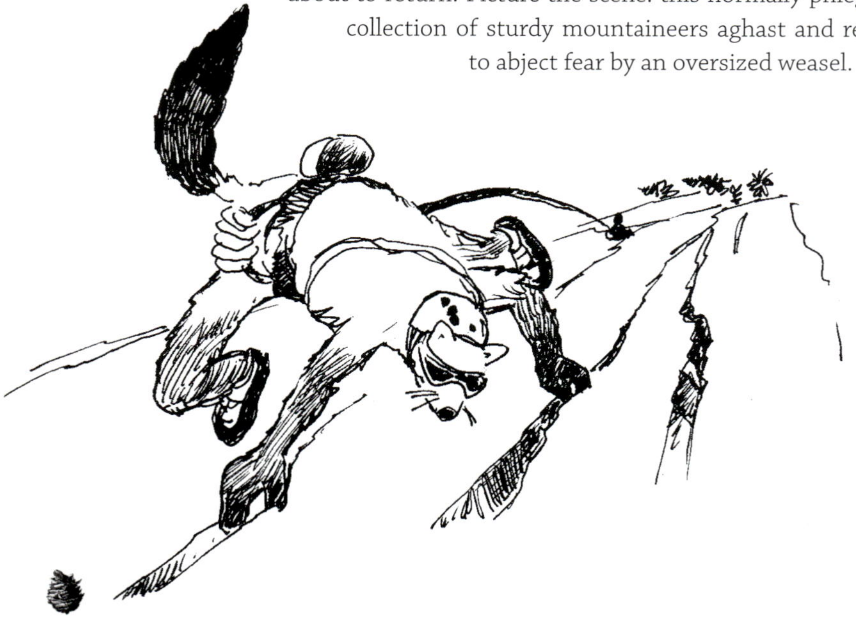

By and by, fully dressed and compressed, the victim was driven straight to hospital where one can only imagine the bemusement of medical personnel. While back at the hostel, all that evening, nervous skiers would venture out to relieve themselves only in groups of three, carrying brooms for self-defense. The night passed without incident, but incredibly, the main event was not over. Extending its reign of terror, the following morning the marten threw itself again and again at the hostel door at about waist height, clinging spread-eagled on the screen, claws dug in. Wardens, summoned to the scene, appeared and trapped the tiny terror. There was no sign of rabies, and no other explanation was ever found. The events of that night have never been repeated. To this day, though, every time I go to an outhouse, I give the seat box a good hard kick just before I sit down.

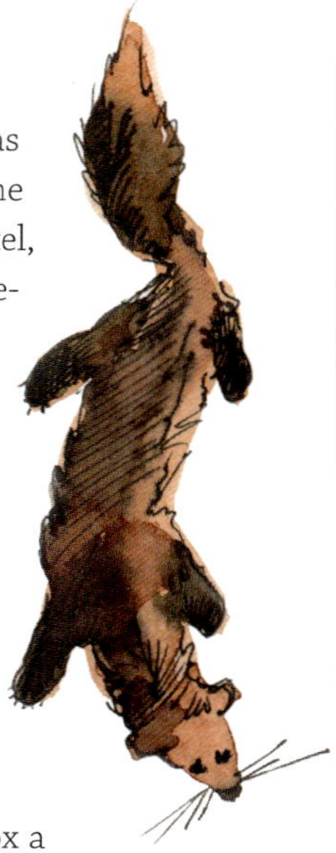

Bearly There

LAKE LOUISE, 1975. Standing at the counter in the national park warden's office, I am waiting to talk to a warden. Retrieved from storage in Calgary, and now in my hand, is my modified 303 Enfield rifle, the stock a varnished warm brown, the workings dark grey. It's the poor man's hunting rifle, but deadly accurate—it can kill at a thousand metres. When I pull the trigger it goes off with a *ka-BOOM* that leaves my shoulder sore and my ears ringing. You wouldn't want to be standing in front of it.

Now, I am not a hunter, and would never take a life in the name of expedience or entertainment. But the grim reality is, at the back country hostel where I work, a grizzly bear has been pillaging the dumpster. I am deeply concerned that this hungry, confused bear is going to pay me a night visit in my small, flimsy cabin. (Keep in mind that bear spray, an effective temporary attack deterrent something like mace, would not appear in my cosmos for a decade or more.) In the event of said guest's uninvited arrival, lacking electric lights in my cabin, I couldn't just flick a switch, point to the door and say "shoo." Moreover, there was no back door and the bedroom window was sealed. The only way out of the cabin was through the front door or two windows on either side. In effect, I would be cornered in a cramped, pitch-black compartment with a 300-kilo animal that, when push inevitably came to shove, very definitely *would be* a hunter.

The wardens' office is all business. Maps, bulletin boards, wall-mounted clipboards, road reports and avalanche warnings festoon the walls. The dispatcher is monitoring a steady radio chatter of warden-speak. Khaki-clad staff come and go from a row of parked pickups out by the loading dock.

Recall that Woodstock, the music festival of the century and the culmination of a new generation's vision of peace and creative hope, is half a dozen years gone. Up here in Alberta, though, the human fallout is still being felt. Weary of the gratuitous destruction of young men in Vietnam and a host of other serious concerns, the Woodstock generation, my contemporaries, have set off from that epicentre of unrest to hitch-hike a continent in search of their own garden. Thousands have drifted up against Banff National Park, bringing with them long hair, skin-tight bell-bottom jeans patched in colourful flower shapes, beat-up guitars, free love and not a dime. The park wardens are duty bound to protect them from their ignorance in a rough wilderness for which they are miserably unprepared. It might even be said the wardens' world then consisted of two human types: themselves—"us"—and non-wardens—"them." With my unkempt long hair and wire rimmed glasses, having just emerged from a beat-up Chevrolet that cost all of $200, I look decidedly like a "them."

On the other side of the counter, a warden approaches. My attention shifts from the dispatcher to this weary wilderness warrior. Government rules require the gun be "sealed," which in a national park, is as it should be. In effect, this means a light cable, secured by a pressed soft metal seal, is threaded through the trigger mechanism. To fire the rifle, you must break the seal.

I explain my conundrum back home at the hostel. The warden is justifiably concerned I will either shoot myself (which is what he expects and would be regrettable), someone else (somewhat worse), or, in the most unfortunate scenario, a bear (true tragedy). From the way conversation is going, it is clear he's sorely tempted to side with the bear, given the steady press of pot-smoking, lunatic park visitors he is obliged to cope with day in and day out.

He relents. "Make noise," he finally counsels. "Give the bear room to get out. Fire a warning shot first. If you aim to hit him, don't just wound 'im. That'll just make it worse. Either way—you miss, or I catch you with that seal broken and you don't have a *real good story*—yer in deep shit!"

With that, the meeting is adjourned. I slink out the door, the now sealed and disabled rifle in hand, and retreat down the steps amidst heavy silence and a hail of suspicious glances.

So. Back at the cabin, alone as usual, after a night of brooding bear-anoia, I concoct a survival plan. With nervous fingers, I attach my old Swiss Army jack knife to the trigger guard of the rifle. That way, if a bear does enter the cabin and all other efforts at dissuasion fail, even in total darkness and blind panic, I will be able to cut away the seal cable, load and fire. Satisfied, I stow the rifle under my bed.

Meanwhile, my arch villain has returned. Next morning, yet again, the dumpster out by the road, normally lifted and emptied with the aid of hydraulics and a huge noisy truck, has been mauled, battered and shaken like a plaything by the male silver tip.

My cabin, a modest dwelling, is divided in two. In the front, is a small combined kitchen/living room, at the back, my bedroom. Spartan by most standards, to me it is beautiful. Every window offers a view of a lodgepole pine forest. When I step out the door each morning, I can hear water flowing and Canada grey jays on their rounds. A short walk will take me to where the Bow River pinches together and flows over an ancient outcrop in licks of vermilion water and white foam.

Not too many nights later, snug in my fancy new, red Swiss-made sleeping bag, I lie awake, looking out through the bedroom door to the kitchen window beyond, admiring the star-packed night sky. The windows are an old fashioned design, divided by green-painted mullions into six square panes. The next minute I am puzzled to find the window has gone completely dark. Hey, who changed the channel? My gaze drops to the propane stove below the window, on top of which sits a big black frying pan lined with a skin of cooled bacon grease left over from breakfast.

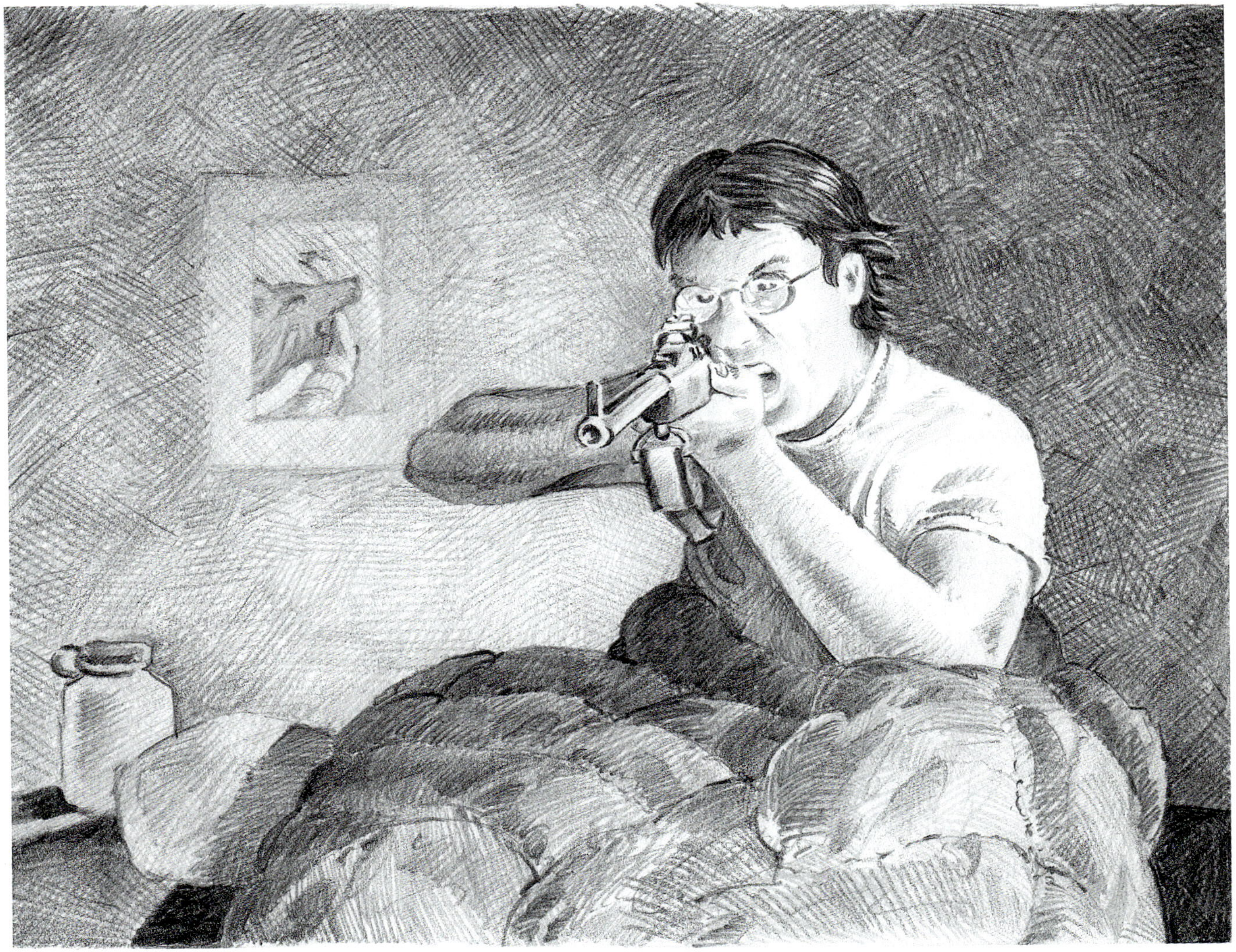

By this time
I'm frightened,
claustrophobic,
half insane.

Now what? A loud thump and a crack, and the air is filled with flying glass. Shards zing all the way across the hard linoleum and in underneath my bed. Now the horrifying truth wends its way into my sleep-deprived head. The mysterious darkness in the window has been my nemesis, the bear, reared on hind legs, blocking the view. Bears' noses are unimaginably sensitive—I knew that. And, like the rest of his kind, this bear has a soft spot for bacon grease—I'd forgotten that. *And now he's on his way in.*

Now, the sleeping bag I'm wrapped in is purpose built, the pinnacle of modern design. To prevent loss of heat, the zipper is a clever half-length affair, with an overlapping flap. Snuggled in up to my neck, my arms are pinned. I pull at the zipper madly, again and again. It jams hard and fast on the clever closure. Stuck, I now resemble a big red Swiss breakfast sausage. By this time I'm frightened, claustrophobic, half insane. Desperate, I wiggle and squirm and work my shoulders and elbows. With a mighty heave, I push my left elbow then my shoulders out of the bag and in one motion reach for the rifle under my bed. Still half in the bag, and unable to stand, I brace myself up against the end of the bed with the rifle between my still captive knees. Fumbling in the pitch black, I feel the jackknife—open. Relief. I've cut the seal. In the chaos of splintering wood and glass I am alternately shouting, "Get out! Get! Go!" then quietly engaging the bear in casual conversation. The warden's warning is flashing in my head like a neon light: "Yer in deep shit!" The rifle is heavy. I work the bolt action that drives a high-powered cartridge into the chamber and cocks it to fire. But, in the blackness, I can distinguish precisely nothing. Absolutely zip. I'm in the worst part of a very bad dream. Is that the tabletop? Maybe bear? Dark coat hung on the wall? Bear? Dammit, cupboard door? Or, Jeesuz, bear?

But wait! At this desperate juncture, my headlong rush toward destruction takes an unexpected turn. The cabin had originally been part of a cheaply built motel, intended neither for its present use or destination. Quick-fix carpentry—a single thin but wide piece of plywood forming the partition between bedroom and kitchen—had readied the structure for hostel use. Rather than fire at nothing, in an act of instinctual self-preservation, I swing the rifle butt at that wall again and again. Tightly nailed, it acts like the head of a huge drum, making a fearful din. Overwhelmed, the bear, in a demonstration of grace and good judgment, backs away and vanishes in the dark.

Afterward, in the cabin, it is absolutely still. The rush of the river, the wind in the pines, a coyote's yap across the meadow—piece by piece my scattered world begins to settle back into place. In the morning, there will be work to fix the window and a drive into town to present a carefully worded explanation to the warden service—a story which is, as it turns out, "real good."

Little do I know what luck I've really had with this bruin: no blood shed, little damage done. What awaits a few years and not many kilometres down the road is another tale. As for the rest of the summer, I will not sleep at all well.

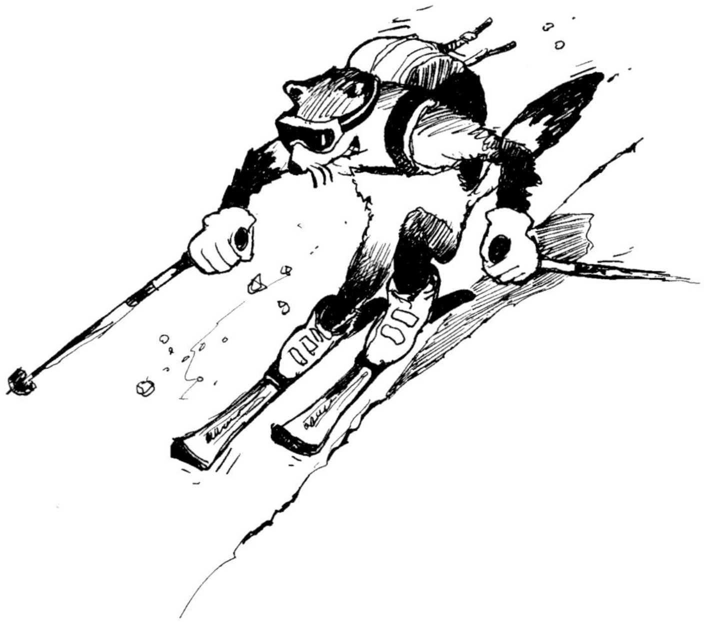

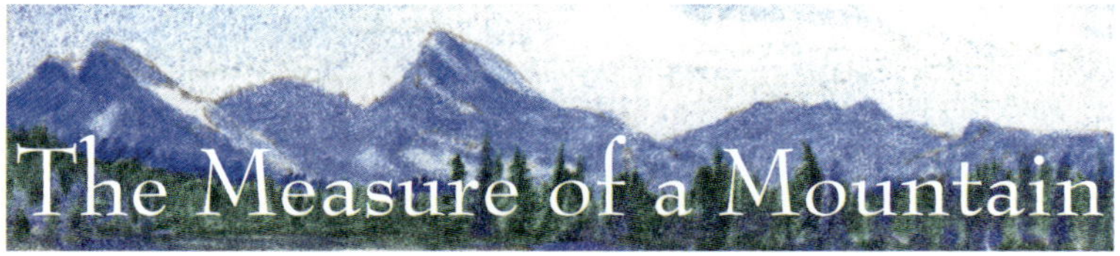

The Measure of a Mountain

ON THE MOUNTAIN SUMMIT A GLACIER GLITTERS—tiny crystal remnant of the passing of the great ice sheets. Suspended far out, on updrafts of earth-warmed air, two ravens, engrossed in a ritual pas de deux, wheel, glide and spin, flashing iridescent silver-black. In unison they fold their wings and drop, spread out again, halt instantaneously. Fold, drop, flare, halt; fold, drop, flare, halt. As though on a fall of invisible fabric, the ravens slide down a golden shaft of light somewhere between the sun and the drowsy forest floor.

Around the mountain's middle, clouds float like boats gently adrift on a blue-green sea. Their shadows skim softly up the rock faces, over sharp lofty ridges and down a carpet of green into the canyons' shadow-throats. Deep in sun-dappled, mossy rock crevices, glacial meltwater rears and tumbles, shaking the very earth. On the great north-facing walls, moisture driven into cracks by winter gales alternately freezes and thaws, loosening the buttress blocks. Then, it's as if the gargoyles on some gargantuan cathedral had wakened in a rage, tearing at the ramparts, hurtling them down. Each impact vibrates the mountain's core. It scars the rock white and expels a sulphurous dust on the air.

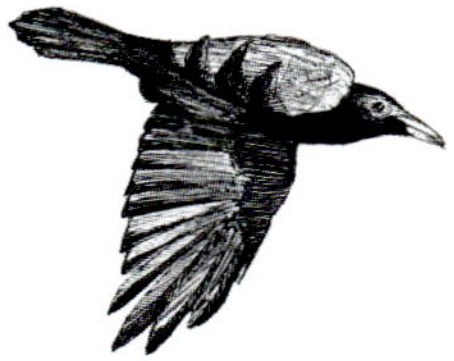

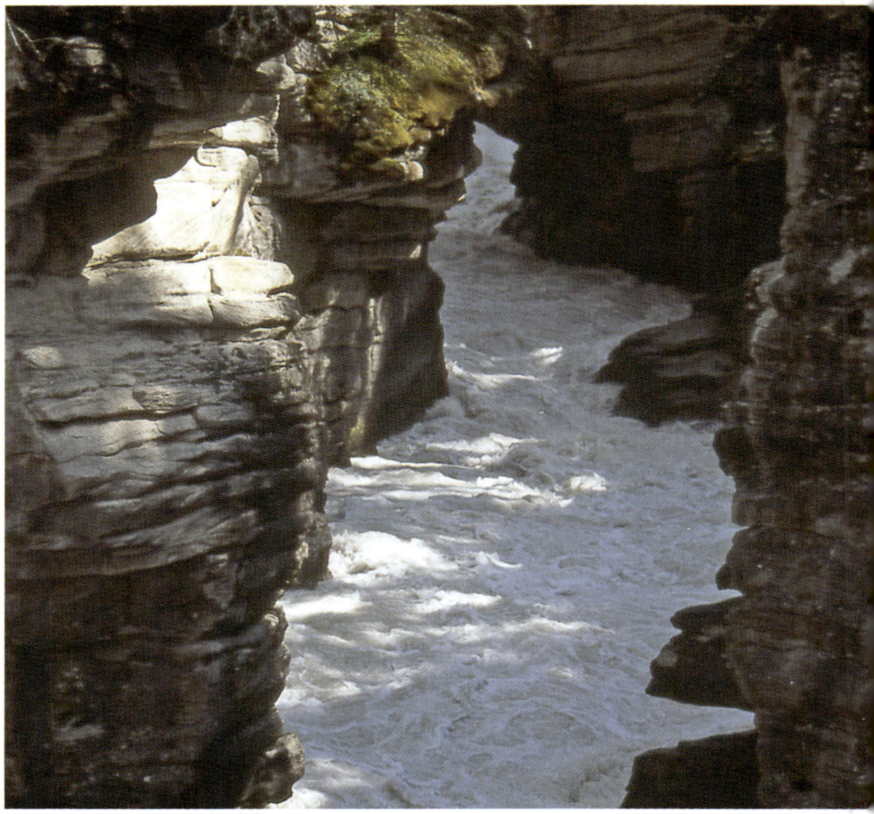

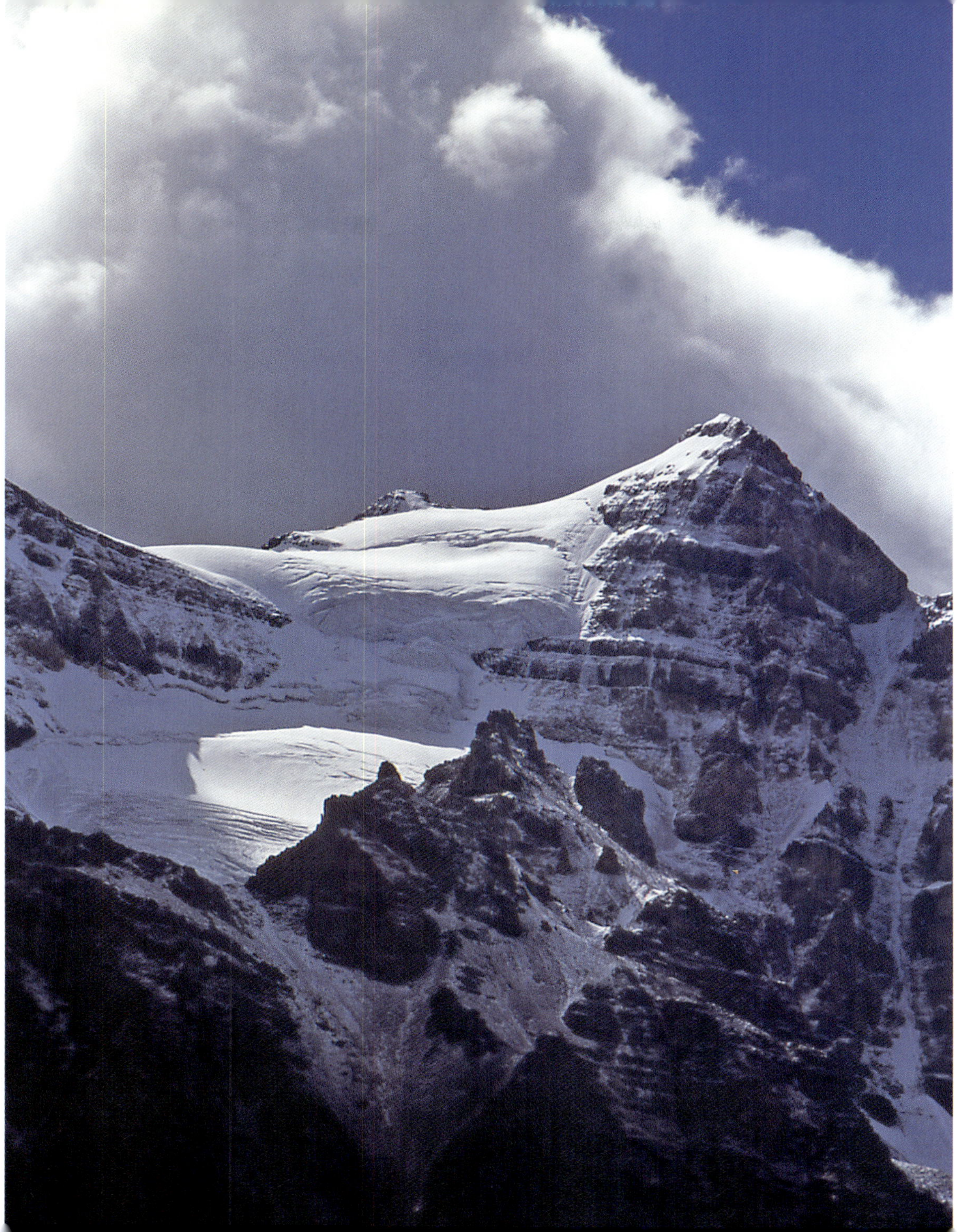

Overnight, an early fall storm has dropped new snow on the summit of Mount Aberdeen, just west of Lake Louise in Banff National Park, creating a stark contrast between the brilliant white glacier and black teeth of the buttress towers.

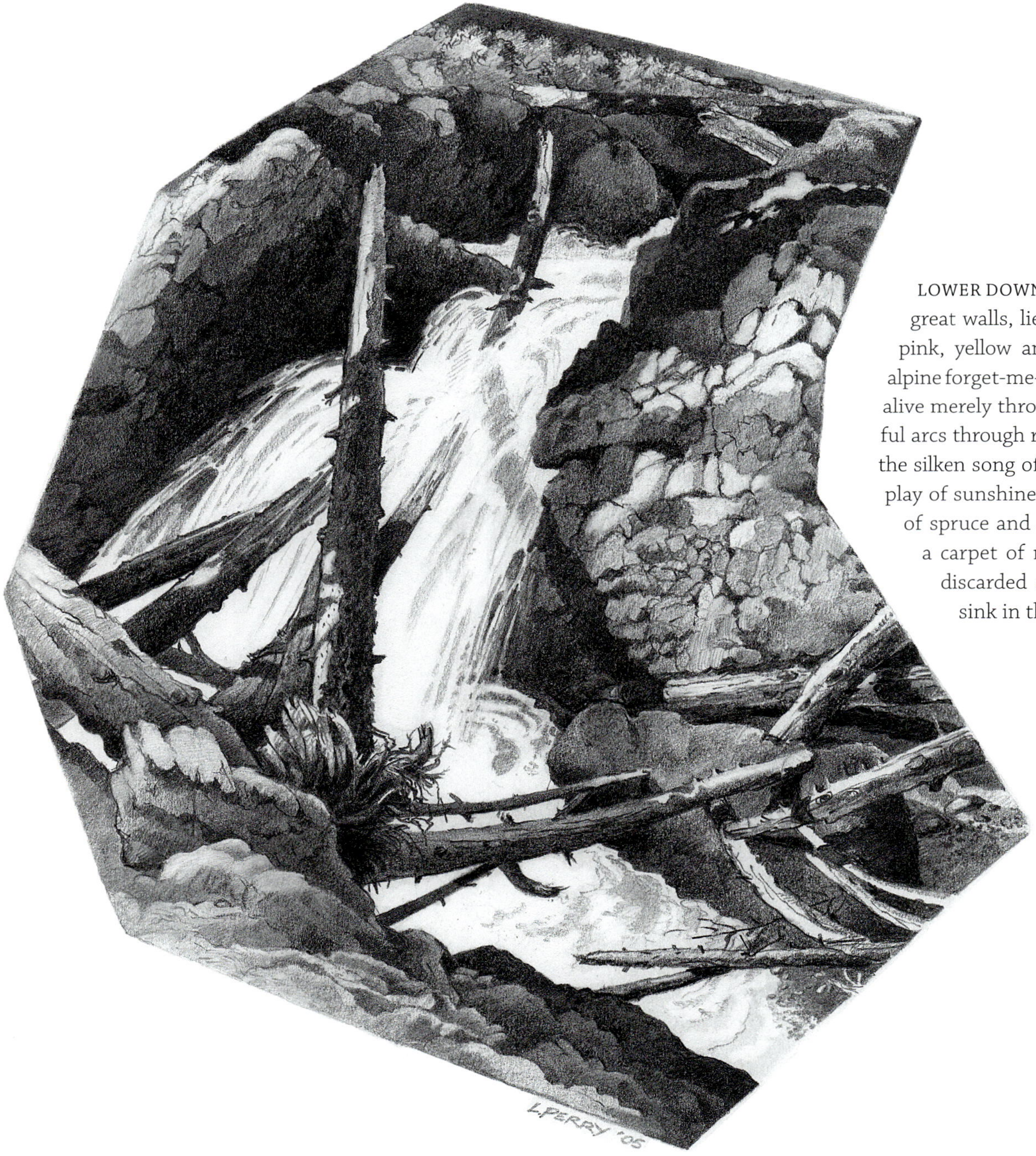

LOWER DOWN THE MOUNTAIN'S FLANKS, at the foot of the great walls, lie green grass meadows flecked with delicate pink, yellow and blue flowers: moss-campion, glacier lily, alpine forget-me-not. In the forest it is cool and moist. Insects, alive merely through the halcyon days of August, limn graceful arcs through rays of light. Woven into that delicate tracery, the silken song of a white-throated sparrow accompanies the play of sunshine on clear streams. Between the thick trunks of spruce and alpine fir, deadfall lies black and rotting on a carpet of moss. The jawbone of a deer, elk antlers—discarded after the rut and chewed by mice—slowly sink in the wet sand beside a spring.

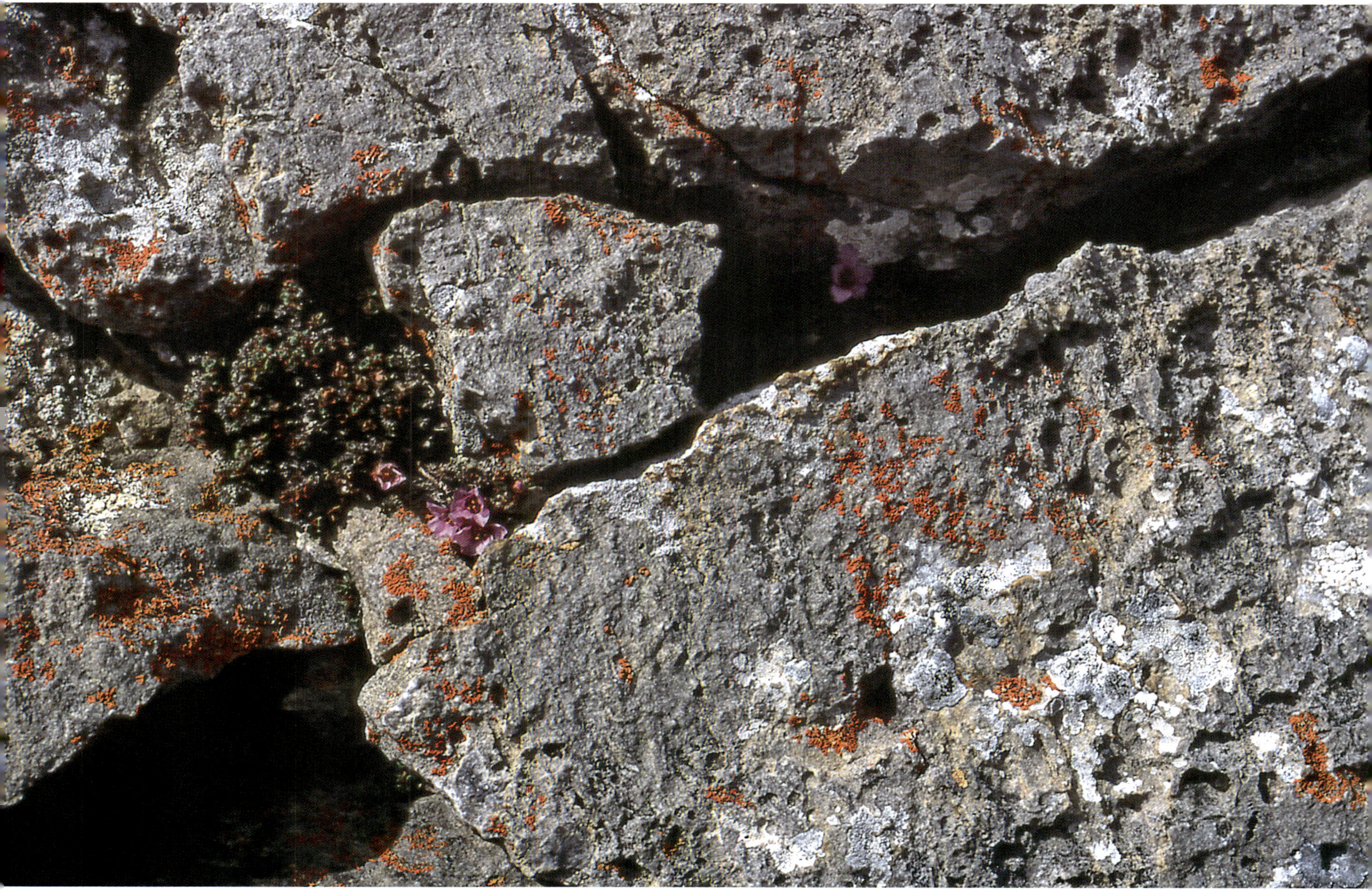

From a high ridge near Balu Pass above Rogers Pass, the ski mountaineer gains a spectacular view of the grand pyramid of Mount Sir Donald and the white plain of the Illecillewaet névé.

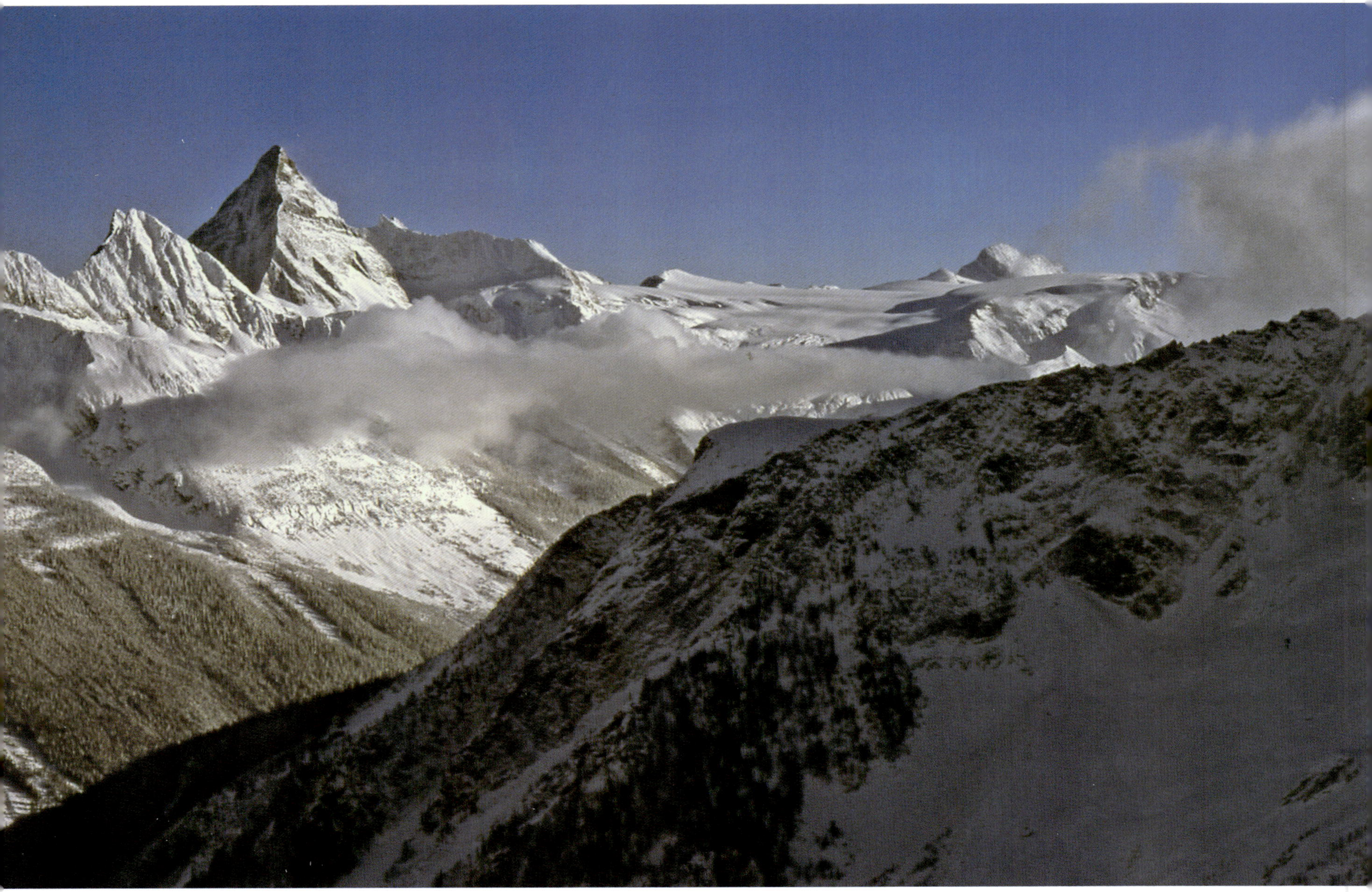

Lords of the dance

CHAPTER 5

"Sicatur ad Astra" (Now We Go to the Stars)

ALPINE CLUB OF CANADA MOTTO

Four hours drive west of Calgary, at the limit of the weekend climber's range, the Trans Canada Highway winds a black ribbon through forest and mountain, gathers itself with a couple of switchbacks and takes a long, hard run out of the Columbia River valley and up over Rogers Pass. In late March, winter's grip has eased, but thin clouds still hang low and grey. A scatter of snowflakes lands on the dark asphalt. Huge growling semis, heaving sooty exhaust, take a quick breath, grind down another gear. From east and west, they labour up the steep incline, carrying oranges from California and plywood to Vancouver. After the long, slow work to the crest, they hurtle down the other side, snorting through gears in a blast of flying snow and whining tires.

Back at the pass, vehicles roar by. Can of pop in hand, stomach just shy of his steering wheel, a furniture company rep westbound for Seattle quells boredom with a bag of chips beside him and non-stop country music twanging in his ear. In a salt- and grit-encrusted SUV frenetic with two restless kids, a mother peers through her windshield wipers' endless sweeping. Snow is banked so high that even as she wheels in at the hotel/service station complex, she still sees no sign of life, just the steep-peaked roofs of buildings. Minutes later, pit stop complete, kids in tow, she climbs back in. Doors slam, the ruby taillight winks. Back on the highway, swallowed up in the gloom, the vehicle rolls on eastward toward its destination: a family wedding in Banff.

All transit this high bottleneck, glancing around at the silent forest mounting the steep valleys into low cloud. All move on, passing blindly in the dark.

While high above, a parallel world prevails. Though physically connected to the asphalt line, metaphysically it's a world apart—an archipelago of the mind. With its topography of water-streaked rock, brilliant snowfield, ice chasm and endless sky, this is the domain of the ski-mountaineer.

I'M AS EXCITED AS A CHILD to be here. In the beam of my headlamp, a wet snow is falling. Like ships leaving a night port, we skied off at about nine, gradually leaving cars, parking lot and highway roar behind. On either side of the trail, snow-cloaked alpine fir rise up to nearly touch each other, leaving a single narrow vault of sky. I stop and swing around, and the pale cone of light falls on my partner. Under an immense, overloaded pack, Jim is plodding happily in the dark along the wide ski track. We are pulling top-heavy toboggans, like sea turtles, that flip over every now and then with a clink and rattle—our weekend supply of Coke, nachos and beer. Our high-tech ski boots sound a steady *plodge, plodge* as the soft snow repeatedly builds under our heels, then falls away in the track behind.

Jim is a thoughtful companion whose life has run somewhat parallel to mine. Long-legged, square-jawed, possessed of a sly wit, he's a veteran climber and skier whose alpine curriculum vitae includes major ascents on three continents as well as some of the most difficult snow and ice climbing right here at home. He has logged hundreds of hours of high-altitude ski traverses. At the core of these accomplishments are the personal prerequisites for ski mountaineering: courage, skill and absolute unrelenting dogged determination. This pursuit is not just physically demanding but, approached carelessly, potentially lethal. We have our plans, but should they go awry, there's no ski patrol to pick up the pieces. Nor, on a glacier, will there be marked trails or signs warning of crevasses. Rescue could be many cold, uncomfortable hours or days in coming.

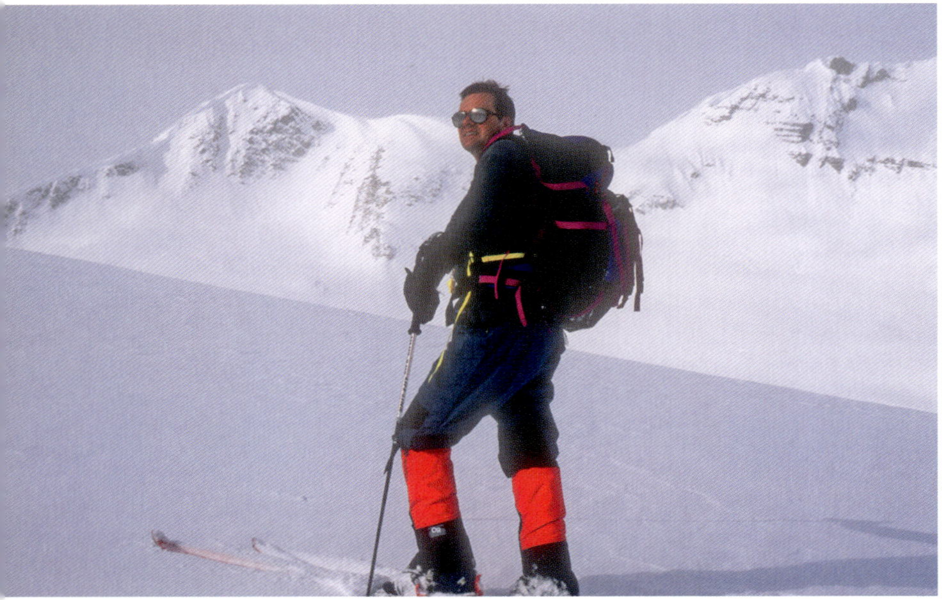

Taking a break on the long grind out of the Illecillewaet valley, Jim is a picture of the ski tourer—plastic telemark skis, gaiters and overpants, poles that screw together to make an avalanche probe, avalanche transceiver strapped to his chest and the indispensable glacier glasses.

And, of course, things don't always go as planned. Two years before this trip, my partner and I were outbound for a high hut at the toe of the Bow Glacier. Where the ski trail makes a sharp turn out of a snow-filled canyon, a man stood up to my left, strangely stiff-legged, rocking from foot to foot. Apparently, something was very wrong. He stared at us, and answered my greeting in a hollow voice. As we approached, I was startled to see his face cut open from inner eyebrow to cheekbone. Spattered on the snow around him, frozen drops of blood sat like red poker chips. Through the pain, in measured words, he told us his story. Skiing at speed, he'd pitched forward, face first, onto a sharp boulder.

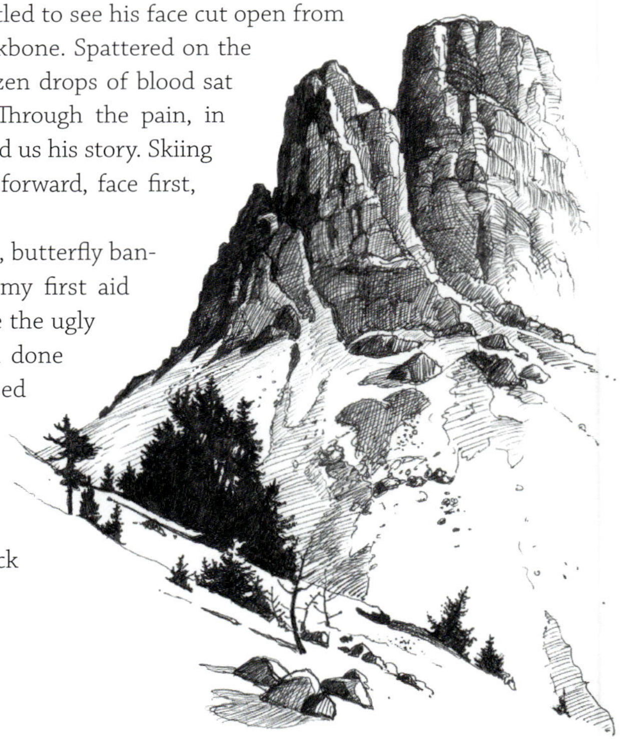

With alcohol swabs, butterfly bandages and tape from my first aid kit, we worked to close the ugly wound. When we had done what we could, I pressed several strong codeine pills into his palm, and he resumed what would be a long, miserable descent back to his car.

THE TRAIL TURNS TOWARD THE CABIN. Built and maintained by the Alpine Club of Canada, this venerable log structure will be the base from which we explore the surrounding glaciers and high passes. At first, the place seems so lifeless—doors locked, chimney smokeless, dark windows a vacant stare. Inside is a damp darkness; the air is cold, stale and smells faintly of floor cleaner. Jim lights a fire, and I hold a match up to the propane lamp, which ignites with a *whoompf*. We leave the doors ajar for a while, then shut them and gradually light and warmth banish the ghosts. We are comfortably ensconced in our own close little world.

Outside sits a deep, heavy darkness. The cabin lamplight draws a warm yellow window on the snow. All is cool, still and silent, the sky a dome of stars, some bright, some twinkling, others lost in the faint glow at the horizon. The moon and planets align in a great arc. The sky silhouettes dark hemlock and slim alpine fir. To the north, aurora borealis drapes a shimmering curtain behind tall peaks. Back in our cozy abode, I see carved in the fireplace mantle the historic Alpine Club motto: *Sicatur ad Astra*—"Now we go to the stars."

AT 4:30, MORNING COMES MUCH TOO EARLY. I crane my neck, shade my eyes from the glare of the lamps and peer out. Overhead a few stars are still floating pinholes in a dark firmament, but behind the black monolith of Mount Sir Donald to the east, the sky glows a soft rose. On spring ski trips, timing is everything; we must not be slow.

The great trick is to arrive at the top of the glacier just as the snow, refrozen overnight, is beginning to soften, allowing the sharp steel edges of our skis to bite the slope. Arrive too late and the slopes in the warm lower valley will have turned to wet hash browns. This makes for miserable skiing, increases the chance of knee injury and loosens the tongue of avalanches that, like wild beasts to the chase, will begin to give voice around two in the afternoon. Hence our goal is to begin descending no later than noon. On the great avalanche roulette table, despite recent research that has sweetened the odds, even the most experienced can lose.

Several years ago, in the lobby of a Lake Louise hotel, I passed a handwritten sign warning backcountry travellers of high avalanche danger. Certain the note was intended for tourists come to take pictures, buy overpriced Nordic sweaters and ski for a few minutes, I dismissed the warning as alarmist twaddle. What could *they* possibly know that I didn't?

I made my way along to the Plain of Six Glaciers under a low ceiling of cloud. There was a thump and a roar, and it was obvious a really big one was on its way down. My scalp tightened; cold liquid fear poured down my spine. I could hear the beast caroming off the canyon walls as it zigzagged lower. At the time, I was answering the call of nature, squatting awkwardly over parted skis. Literally "caught with my pants down," I frantically grabbed and managed to pull them up just to my thighs. Bare rump and family jewels to the cold wind, spruce trees plucking maddeningly at the pants' flapping braces, I pointed tips down and skied for my life.

Out of the cloud just above and behind me, several thousand tons of snow burst into my world. Entirely airborne, this malevolent hissing force struck a grove of mature spruce. *Crack! Crack! Crack!* Trees thick as telephone poles snapped off like matchwood, their upper halves gone. As I stood gaping, the heavy white mass turned, burying my ski tracks before dispersing on slopes lower down. Chastened, I had to admit a new-found respect for the concierge back at the hotel, who had taken into account what I had not: that *above* the low cloud that had hovered all morning, the unrelenting sun had been warming the steep, snow-loaded slopes.

Even the animals make mistakes. Several years ago, above Highway 40 in Kananaskis Country, I was struggling over uneven snow blocks, the debris of an avalanche come to rest at the bottom of a long, narrow chute. On the breeze I caught the instantly repellant scent of putrefaction. Clumps of hair told me a wolf had been entombed in the wet concrete of a big spring avalanche. Over a wide area I sighted shreds of skin, pulverized rock, broken branches and bone chips. The largest piece of the unfortunate animal I found was a slightly yellowed, unmistakably canine tooth.

IN LIGHT OF SUCH CONSIDERATIONS, deciding where to go, and when, is a question of considerable importance to the backcountry skier: decisions can be literally life or death. The most significant factor in these

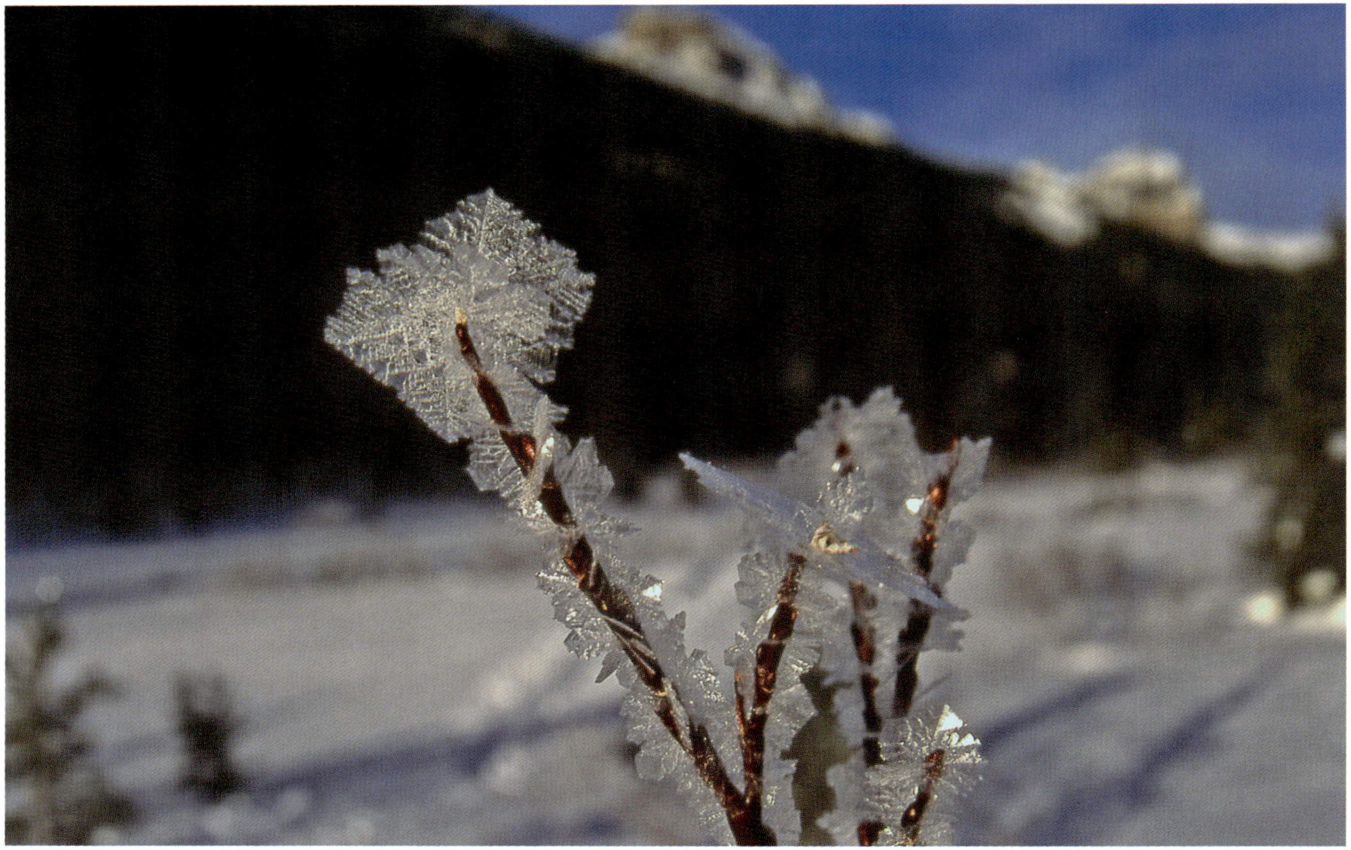

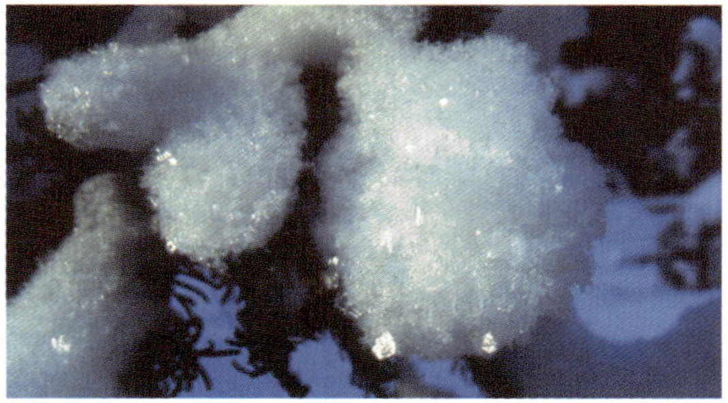

A ptarmigan has taken off, leaving behind a transient calligraphy—a delicate fan of depressions created by its tail and flight feathers in the soft, new snow.

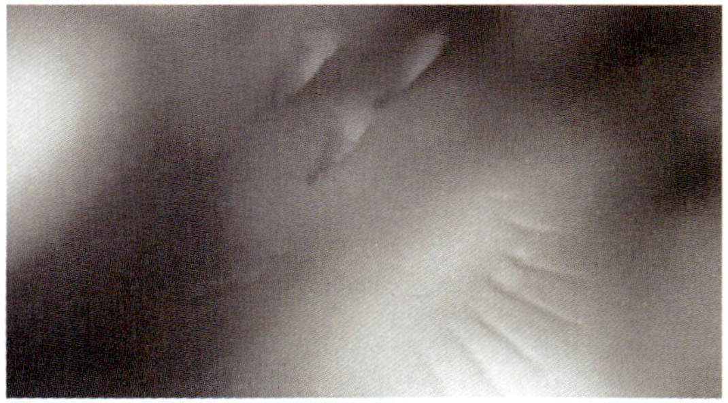

decisions is the white stuff we take for granted, specifically its structure. That pretty Christmas-card snow crystal is actually an unrepentant shape-shifter, equally able to form benign snowmen and kick down huge power lines and towers. Some tiny hexagonal crystals stack like dinner plates to form columnar depth hoar crystals. As one might expect, this very fragile structure is responsible for many snow slides and, unfortunately, deaths. When the temperature rises, snow crystals can evolve into fused, misshapen kernels. At really warm temperatures, close examination reveals something like wet micro-hash browns—dangerous on steep slopes and impossible to ski.

The architecture of the frozen water crystal reflects elemental molecular forces manifest in every structure in the universe. At the core of every snowflake there must be a minuscule piece of dust around which it can form. No dust, no snowflake. And, in a display of incredible natural complexity, the flakes are never alike. Add the capricious mix of daily events in the mountains—storms, heavy snowfall, sunshine, early season rain. It all has an effect. The big question is *what effect?* Ultimately, no matter how the mountaineer makes a decision, whether from intuition born of experience or information gleaned from books or courses, it's got to be right. Remember the wolf.

Rogers Pass, where Jim and I are now, is notorious for avalanches. In March of 1910, a huge one swept down the mountain and buried the railroad tracks, which, at that time, ran through the pass. Shortly thereafter, a second avalanche ravaged the same path, killing the 58 men who had come to clear the route. More recently, in February, 2003, just across the valley from our cabin, a school group skied into the shadows of a narrow valley threatened by numerous avalanche slide paths. A season of wild weather swings had left the snow ominously unstable. High on the mountain, deep within the snow pack, some tenuous bond snapped. The released juggernaut engulfed 14 Calgary school kids and their teachers at the valley bottom before rushing up the opposite side. Seven did not survive; those who did were lucky.

When a big one breaks off, it rumbles down the steep gullies, building friction and heat. The snow, thus melted, finally swirls to a halt and freezes, sealing all it has overtaken in an icy tomb. In guidebooks, such events are referred to as "objective hazard," meaning one can't do a damn

Jan 06. 03
Dolomite Pass.

Warm day, clear views all the way to Lake Louise. A bright sun keeps body from freezing. A spectacular view of Helen Creek drainage. I was able to draw for about Twenty minutes before my fingers froze.

Snow Science

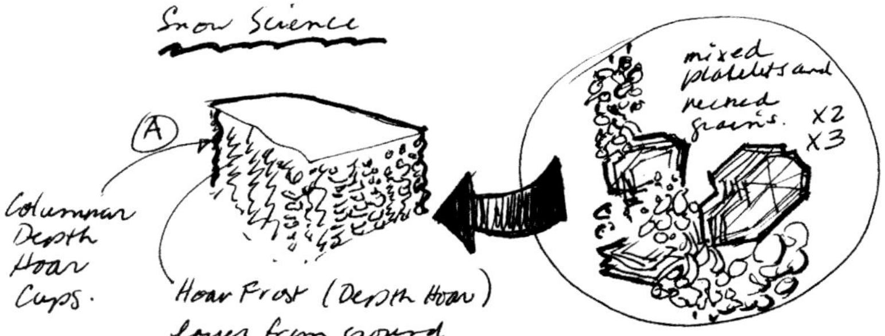

Hoar Frost (Depth Hoar) layer from ground layer at ridge top above Helen Lakes. Note small platelets and rounded particles mixed.

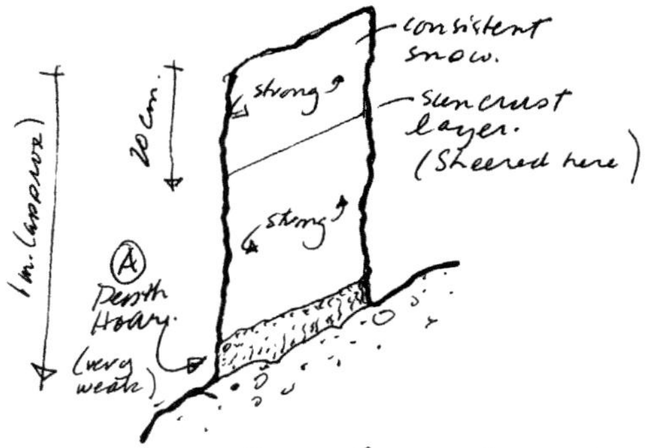

Upper layers seemed relatively solid. Shovel Shear test broke at sun crust layer.

thing to change it. Here, objective hazard abounds. Still, if Jim and I are unlucky—injury, avalanche, a fall in a crevasse or any number of other possible disasters—I know Jim can be counted on. Complete trust and competence are essential kit. The freedom to pursue our goals and the concomitant necessity to accept absolute personal responsibility are powerful antidotes to our daily urban world of stoplights and gridlock, bleak cubicles, computer slavery and endless multitasking.

THROUGH THE CABIN WINDOWS, I can see a brightening; first light tinges the snow a soft mauve. My backpack is on. The avalanche transceiver strapped to my chest is generating an unseen magnetic field very like that classic textbook illustration of a bar magnet emanating curved lines at either end. If I am buried, Jim will switch his own transceiver from "transmit" to "receive" and follow these invisible lines to home in on my body. From a distance he would resemble a fast moving hunting dog, zigzagging across an open field.

Even if the outcome is happy, it may not be immediate. I may be buried deeply, which is why we both carry folding alloy shovels. The faster Jim digs the better the likely outcome. It's a classic race against time. If I'm extricated within 30 minutes, statistics tell us there's a 50/50 chance Jim will find me alive. If I am buried more than two metres under the surface, by this time tomorrow he'll be driving eastbound on the highway alone. In the back of his van, along with his own equipment, would reside a bent ski pole, skis (if they were found at all), and an ownerless rumpled backpack containing a journal that had seen its last entry. Ron Wright in *A Scientific Romance* describes

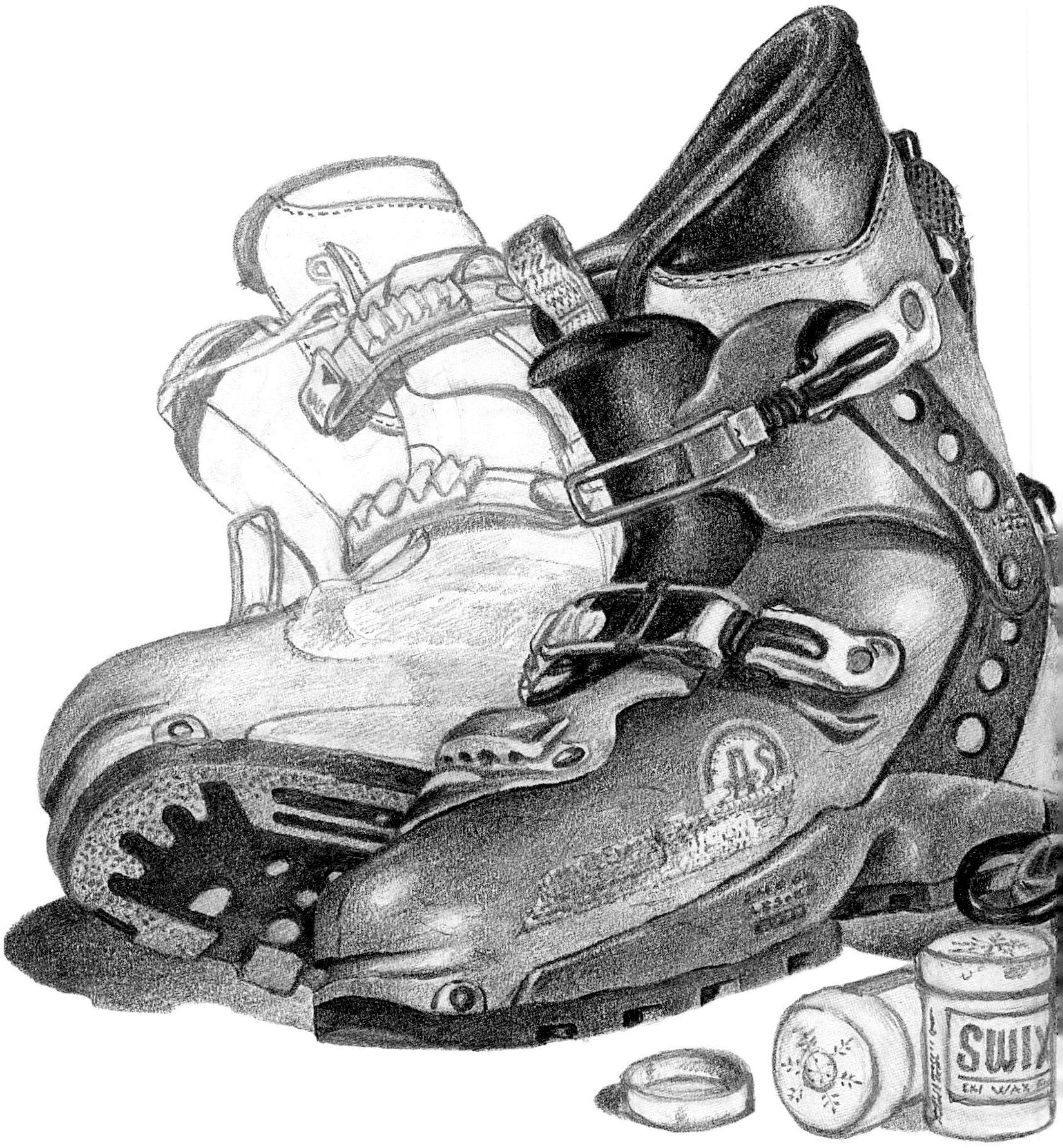

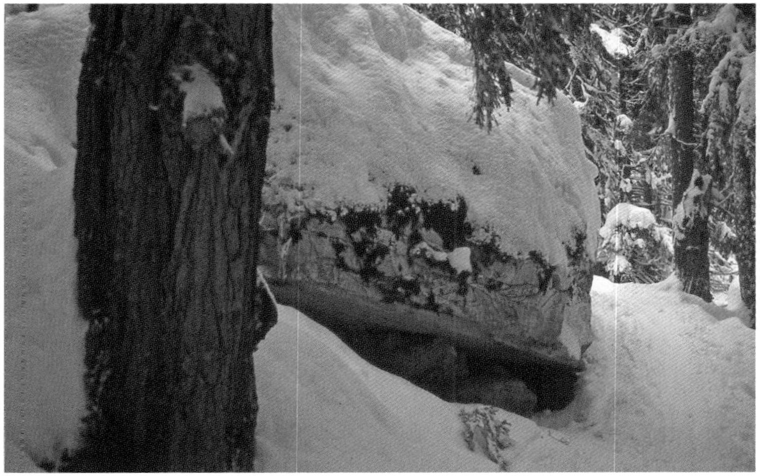

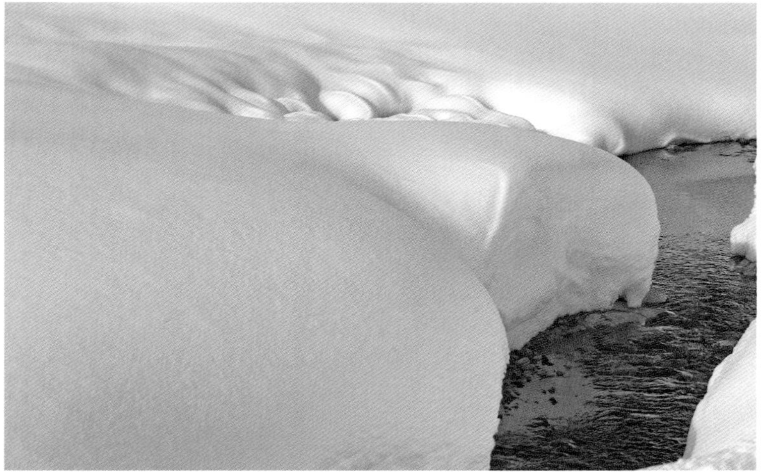

death's strange close separation in time and space: "I sat on a stone and wept, unable to believe, still hoping... that somehow we were simply out of phase, hidden from one another by a veil it might be possible to tear aside." The price of error in the high country.

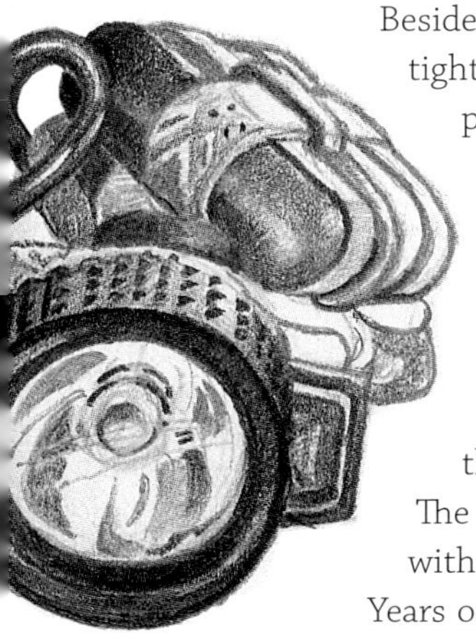

Beside the boot rack on the cold cabin floor, I carefully tighten the laces on my soft inner boots. Standing up, I push each into its hard-shelled outer boot, wiggling forward and back until it slips in with a *soomf*. I close each engineered buckle with a satisfying snap, having adjusted for perfect length and tension. We turn out the lamps, check the stove and stomp out of the busy, warm closeness of the cabin into the cool blues, pinks, greys and blacks of the predawn. We are dark shapes crunching on snow. The air is cool on my face, cold on my fingers as I fiddle with frost-covered alloy bindings and climbing skins.

Years of experience and attention to detail ensure that the equipment is exactly right. A slightly loose binding will quickly destroy its mounting, necessitating a jury-rigged repair and a cold, laborious descent. The wrench of a hard fall could break a worn safety retention strap, sending a ski a long way down the mountain, where, after a lengthy search, it may or may not be found. Poorly fitted plastic boots will amplify an innocuous lump in the lining to a medieval torture instrument in an alarmingly short time.

As Jim leads off, following a vaguely marked trail up through the old-growth forest, I look back over my shoulder. The cabin has resumed its introverted stare. We ski over snow-covered boulders the size of cars and around the bases of huge cedars. We traverse avalanche slopes at present mercifully inactive. Down to my right is the Illecillewaet River. I revel in the fluid beauty of clear water over smooth stones. In the early morning calm, its steady rushing is a mellifluous sound landscape on which our tap-tapping ski bindings drop a staccato syncopation.

We emerge from the forest; our ski poles scrunch in the hard crust, and the dark valley floor begins to drop away. The slope is now barren of trees and dramatically steeper. Beneath the deep layer of snow we ski on, the rock is smooth and glacier-worn, as today's shrunken glacier still reached here as little as a century ago. Each irregularity in the terrain has become a sculpture. We push past black and green lichen-covered boulders whose snowcaps have been curled by sun and wind into fantastic mushrooms, fat curled snail shells, fedoras, huge crooked pillows. On another

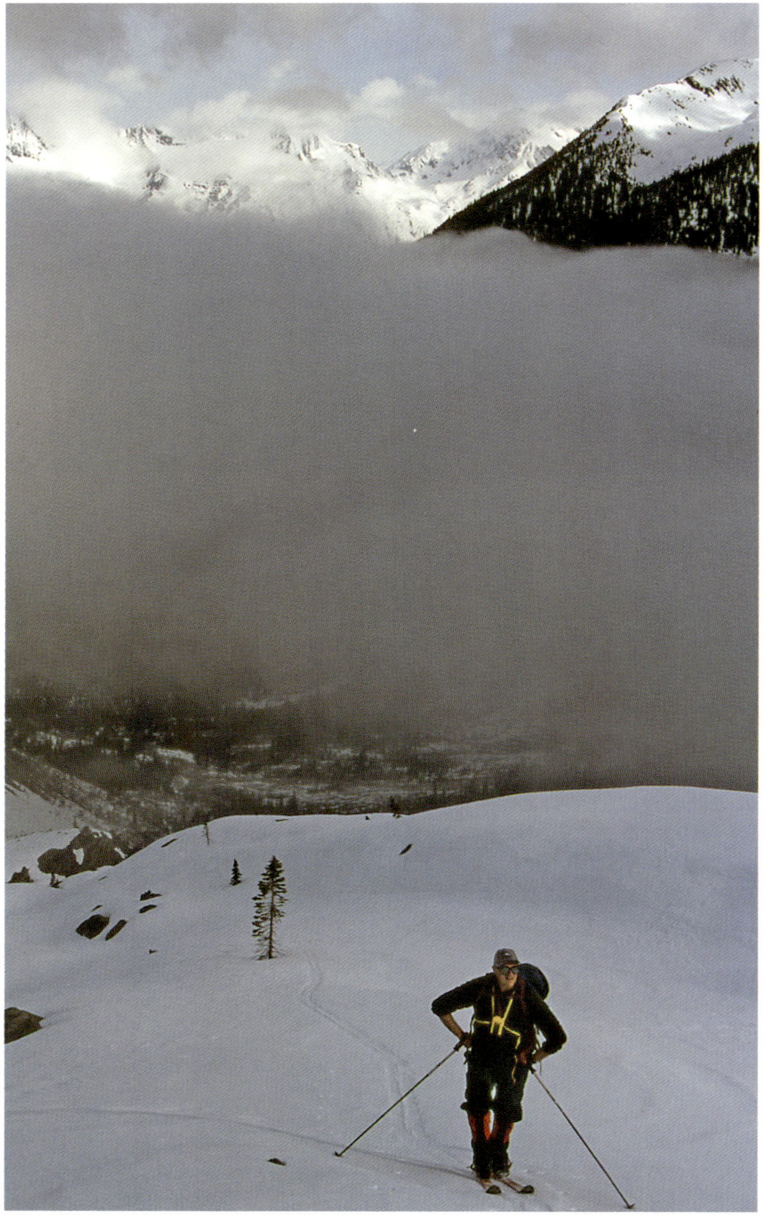

occasion, near a creek not far from here, I will come across a flight of tiny grey birds that appear as an ever-changing yet precise calligraphy on soft snow formations like these.

We have been on the trail an hour and the sky has lightened. Soon the sun will turn the upper slopes gold, pink and silver. Now the hard work is starting. My sweat carries bits of stinging sunscreen into my eyes. Maintaining stride, I pull the hanky I always keep in my ski pants' pocket and wipe nose and eyebrows dry. The inner cuff of my right boot chafes just above my ankle. Without slowing, I lean down and in one movement adjust the buckle just a fraction. Two hours. Three hours. Conversation consists of single short sentences squeezed out between deep breaths. Four hours. Time is passing, and Jim and I know that, far below us, the valley snow is beginning to soften and collapse.

A light breeze has sprung up. The sky is a jumble of clouds in motion, bringing first snow flurries then patches of blue. Playful snow devils whip among the trees leaving them nodding in agitation. Ice crystals, sparkling prisms, blow tinkling between my skis and out across the hard pack like tiny chimes. Stride follows stride, pole plants succeed each other, higher and higher, measuring the immensity of the glacier in the ache of muscles, the rhythmic sound of my own breath and the steady felt thud of the pumping in my chest. The sweat builds again ... and again is swiped away.

The slopes steepen, forcing us to zigzag. We make awkward step turns as we pass beneath great slanting rock walls ground smooth by the ancient passing of ice. To our right is the steep face of Lookout Mountain, its avalanche voice frozen quiet in the early morning cold. To our left is a jumble of cliffs, outcrops, ravines and crevasses. We'll be absolutely certain to avoid these on our way back down.

Spirits are rising, but energy levels are dropping. We've stopped only once to down great gulps of water coloured green and orange with flavour crystals. From the right pocket of my ski pants, where I always keep them, I extract a lime-flavoured candy. Breathing too hard to chew, I hold it between gum and cheek and let it slowly dissolve. The tangy liquor trickling down my throat seems extraordinarily delicious.

Now far above the highway, we look down to see moving dots wind their way along the valley floor. Surveying the islands of snowy pinnacles that poke up from the ocean of ice, I sense that some curious dimension

At ast, Jim skis out of the valley shadows and onto the open Illecillewaet Glacier. Just visible below is the bold line of the Trans Canada Highway at the high point where vehicles traverse Rogers Pass.

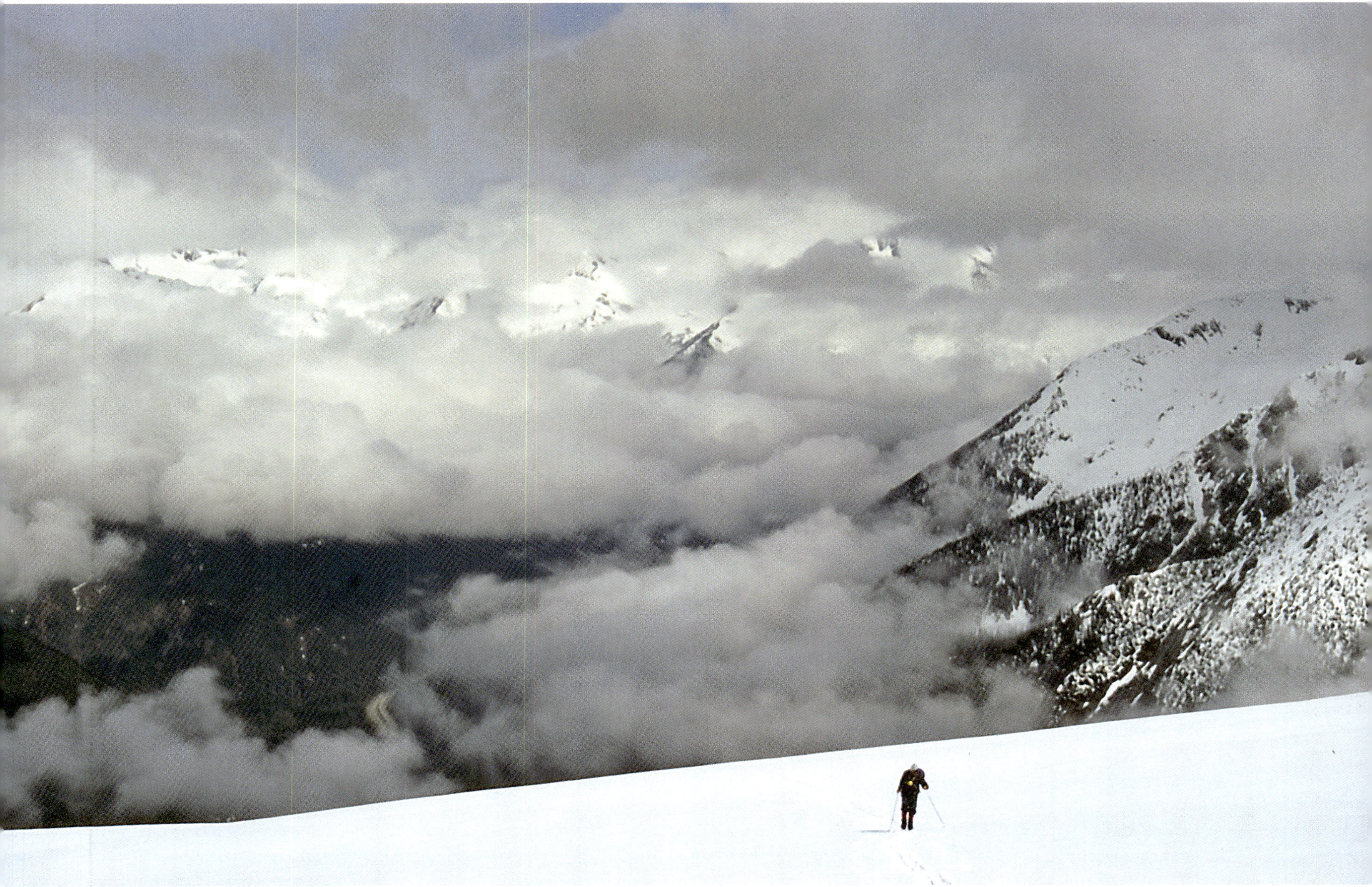

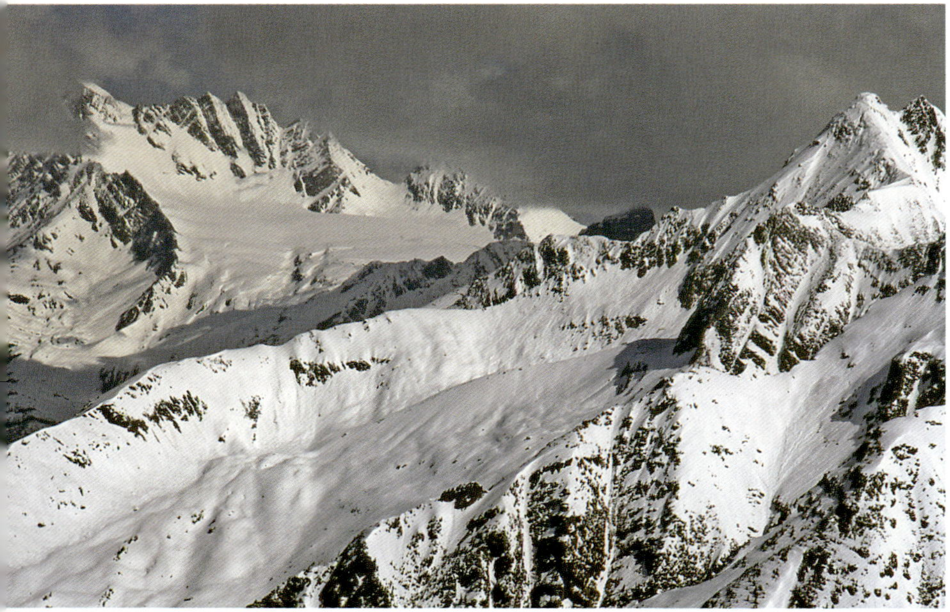

has been crossed. Across the valley, early morning cloud is dispersing to reveal a dramatic symphony of grey peaks and precipitous snow slopes.

At last, the steep climb is over. We emerge from deep blue shadow onto a brilliant glacial plain. Although my legs are leaden and I'm wondering how I'll keep up, our spirits are flying. The last kilometre, I follow Jim to a short, steep-sided outcrop that is our objective. Among the jumble of lichen-dark boulders, I drop pack, release bindings, and the world is at my feet. Jim pulls out the map. We identify the magnificent palisade in the distant west as Jupiter Peak. To the north, in a grand series of rock walls is the Hermit Range, the scene of many guided climbs at the turn of the last century. East, across the glacier we've just ascended, is the rough pyramid of Mount Sir Donald. And behind us is the vast glacial plateau of the Illecillewaet névé. Just beyond my outstretched legs, the rocks lunge straight down to the Asulkan River valley.

I arrange my gear so nothing will spin off into space and sit down. Blessed relief. During lunch we continually monitor conditions; in a couple of hours, we know, the snow in the valley will no longer support a skier's weight. So, reluctantly, we begin packing up. We peel off the climbing skins, don packs, and I step into the special bindings that allowed my heels to swing up and free in order to climb, but now, for the downhill run, will grab hold with a solid thunk. My stomach takes a couple of nervous hops.

Sunglasses are exchanged for goggles, which will protect my face, keep the wind off my eyes and snow from behind my glasses. I tighten the adjustable chest- and waistbands of my backpack to prevent it swinging side to side. With its contoured fit, the pack should move with and not against me—an extension of my body.

In contrast to the packed runs of resorts, the soft snow here will make skiing a little like riding a big ball. To maintain balance, my foot must be held very firmly in place, allowing every steering action to be precisely and positively transmitted from my legs to the boot/ski combination. I'll need to feel the pressure of my toes up toward the roof of the boot or down toward the sole. The subtle difference will, in soft powder, spell the difference between a great ride and a disastrous face plant. Taken with a sequence of knee flexion and extension to change the skis' shape on the snow, and a rotation and rolling of the knees to direct the steel edges, all together make it possible to overcome the apparent physical impossibility of turning two long, inanimate "boards." Which, of course, are not just boards, but highly specialized, bow-taut instruments of polycarbonate, fiberglass and steel.

But what is truly wonderful is that at a certain point on the descent, *we will be conscious of none of this.* All the hours of practice, years of fitness training, trial and error will vanish. Lost like master jazz musicians in a world of improvisation, we'll cross that mysterious juncture where analysis and techno-chatter become meaningless and nothing but the melody remains.

I try a couple of conservative turns to get the feel of the snow. My skis are restless, jumpy, a bit hard to handle. The little green LED on my avalanche transceiver winks at my chest like the belly light on a taxiing plane. I'm the pilot checking his preflight plan as I talk myself through my powder skiing checklist. *Arms down and flexed. Hands a little higher, wider apart. Should see your hands. C'mon, let's see the hands. Round shoulders a bit. Bend knees. Waaaay down. Drop butt. Suck in belly. Focus.* Wind on my face, I'm picking up speed. So far, we've been slipping down a gentle slope, crisscrossing our up-track. Ahead, and fast approaching, the slope takes a steep plunge. *Legs together, toes pull up, equal weight on the skis to start. Okay, let 'em run.*

And do they! They not only run, they hiss, each turn I carve shooting white spray arcs. I've crossed the boundary. I'm yipping. Wahoo! Faster. Vibrating. Smiling. In my head, there's music—all rhythm, no blues. Jim appears to my left, gaining then dropping behind, reappearing as we

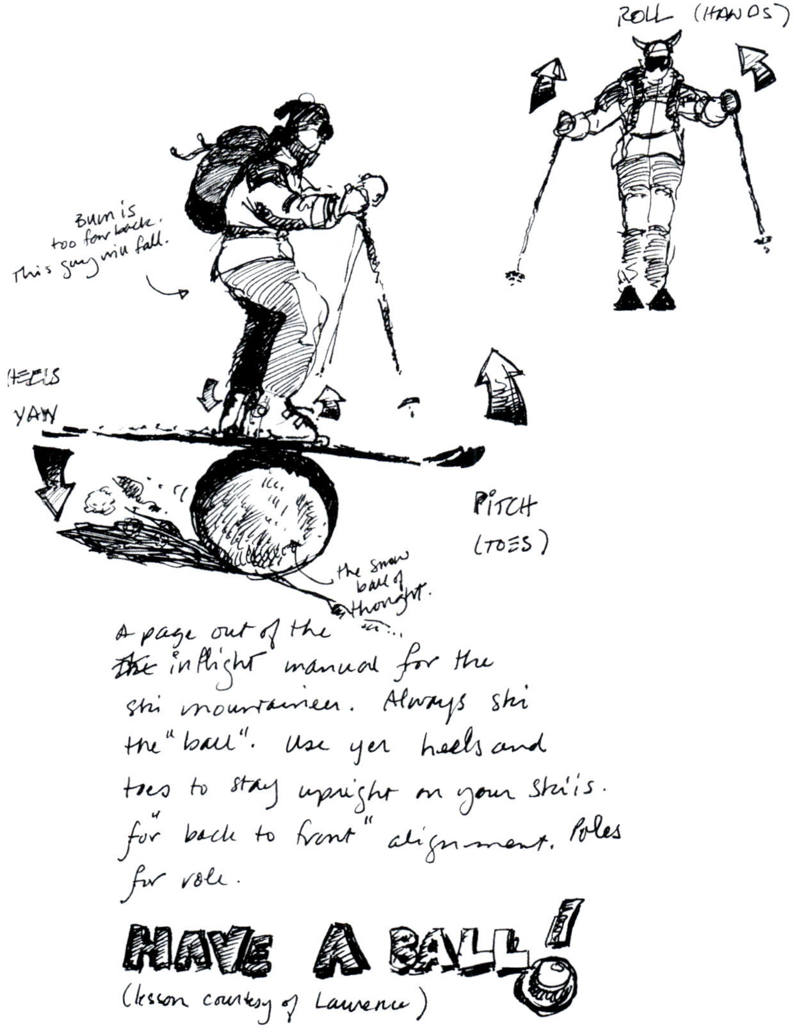

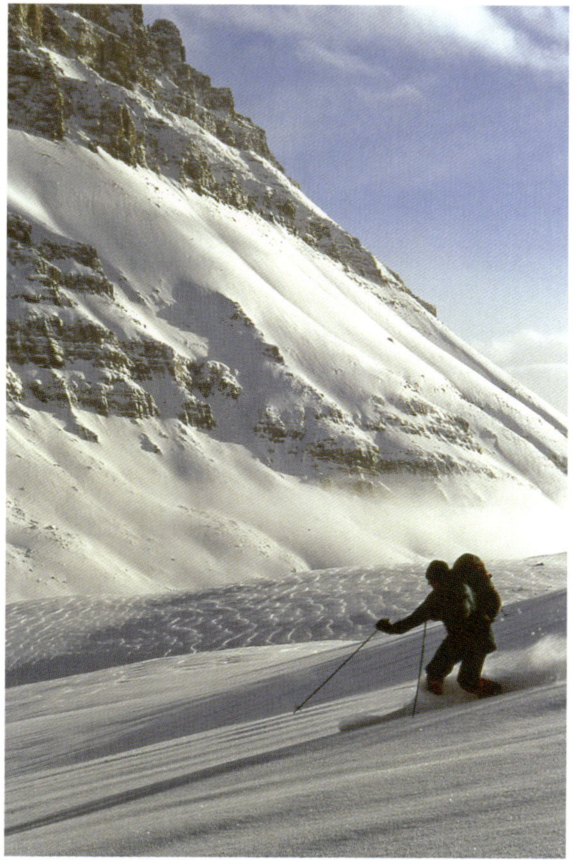

A telemark skier comes to a halt below the cliff bands of Dolomite Peak near the Banff-Jasper Highway.

Dr. Patrick Clarke, my ultra-fit mountain-biking next-door neighbour and sometime ski partner, is pedal to the metal and downward bound on the Asulkan Glacier, Rogers Pass.

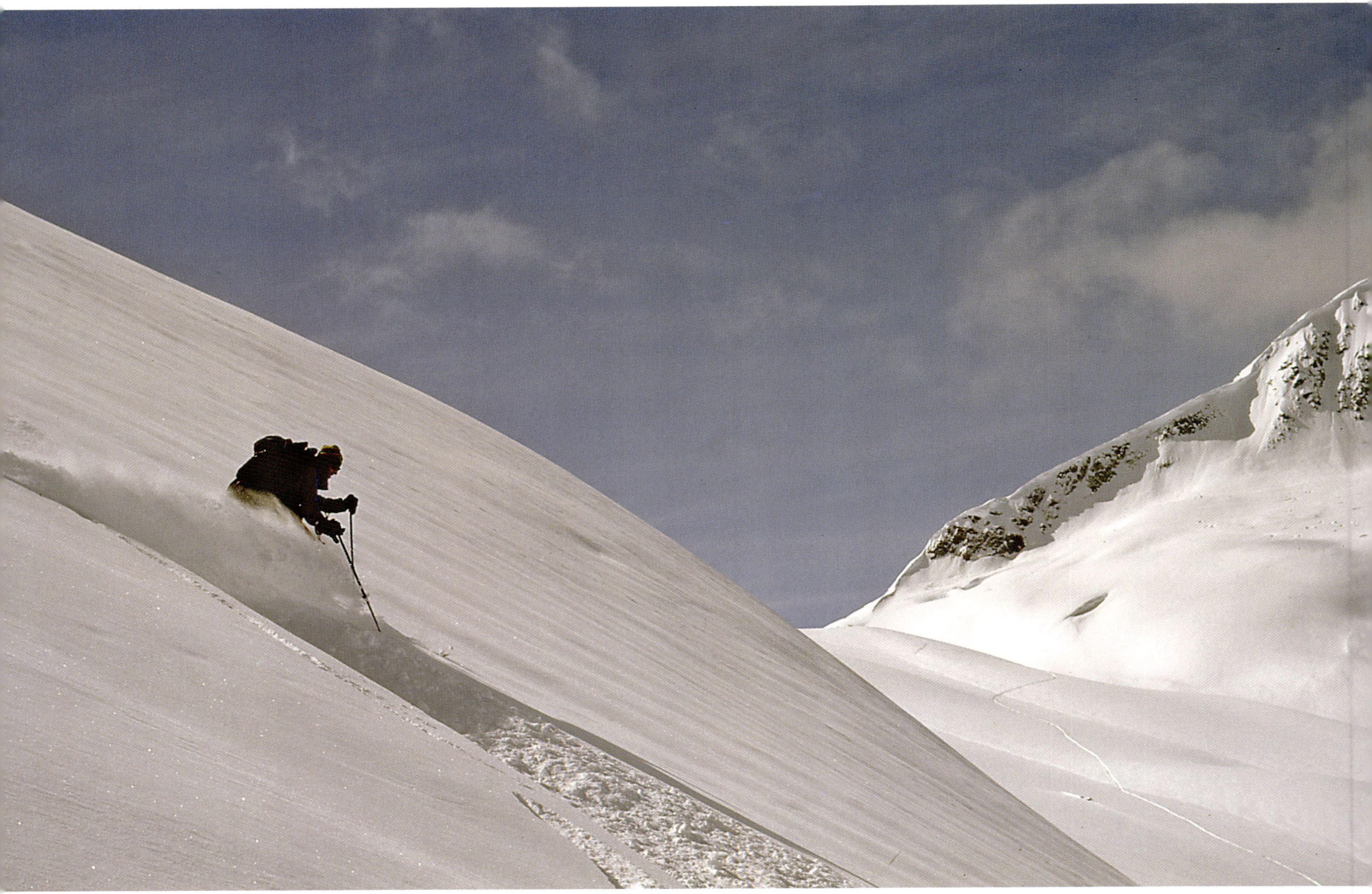

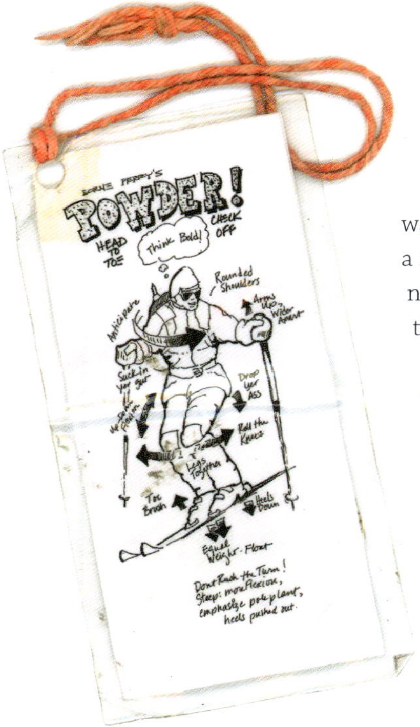

cross paths. Knees bend, skis flex—another turn launched. Faster still, galloping, full-tilt boogey. Green ridges once far below us mount upward. My jacket sleeves flap. I'm flung on a single trajectory from one turn to the next. We are lords of the dance, riding the rim of our white world.

The crevasses previously noted flash past on my right: zoooom, zip, zip and they're gone. To my left, ah yes, that extremely steep slope with its hidden holes. I steer centre. Turn, turn, turn. My muscles burn with exertion, and still the skis are drawn down. Up ahead the route vanishes over a steep-sided ridge. Flexing deeper, pressing harder on the heels, I force the skis' keen edges in deep and jump from turn to turn. Edge, jump. Edge, jump hard. The G-force sucks down, legs and skis power off again. Further and further down the valley we drop while around us the peaks grow steadily up. We ski a rapid rush of turns through shaded blue glades then down bright white open slopes. One minute we're twisting sharply through fissures in rocky outcrops; the next, dancing long easy S-curves over undulating terrain. At times we slow-pick our way down, stopping altogether to peer over a cliff, backtrack, find another way around.

Over to the left, Jim bounces and thumps along a fringe of old avalanche rubble. The air becomes warmer, the snow has softened to the point of being wet. A sticky quagmire, it sucks and slows our skis. When it tries to pull them apart, I fight back, pressing my boots tight together to form a ski toboggan. The result is what feels like a hip-swinging rumba. My knees are so deeply flexed I could be sitting on a low bench. Slide alder, fir, exposed rocks come and go.

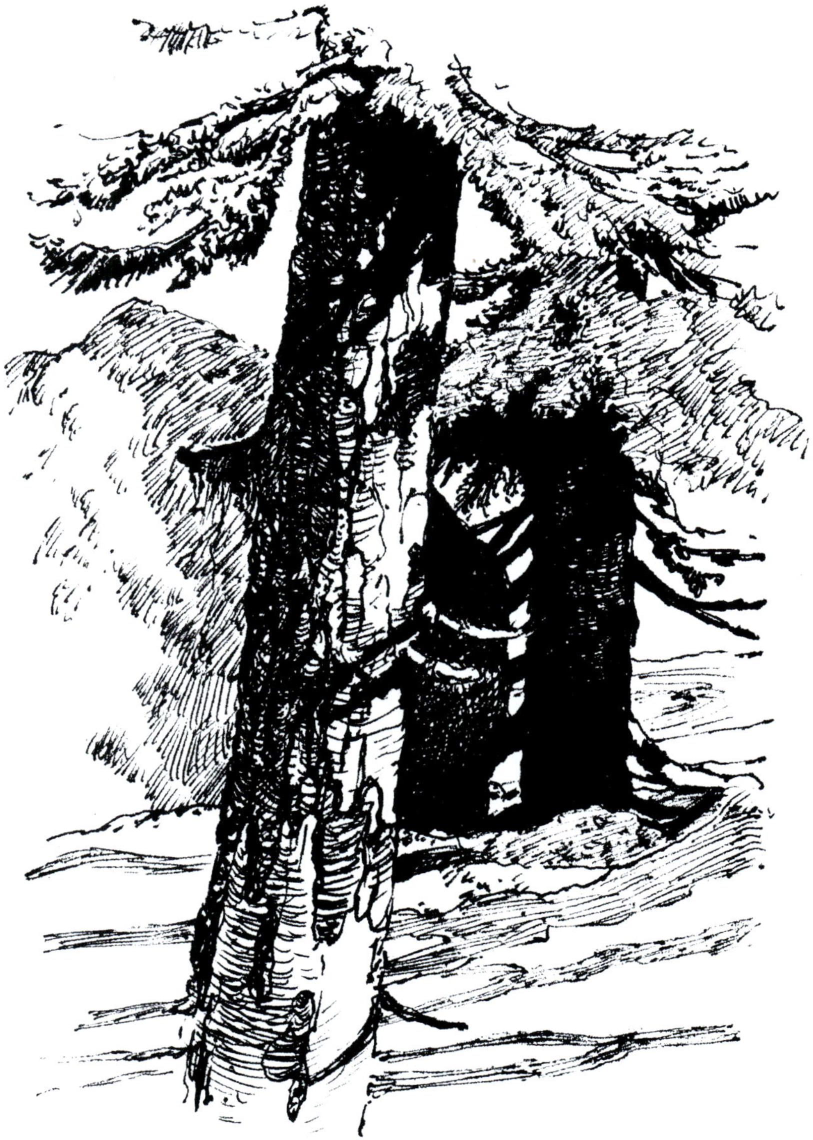

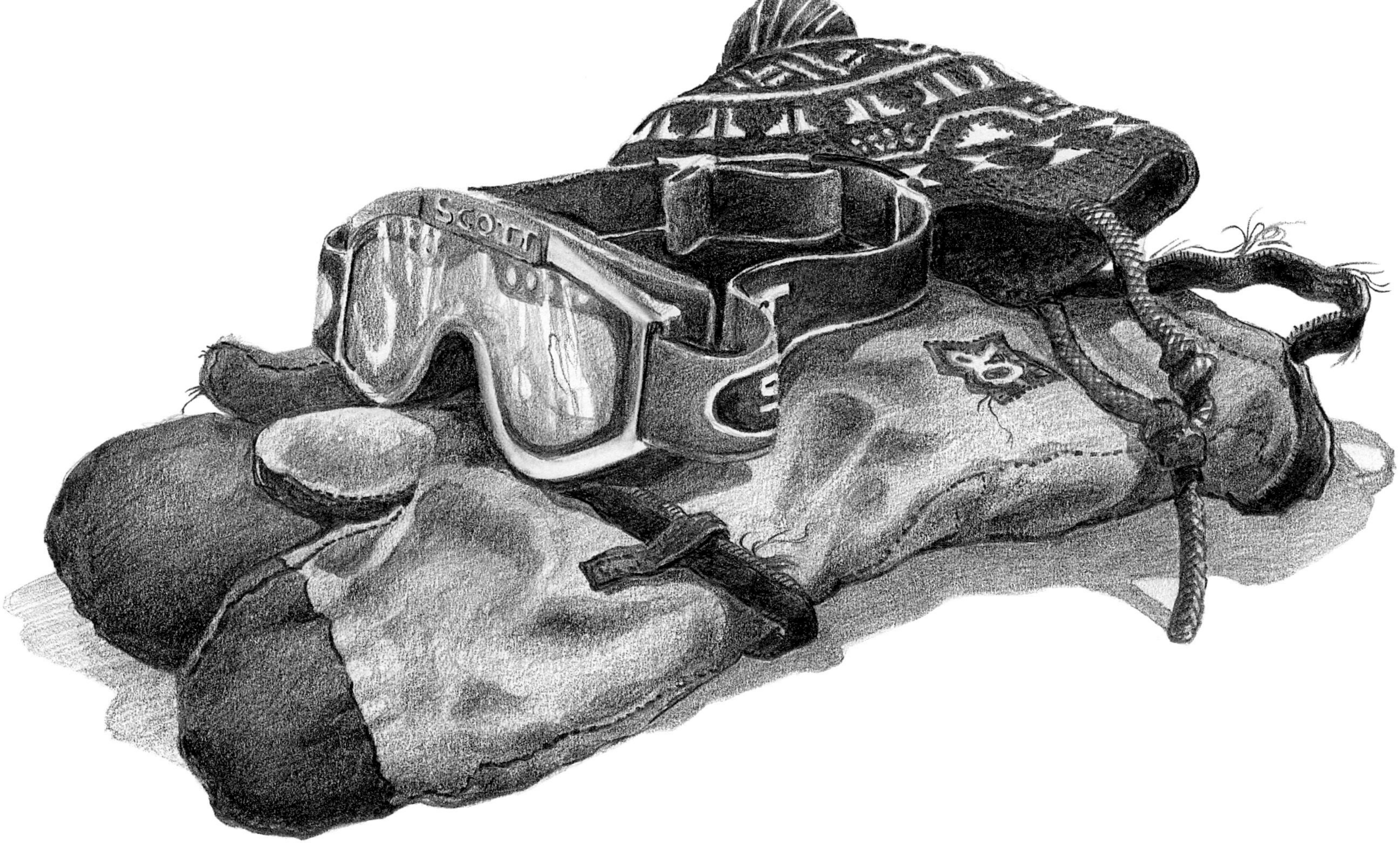
SCOTT

The slope gentles out. Like a bird flaring wing and tail feathers to come in for a landing, I make several fast, sharp turns, leaning the full length and breadth of the skis against the snow. In the same moment I come both to a halt and down to earth from paradise. Trees envelop me. I smell sweet alder buds and the tang of cedar. I pull off my goggles, blinking at the brilliance. Gone is the glacier's crisp chill. The big ride is over. In a matter of minutes, I've emerged from winter into spring.

So toque, mitts, jacket and goggles come off, replaced by sunglasses and baseball cap. Jim bursts into view on a wave of snow and flying branches. Puffing hard, working left and right in those quadriceps-killing, deep-genuflecting telemark turns, he swoops to a stop just upslope, filling the air with a damp snow-spray. He is smiling broadly. Like a pair of excited kids, we swap close-encounter stories as we slide off into the thick forest, following clearings and faint trails.

My throat is dry, and I'm thirsty. My thighs burn; I can barely hold myself up. But my senses are extra keen. The sun slants through the trees. Our skis cruise the shade-shot snow, with its straggle of twigs, wet lichen and cedar sprigs. We pass through invisible wisps of cool air and rich scents. At a bend in the trail, a steep bank reveals water below, clear and bright in the sun. A ginger-ale river slips silent over water-worn rock, then tumbles noisily into deep green pools, where it mumbles away to itself. Long shadows, green and navy, draw contours on its surface, not quite hiding the gold-flecked amber rocks beneath.

We drop through the forest, twisting and turning to avoid trunks and low-hanging branches. It's a quick partnerless polka: with pole plants and kick turns, my skis ride up and over large snow pillows, swish down chutes and suddenly are free of the forest and out on the open glades. I reach down, release the toe bindings and, on legs that may soon refuse to function, take the last strides to the cabin. I can smell its warmed logs.

A fresh breeze stirs the treetops. Off with the heavy touring packs and boots. On the sun-warmed, south-facing deck, I pad barefoot about the rough timber floor, wiggling my now-joyous, emancipated toes. From a snow bank cache, we extract ice-cold beer for Jim, Coke for me. After a long swig, Jim raises his eyebrows, smacks his lips. He casually examines the can as if it might contain some magical ingredient hitherto unknown to him. I pull on the tab of the pop can, which looks, at this moment, to be a work of art. It opens with a *pssshhht*. The sparkling liquid—exquisite elixir—pours down my throat. Settling down into old wooden chairs propped up against the cabin, feet resting on benches, we sip, talk and watch.

A black and amber butterfly flutters in to investigate, stopping now and again to examine our happy squalor. Strewn across the deck are wet gloves, toques, empty packs, a ski boot lying on its side, plastic bags, a half-eaten peanut butter and honey sandwich, jacket, goggles, an open bag of nachos and sodden climbing skins. The butterfly comes to a delicate

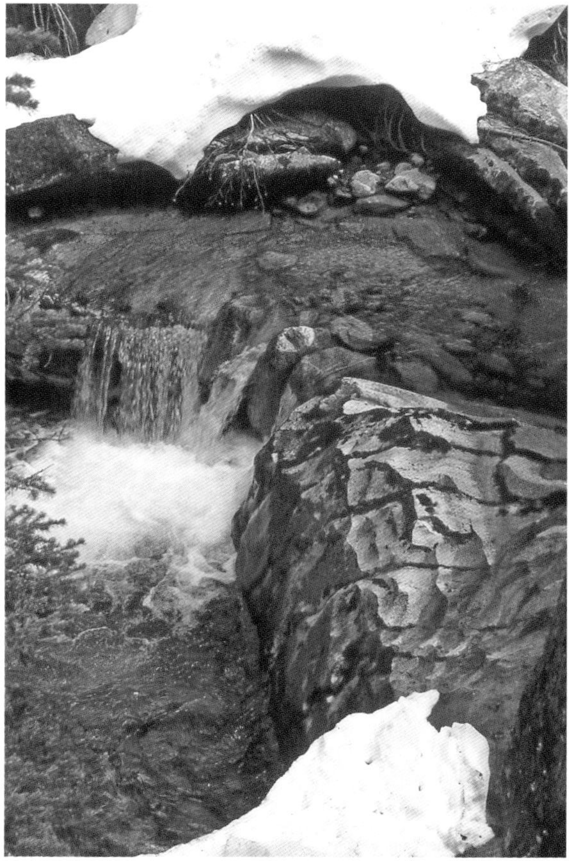

A ginger-ale river slips silent over water-worn rock, then tumbles noisily into deep green pools, where it mumbles away to itself.

stop on the cuff of Jim's ski boot, tasting the salty material with its long black proboscis, wings folding and unfolding. The Zen philosopher's paradox comes to mind: am I a man dreaming I am a butterfly, or the butterfly dreaming I am a man?

In the pensive late afternoon, time's passing no longer worries Jim and me. High above our heads, high above the darkening forest, shadows stretch long wings across the snowfields. Left up there, the electric sizzle of our preoccupied urban thoughts has ceased, blown away with the clouds over a wide, glacial plain. All that remains in their passing is this abiding peace.

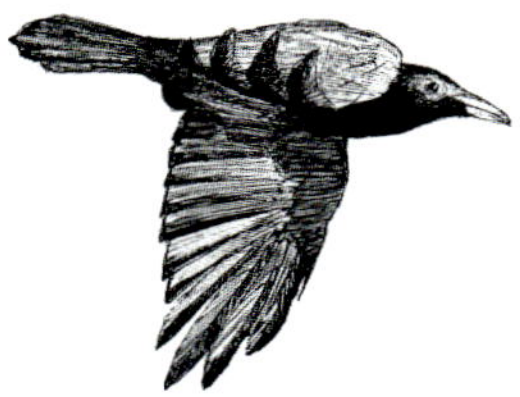

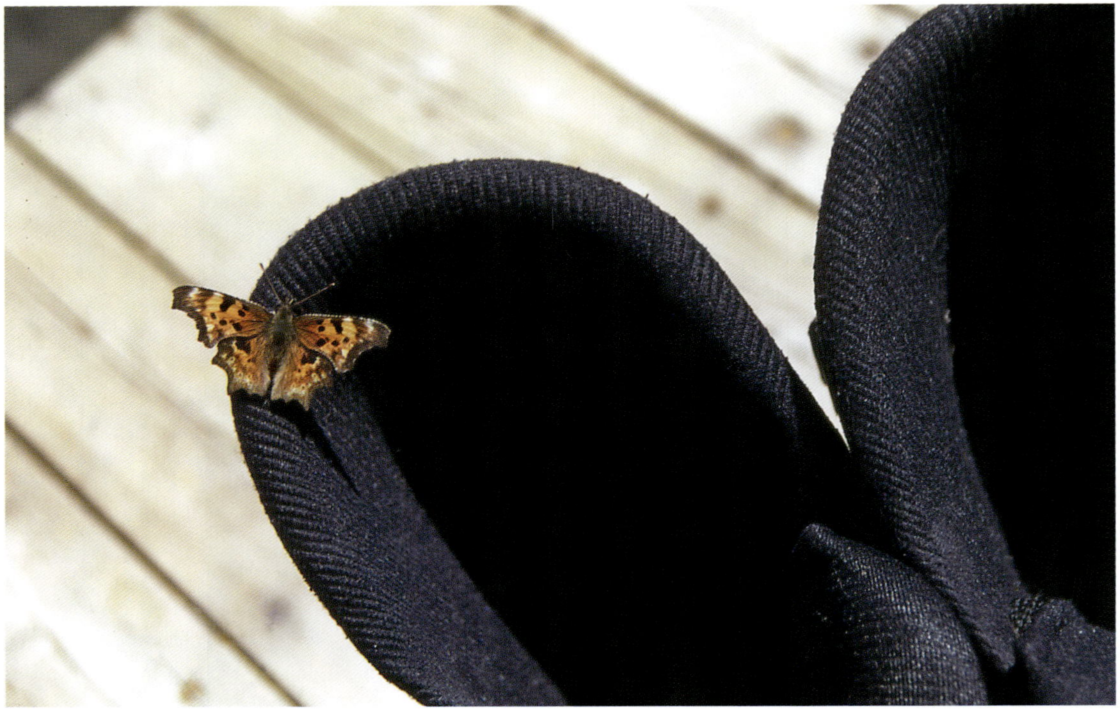

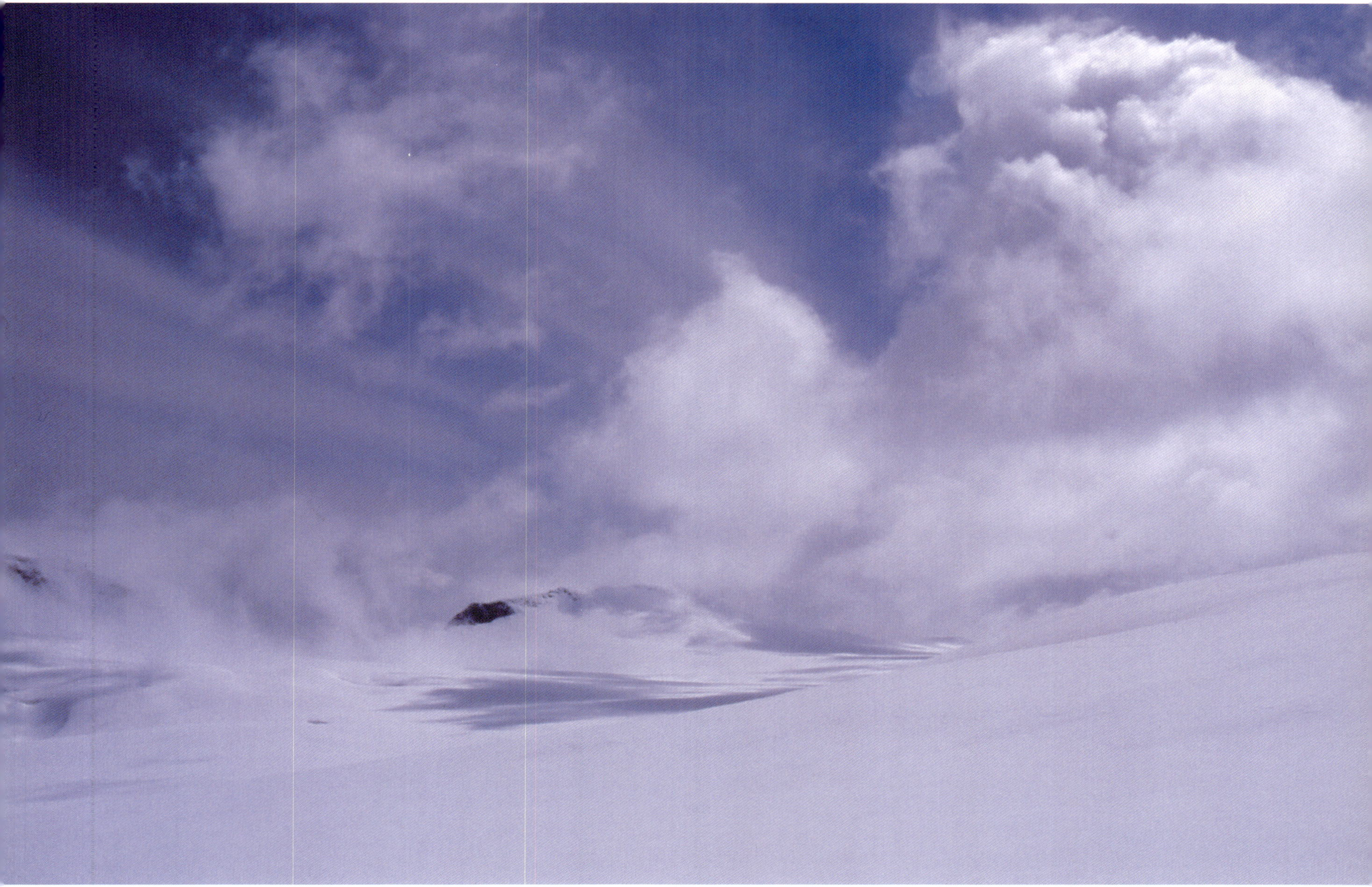

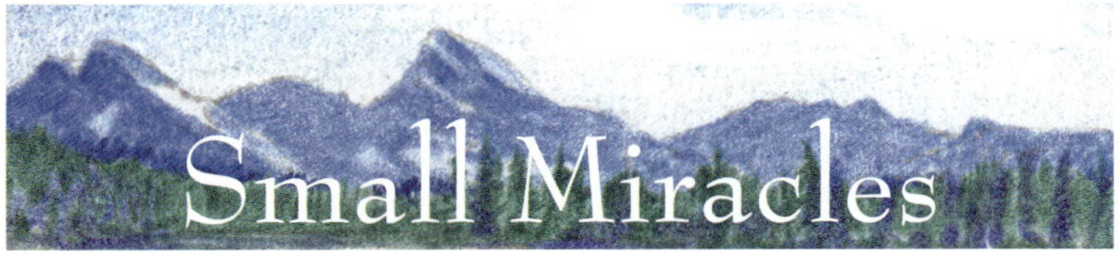

Small Miracles

THE SNOW CRUNCH, CRUNCH, CRUNCHED under my red mountaineering skis as I moved steadily along the crown of a snowy ridge. On a typical early spring morning high in the Rockies, the temperature was still a few degrees below freezing. Little Frisbee-shaped chips of snow, broken loose by my ski tips, upended and sizzled away down a precipitous gully. Glancing downward, my eye was drawn to a tiny speck—an insect—clambering across what must appear from its perspective a limitless, up-ended glacial plain studded with cliffs (pebbles), trees (pine needles) and arctic-like up-thrust ice ridges (crystalline snow). You'd think it would be dead. Frozen solid. Yet, there it was, pursuing its course, gamely defiant of the laws of science as I knew them. I stopped, released my ski bindings and knelt in the snow for a closer look.

What was this? Shouldn't this bug be dead or hibernating or maybe a larva or an egg or something? Unlike warm-blooded animals, insects have neither exothermic chemical reactions to keep muscles warm nor fat and fur to insulate them from the cold. Technically, it seemed, this little explorer should have been as solid as an ice sculpture. What kind of living thing could deny cold physics?

With my gloved hand, I picked up the intrepid traveller along with a little ball of snow. Using the ten power, hand-held magnifying glass I keep in my anorak pocket, I drew closer, until the subject filled my entire field of view. Truly bizarre. Fascinating, oddly repellant. My bright mountain world receded as I shrank in size and slipped into another dimension. I became the camera eye on a desolate, wild ice planet.

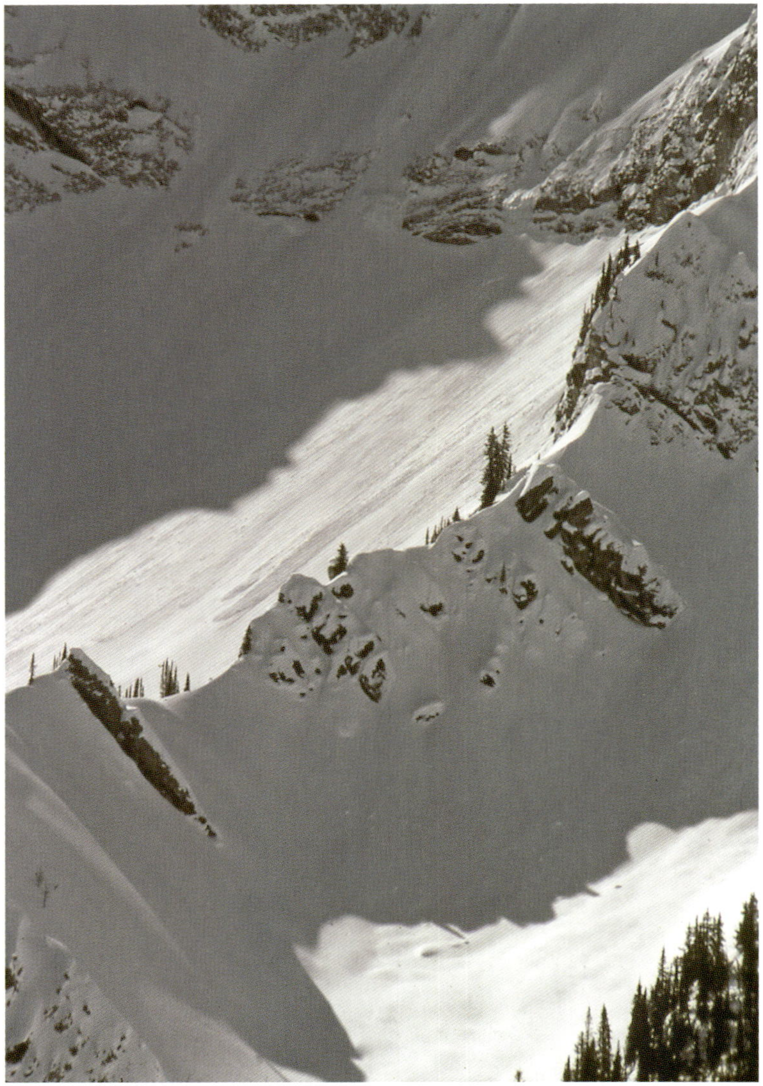

In the early spring, Mount Black Prince in Kananaskis Country offers the ski tourer spectacular open-slope and glade skiing. All, however, avoid the very steep slopes, which are prone to avalanche.

Background audio: low continuous rumble. Point of view: below and beside, panning the hull of a gargantuan insect, itself like a strangely organic intergalactic exploration craft. From the molded body armour protrudes an assemblage of mechanical and menacing devices: sharp bristles, projecting spheres, levers, domes and hooks. Long segmented legs obtrude high above the heavy hull. Like a monster mosquito minus wings, the brownish-grey translucent creature sports an upturned amber "horn" nearly twice the body's length. Between its expressionless eyes jut four segmented protuberances. The upper pair, probably navigational and sensing antennae, are tipped by two nodules. The mouth parts, similarly tipped, curve out and down. Short, sharp hairs poke from between the segments of its scaly carapace. At the juncture of thorax and abdomen on top of its hull sit two large, milky brown bulbs like radar domes, likely once wings, now apparently modified to assist with the complex job of maintaining balance on rough terrain.

The strange craft swayed slightly from side to side with each step, suspended on impossibly gangly legs that marched in triplicate on a deliberate northward course. Jolted out of my reverie by the imminent loss of the creature as it threatened to topple over the abyss of my palm, I detained it briefly in the service of art and science.

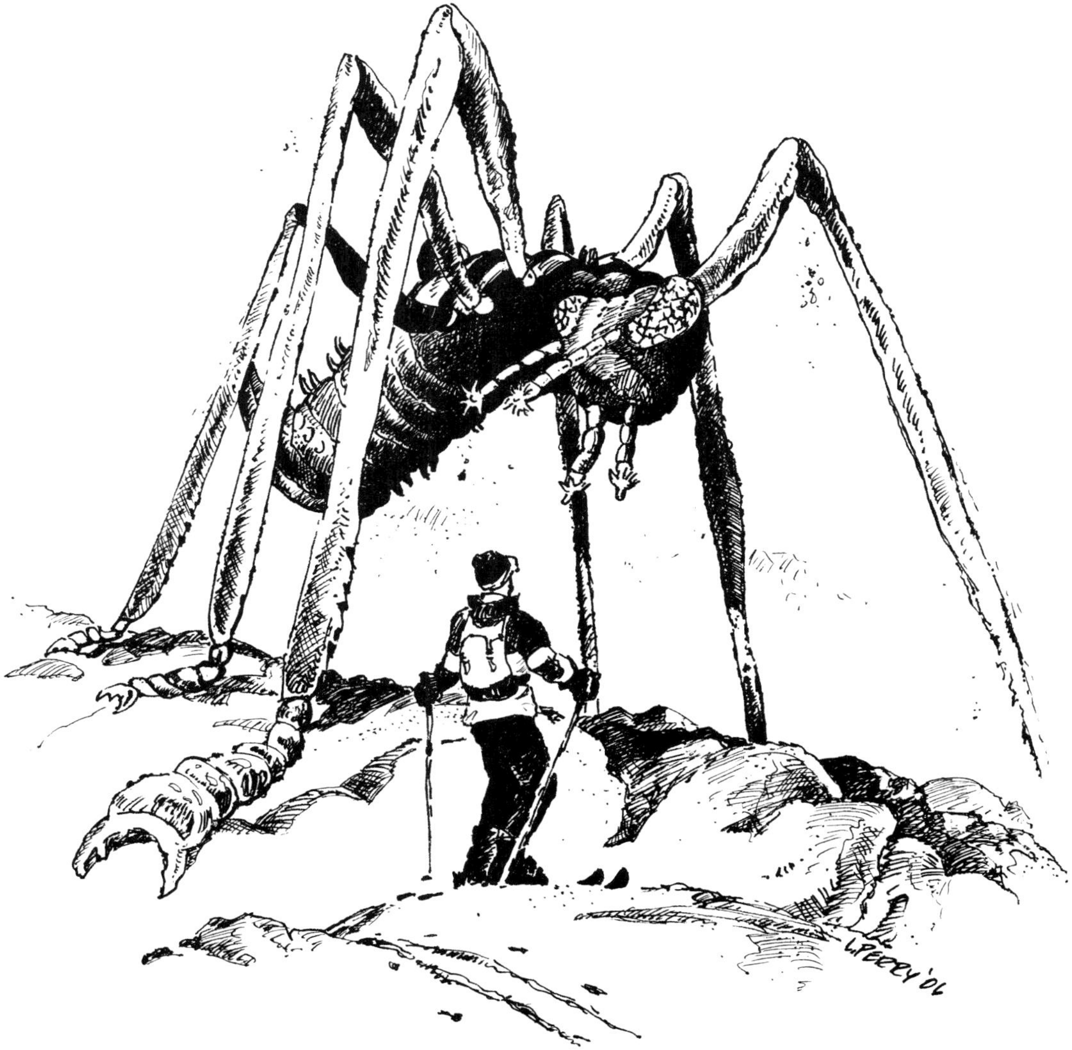

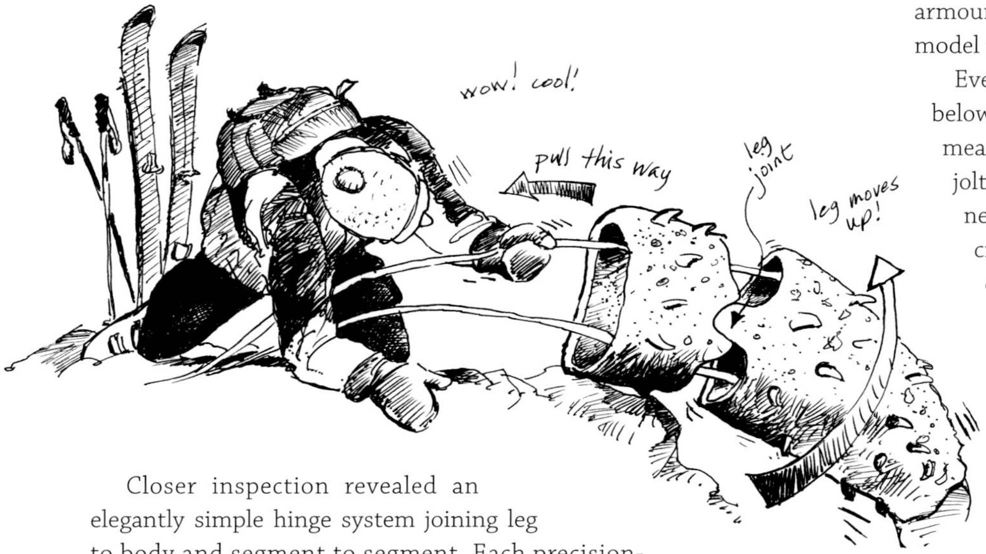

Closer inspection revealed an elegantly simple hinge system joining leg to body and segment to segment. Each precision-engineered joint consisted of a double hinge with attachments on either side that, when pulled, formed a lever that swung the leg. These in turn were set at angles to provide the correct propulsion with each stride. Instead of feet, a series of shorter, articulated segments terminated in a double crab-claw hook.

Subsequent thumbing through Ben Gadd's *Handbook of the Canadian Rockies* revealed this as one of the Rockies' small miracles. To skiers, the wingless snow crane fly, or chionea, is an innocuous (it doesn't suck blood or sting) small, dark bug about 10 millimeters long, usually found crawling over the snow's surface between October and April, sometimes at remarkably low temperatures. In other seasons and at lower altitudes, it's darkly reclusive; literally "going underground," it hangs out in the form of egg and larvae in the burrows of ground squirrels and other small rodents. Exquisitely adapted for cold, mountain winters, it literally "can't take the heat" in sun-warmed valleys filled with ravenous predators.

The fly's astounding ability to remain active in extreme cold (as low as -20°C) is due in part to its ability to flood its tissues with glycerol, a thick liquid. Basically, antifreeze. Miracle one. A similar strategy is employed by a less successful terrestrial exploration device, which also claims body armour and no insulation. In design features, though, the contemporary model of snow crane fly has a few million years on the car.

Even more bizarre, Gadd reports that, in fact, "at temperatures well below freezing the body of the snow crane fly is super cooled. This means that the insect is subject to instant and complete freeze-up if jolted." Picture this. It's winter. You're walking along with your partner, when s/he trips on a small rock. If humans were like the snow crane fly, *boink*, your partner would instantly freeze, rigid as an ice cube. For the fly, avoiding the above scenario requires the techno-magic of walking *carefully*. Typically, insects use their six legs in alternating groups of three. The front left, middle right, and back left move simultaneously with each step, roughly forming a triangular support on the ground. Likewise, the remaining three legs. Replace feet with hooks, and insects become the ultimate all terrain vehicle, able to traverse extremely rough ground right-side up and upside down with equal ease. Maintaining the stable platform at all times, the body avoids jolting.

Miracle two. Envious of Mother Nature's success, and imitation being the most sincere form of flattery, resourceful NASA design engineers, in fact, tried the same thing with the prototypical Mars rover. Eventually, though, the idea was abandoned; the design was simply too complex.

But wait, that's not all. Dr George Byers, clearly a man to revel in the exploratory journey and undeterred by just plain weirdness—even while it involved crawling around in the snow—is reported by John Schrock in the *Kansas School Naturalist* as having made an even stranger discovery about one species of crane fly. He noticed "a ring-like capsule around the neck, thin walled and somewhat the shape of an inner tube of an automobile tire." A microscope-assisted drawing clearly confirms this detail. Using a needle, he discovered that the necklace-like object could be rotated freely but could not be removed from the head. Further probing revealed that the mysterious tube was full of tiny, developing round worms. Nematodes,

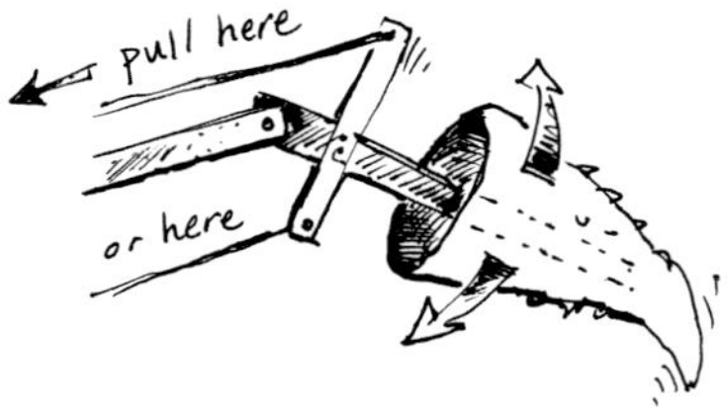

specifically. The theory goes that these tiny freeloaders slowly mature while in transit. Having thus been transported to an appropriate ground burrow, they hatch and parasitize the resident rodents. Miracle three.

Still, nothing in the scientific literature could have prepared me for the tiny life drama that played out on my gloved palm. I expected the insect to find the black fabric of my glove a welcome, warm island in an icy world. But no. Each time its carefully extended front leg moved off the ball of snow to touch warm fabric, the fly recoiled as though burned. Repeatedly, it took tentative excursions from the periphery of the snow microcosm, and repeatedly performed the same sequence: reach out, explore tentatively with left front leg, recoil from the heat of my hand, move one step counter-clockwise, try again. The whole sequence took the fly completely around the snowball's equator. The circumference fully traversed and having detected no opportunity for escape, the tiny explorer retreated to the highest point of its known world and stood motionless.

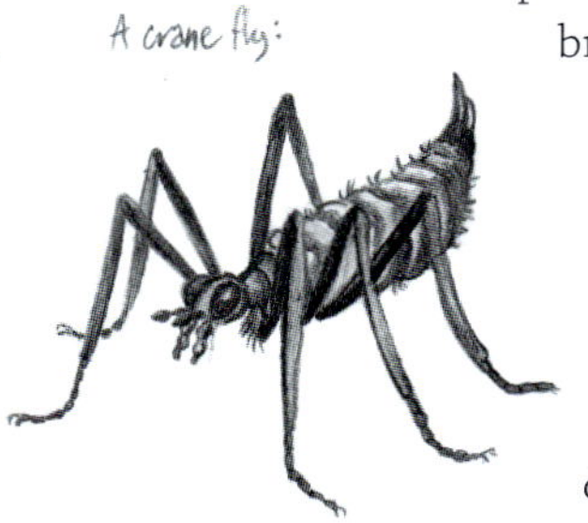

How to interpret this? A miniature robot, product of an artificial intelligence somewhere on the other side of the galaxy? A machine whose organic on-board computer, having exhausted all memory-banked options, had simply powered down? Yet, I felt some distant brotherhood with this mechanical thing. I intuitively understood its search for freedom, its resignation at discovering there was none. I sensed we were variations on a distant but related theme—cut from the same cloth, just different parts of the pattern.

This tiny creature, mini sojourner from the dawn of time, finding every route to safety blocked, was now utterly devoid of solutions. As though its senses had imploded, it could only wait on the margin of its own consciousness for fate to intervene. I set the snow crane fly and its little white asteroid down on the snow and resumed my journey. As did the crane fly, on exactly the same heading as when I had so rudely interrupted its day. How did it know which way to go? Just another small miracle.

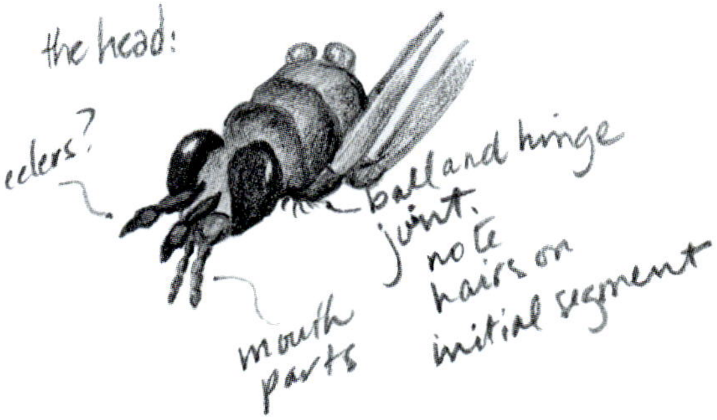

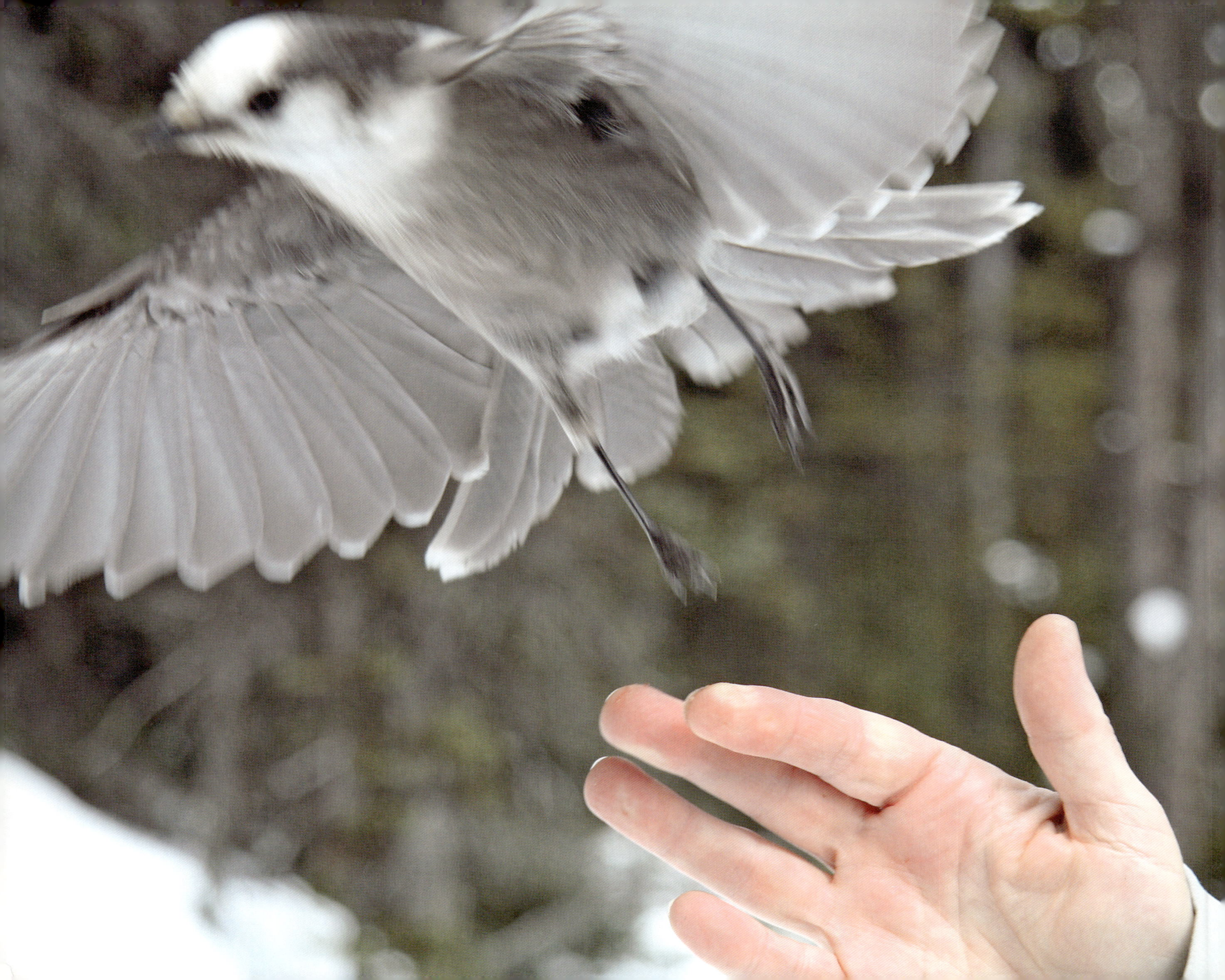

The power of one

CHAPTER 6

"To get some of the spirit power of nature and to find a protector through life you must go out alone on a guardian spirit quest."

CHIEF JOHN SNOW, NAKODAH

"I wish you wouldn't do that."

ALICE PERRY, MY MOTHER

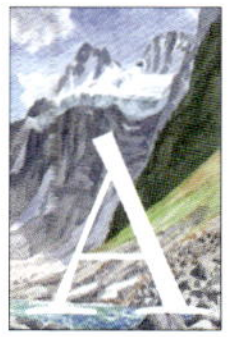

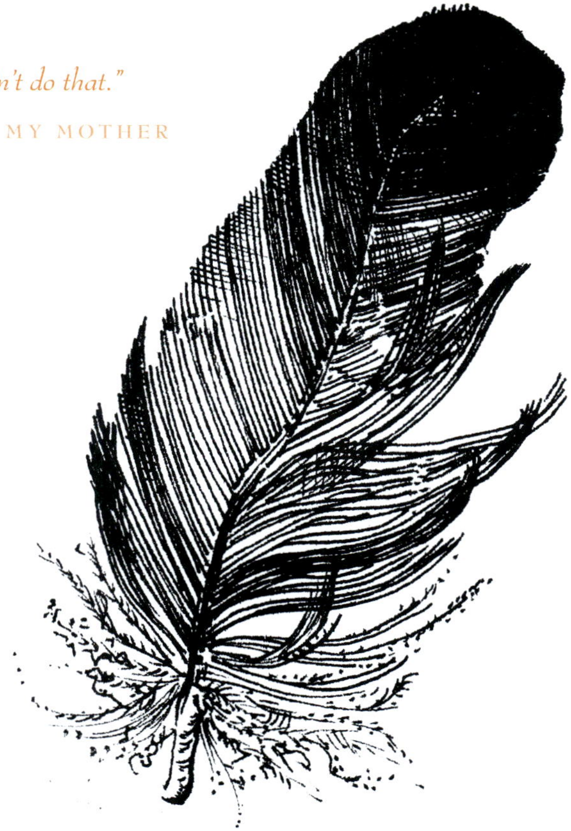

Alone in my old Dodge van, I pulled in at the trailhead and cut the engine. The whine of tires, gravel hammering on the rusting undercarriage, wind whistling through the duct-taped roof rack abruptly ceased. Complete peace. I became aware of the soft wind sound in the treetops, warm sun on my face, the scent of spruce gum on the cool morning air, bird song. Grey jays, known as "whiskey-jacks" from the Cree mythological figure Weesakejac, were patrolling the forest perimeter, one eye open for unguarded lunches provided by the occasional human visitor. Whiskey-jacks belong to the corvid family, which includes the raven, crow and Clarke's nutcracker. Brazen, precocious, seriously smart, whiskey-jacks co-habit well with humans in the backcountry thanks to their special talent for "working the crowd."

I sat down on a high bank of snow left by the plow and opened my lunch. Knowing one of the whiskey-jacks had sensed opportunity, I held out my hand, index finger extended. The jay turned its head one way then the other, fixed me with a single, shiny black eye. Then it made its leap of faith.

What followed took my breath away. With a few wing beats his body rose. Flight feathers outstretched, in a flash he made a quick gliding dive,

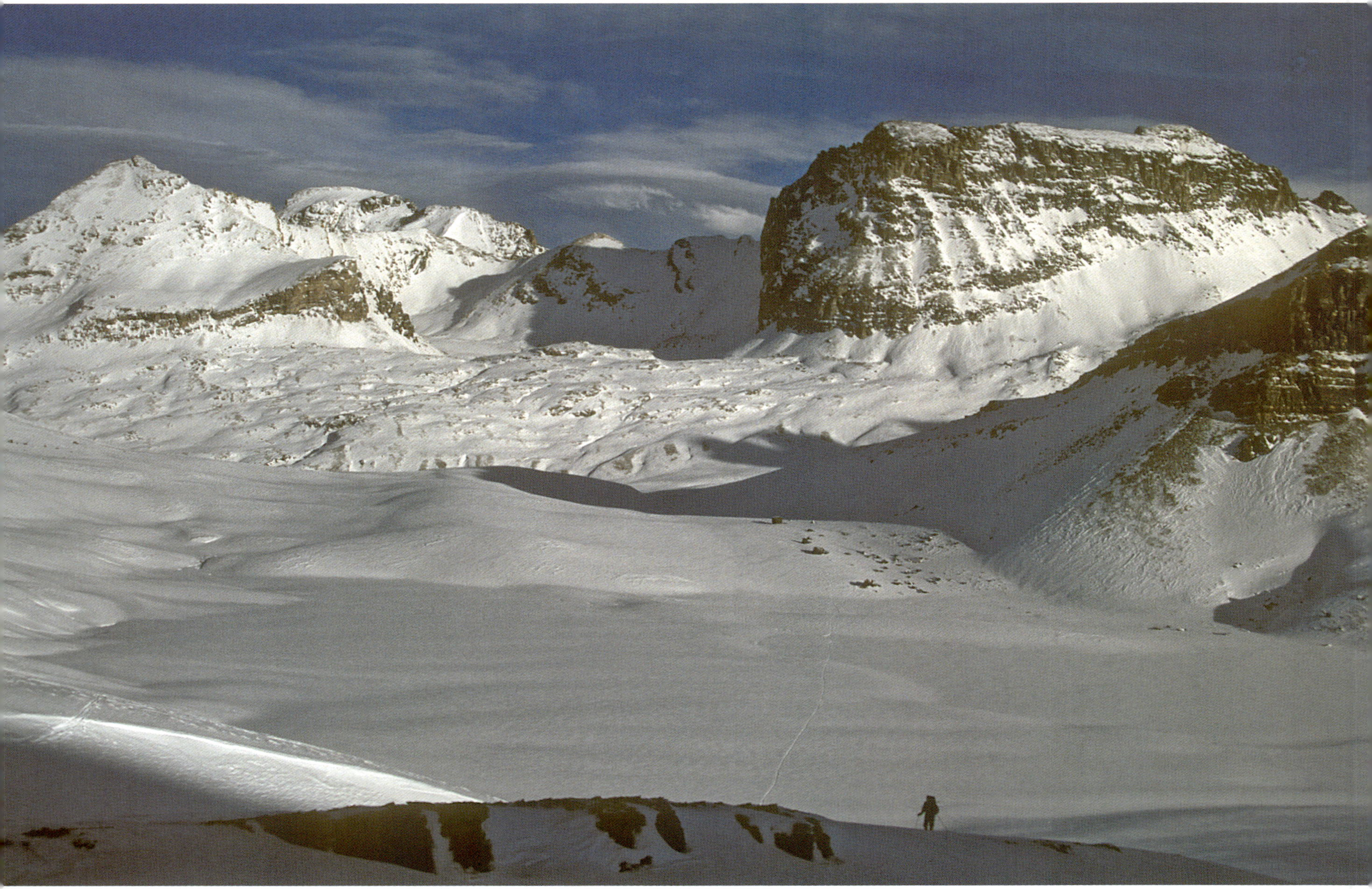

rose up and flew straight toward my hand. This glide, dive, flare sequence was repeated several times in short succession. It was clear the jay knew even at speed and distance exactly where he would land. Precision and grace—his path was a perfect arc, a calligrapher's master stroke. As the jay approached, those black-trimmed grey and white feathers were busily adjusting his trajectory mid-flight. Then, with a quick nervous feint left, a little right, tail down, feathers spread, legs extended, he landed. And with a surprisingly light touch—this tiny feathered body no heavier than a few coins. All eyes, flapping energy and action, without invitation he helped himself to my lunch, hastily breaking off bits of bread, rolling them between tongue and bill, coating them with a drop of saliva then fitting one piece after another into the impossibly large stash of plunder in his bill. I watched his black, wrinkled legs and felt the tight nip of his claws. I could sense the vibration as he posed nimbly on my finger, bobbing his tail now and then for balance. Curious about his trust and tolerance, and somehow fundamentally wishing to shrink our communication gap, I raised and lowered my hand with the jay still on board. He hunkered down, deploying wings now and then for balance, tightened his grip and merely glared. With my thumb I gently pressed his toes, one foot then the other, momentarily to my finger. He shifted his weight from one leg to the other, freeing each lightly pinioned toe—tug, tug—before fixing me anew with those bright eyes. I drew my hand up close to my face. We eyed each other, and for a brief moment there were just us two.

Another leap and he was gone—a progressively smaller and smaller figure in the forest. After a few seconds' search he found the perfect spot high in a spruce. Prying a scale of bark out just a little with his beak, he deposited the ball of food. And repeated the process. Hundreds of future meals would be stored this way and, according to biologists, very few forgotten.

What's a moment like that worth? Would it have even happened had the parking lot been full of cars and people? And if so, would my experience have been as memorable or intense? On several solo trips in the mountains I've noted the remarkable difference it made to be alone, intrigued by the unique, strong insights this point of view brought on. With the jay, as I stood still, I grew conscious of his grace of movement. As I stayed absolutely quiet, I took in his *wheer-oooh! wheer-ooooh!,* heard the wind in his flight feathers and the *click, click* of his working bill.

What was it that makes being alone so different than being in company? Is it that I customarily define myself against others' reactions? Or that, with others, I focus on them? Both reasons have merit, but there's more: when I'm alone I somehow become just another part of the picture, another shape, another form, like a rock or tree. Neither separate nor different.

That day in the remote parking lot, as I stopped moving quickly, I became aware of elemental movement all around. Being still, I sensed motion. As I became silent, I grew that much more conscious of sound. And I heard well. I could hear other things speaking to each other and, if

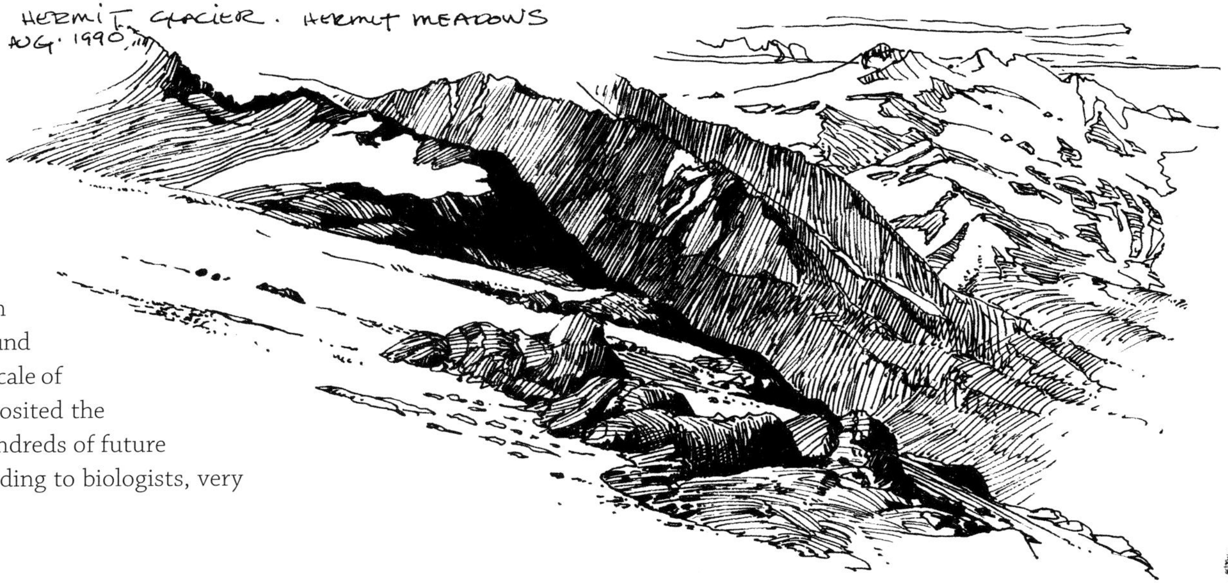

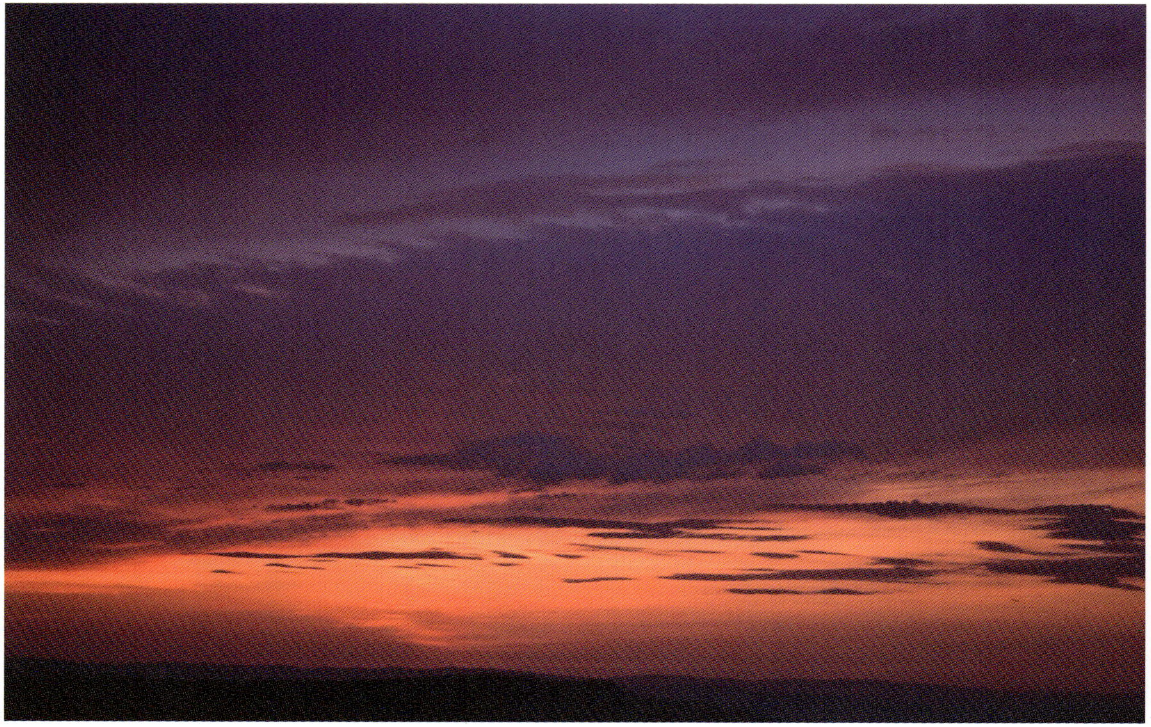

very fortunate, to me. My language of words abandoned, I could listen to the languages of other living things. Of course, my experience was nothing new. Many walk a similar road, and have done for a very long time!

Imagine yourself a creature possessed of flight, resting momentarily in the upper limbs of the old spruce trees on the lower slopes of Mount Yamnuska, at the place where the prairies and foothills roll up against the grey limestone wall of the Rocky Mountains. It is just before dawn, summertime, and the air is cool, moist and redolent with pine. The stars are vanishing, and the blue-black sky is slowly turning from soft rose to brilliant yellow. Fly north, skimming the treetops, up over the long open shoulders of the foothills then down into the dark vale behind. Ride the cool breeze up again to a place where the sheer cliffs meet dark forest ridges. Circle down and find a small, flat rock balcony facing east just at treeline. All creation is spread below you—tan prairies, gold rivers, gray green forests and ridge upon hazy ridge stretching out to the horizon. The mountains at your back raise an immense protective wall, while the distant, eastern rim of the earth drops away at your feet. The first rays of white-hot sun warm your face and throw long beams across this ancient site.

To this place, and others like it, many have been drawn on a guardian spirit quest. Alone, through fasting and contemplation, they've sought personal strength and guidance. On this solid limestone esplanade you can see the evidence: a small circle of stones encompassing the charred coals of a fire long cold. Nearby, a smaller stone circle rings a few special objects—a brightly coloured pebble, a feather matted with morning dew,

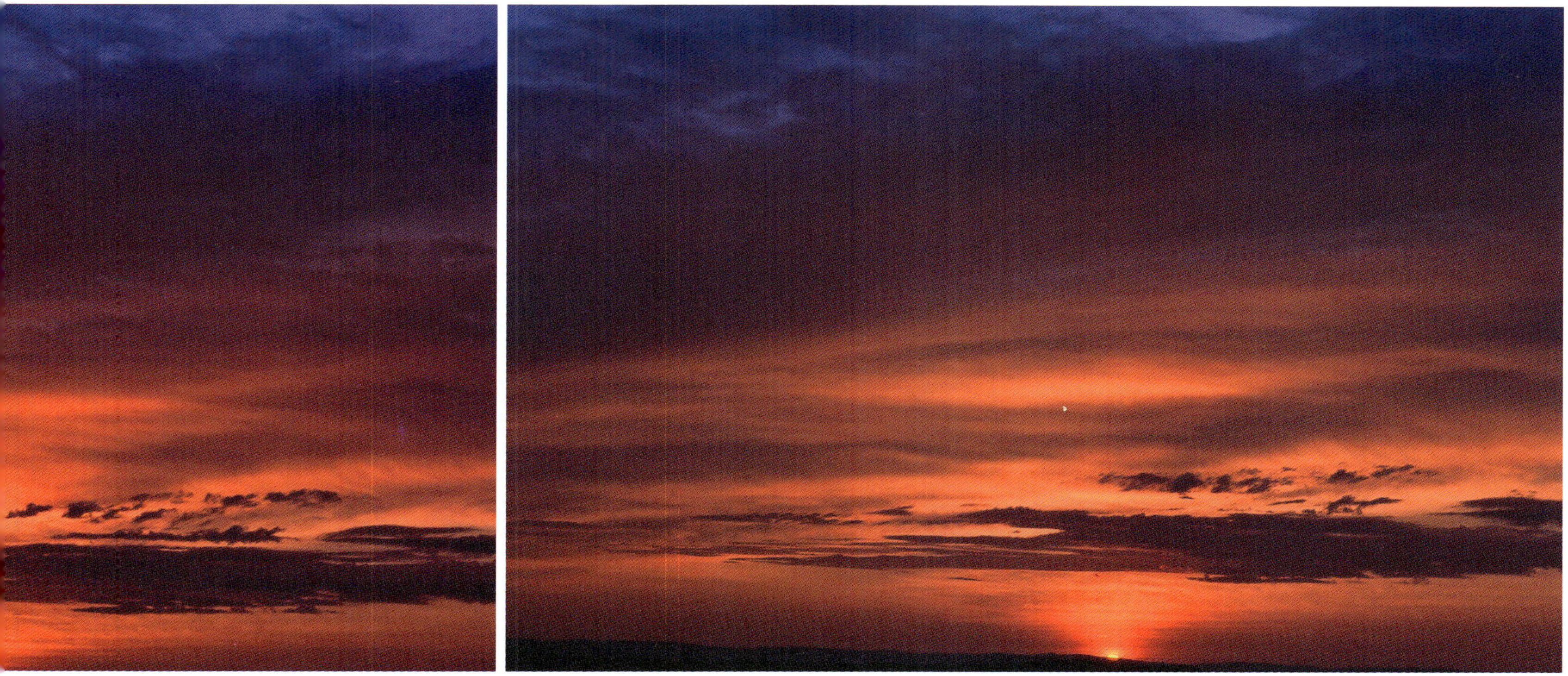

Alone on the east ridge of Mount Yamnuska, I am sole witness to this spectacular daily event known as sunrise. Admittance is open to all and absolutely free.

some weather-worn wood. For personal growth, special communion, self-realization and renewal, the solitary quest has for millennia been a required course on the First Nations' curricula of life.

BEING ALONE IS A POWERFUL INSPIRATION TO CREATIVITY. "The act of recording a life," writes Hannah Hinchman in *A Trail through Leaves*, "is also the act of creating a life." A master of the illuminated journal, Hinchman describes her work as a path to place. Not just any place, but *place*—that is, a place in the heart. For me, that is the limestone triangle. I love the light on the mountain shapes: the contrast of light and shadow on high cliff faces, the subtle blue-greys and deep greens of icefields, the hazy blue of high peaks on a fall afternoon. These I experience as moments of crystal clarity. And I'm driven to record them—as photos and journal entries of pictures and words.

Often my subject is evocative but fleeting, an effect lasting just a few seconds. Then there's a mad rush to set the camera, jot the idea, sketch the lines. Sometimes I sit for hours, long after the shadows I'm drawing have vanished, until I can barely see the page in the fading light and stiffened muscles refuse to let me stand up. Creating art fosters an immediacy—instantaneous, tactile feedback. I feel my hand brush the soft, textured paper as a tree, cliff or feather emerges in expressive graphite lines. And simplicity—all I need is a pencil and paper. Because the act of drawing obliges me to halt my incessant movement to first assess, gauge, reflect, test and observe, I see much more than I would otherwise. In marked contrast to my average urban day, this is a sensually rich experience. An artist must proceed as if there were all the time in the world, and the result is the great pleasure of knowing a particular view well, of seeing the world in a blade of grass. I rarely forget the places I've stopped to draw. Each drawing forever marks that place as special, giving me the sense I've captured a small piece of time. Years later, these drawings allow a new kind of communion—with the younger person who set them down.

MIDNIGHT ARRIVAL. I turn into a side road off the Banff-Jasper highway. Tomorrow's goal: to ski alone to the summit of Mount Olive on the Wapta Icefields. The moon casts long shadows across the silver-grey snow. Between the tall, dark shapes of spruce, a porch light glows. Just audible above the creek's gurgle is a diesel generator's thrum.

Inside the elegantly simple Num-ti-jah Lodge (a log structure on a stone foundation built by Jimmy Simpson, an early guide and outfitter in the area), cheery light illuminates the rustic interior with its red-upholstered furniture. The sitting room is filled with comfortable old chairs; photographs and paintings of the mountains hang on the walls. I move around, peering at the soft black and white photographs framed in dark hardwood hung here and there. Faces, stopped in time, peer back, the folk who built the lodge and their family—direct and hardworking, tough and courageous, unpretentious, hopeful, free of doubt. That faint tink and click is the rock and metal fireplace beginning to cool, its last red embers collapsing in white ash. It is easy to imagine this place back when travel was more genteel, a lively evening soirée having just adjourned. All the guests from New York, London and Montreal, replete with dinner and aperitifs, have retired to their rooms, leaving behind just the spirit of the evening in the dying fire.

In the van that night, steadily inhaling and exhaling the cool night air, warm in an eiderdown sleeping bag, I am gently adrift in a child's painting, The stars are so clear they could rush into my mouth, like effervescent celestial candies. My mantra is the ancient names of constellations—Deneb, Vega, Draco the Dragon, Cassiopeia. Sleep is deep and dream filled, floating me out beyond the mountains' rim to orbit the eerily moonlit peaks across the lake.

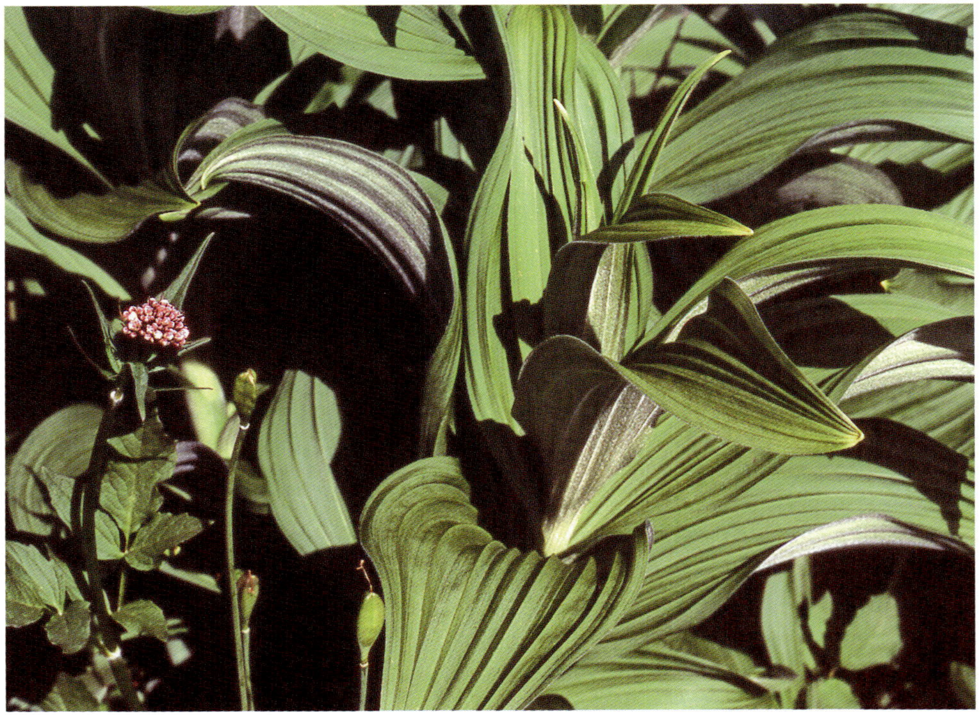

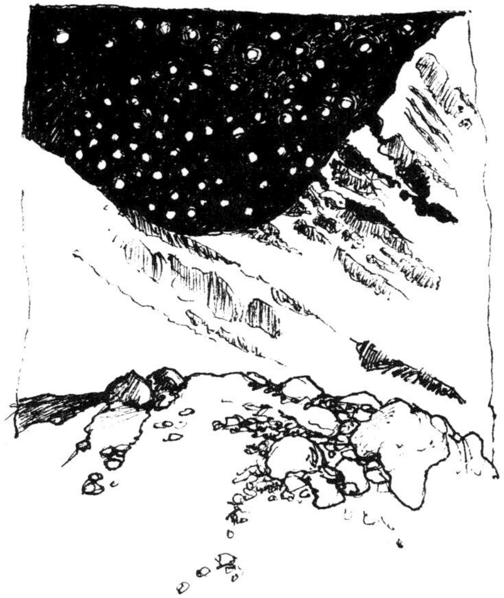

I wake with a start. Having missed the beeping of my tiny Timex taskmaster, I'm half an hour late. Through the frost build-up on the back window, the sky is turning bluish grey. I should already be away. There follows a flurry of activity as I shiver and squirm into cold ski pants, squeeze and hop into frozen ski boot liners. For breakfast I bolt down rock-hard cheese and wooden bagels washed down with draughts of slushy water.

The complex sequence of getting frozen gear together in dim light is finally accomplished and I'm ski-skating across the lake, each stride bringing me closer to the wind-whipped trees on the far shore. It's late in the season and I'm concerned about the safety of the ice. Now and then visions of a cold watery death worm into my consciousness. I've decided to cross rather than go around to save time, and it's up to me to find comfort in this judgment. Nevertheless, I'm haunted, compelled to speed as though pursued by ice demons, and I double pole till my arms and legs ache. I concentrate on watching a single tree, a lone dark marker, grow larger as I draw near.

On solid ground, my pace slows. Having regained my breath, I experience that "out of body" state I've come to associate with travelling alone: fully alert, taking everything in, devoid of a sense of corporeal self. In the half-light, I have the bizarre sensation that my lower body and equipment are functioning completely separately and without apparent direction, taking orders from some consciousness elsewhere. I'm quite comfortable carrying on a silent conversation with my legs, left and right, then boots and skis. Timex time vanishes, and I'm governed instead by the steady brightening of the eastern sky.

Distant, amorphous shapes appear, approach slowly and resolve into wind-blown ridges, gravel outcrops that are then left behind. Sunrise announces itself on the upper peaks with a brilliant fanfare in yellow and orange, inexorably creeping down the mauve snow slopes to the valley floor. At the glacier's snout, on the roof of the world, I begin to travel more carefully, constantly scanning the snow's surface for subtle changes of shape and tone that might indicate hidden crevasses. In my solitary state, it would take only one wrong step for the door to open, plunging me into the frozen abyss. If unlucky, my end could be a long, lonely vigil deep below the surface, far from light and warmth, waiting for the tiny flame of my own consciousness to flicker and go out.

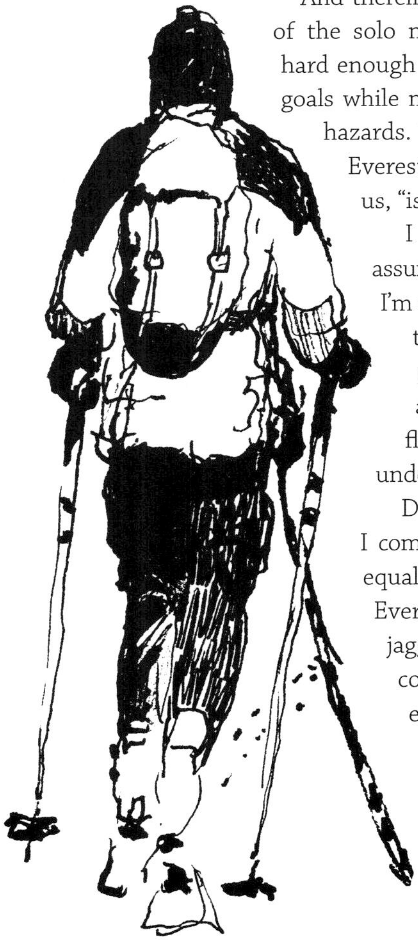

And therein lies the dilemma and responsibility of the solo mountain traveller, who must work hard enough to succeed in reaching the toughest goals while maintaining sufficient focus to avoid hazards. "The finish line," as the Imax-toting Everest veteran David Breashears reminds us, "is at the bottom, not the top."

I quit pushing myself to go faster and assume a more harmonious pace. Suddenly I'm no longer "working." Rather, the mountain landscape seems to simply travel past. Unconscious of effort, I experience a steady dropping away of the valley floor. High ridges move toward me, roll underneath and are lost behind in waves.

Despite the plain hard work of ascent, I come to enjoy every moment, savouring equally small things and grand vistas. Every rock, glaciated peak, shadow and jagged horizon becomes an Ansel Adams composition in light and dark. Hard effort, but not. Alone, but as high as I can be. Totally in the moment, living for the moment—there's nowhere I'd rather be.

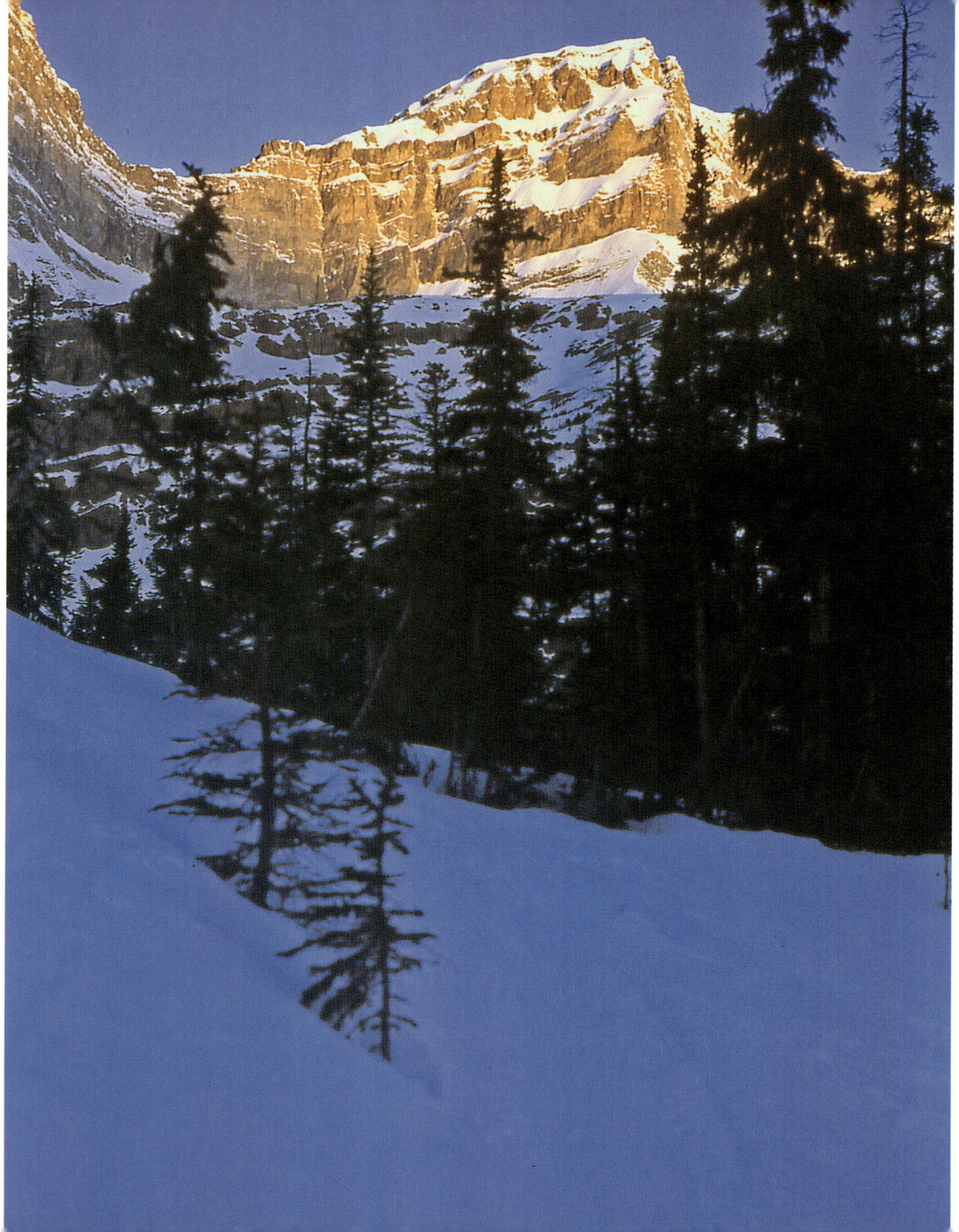

Below the steep cliffs of Mount St. Nicholas on the Wapta Icefields, 20 kilometres north of Lake Louise, I stand alone on a perfectly smooth counterpane of snow.

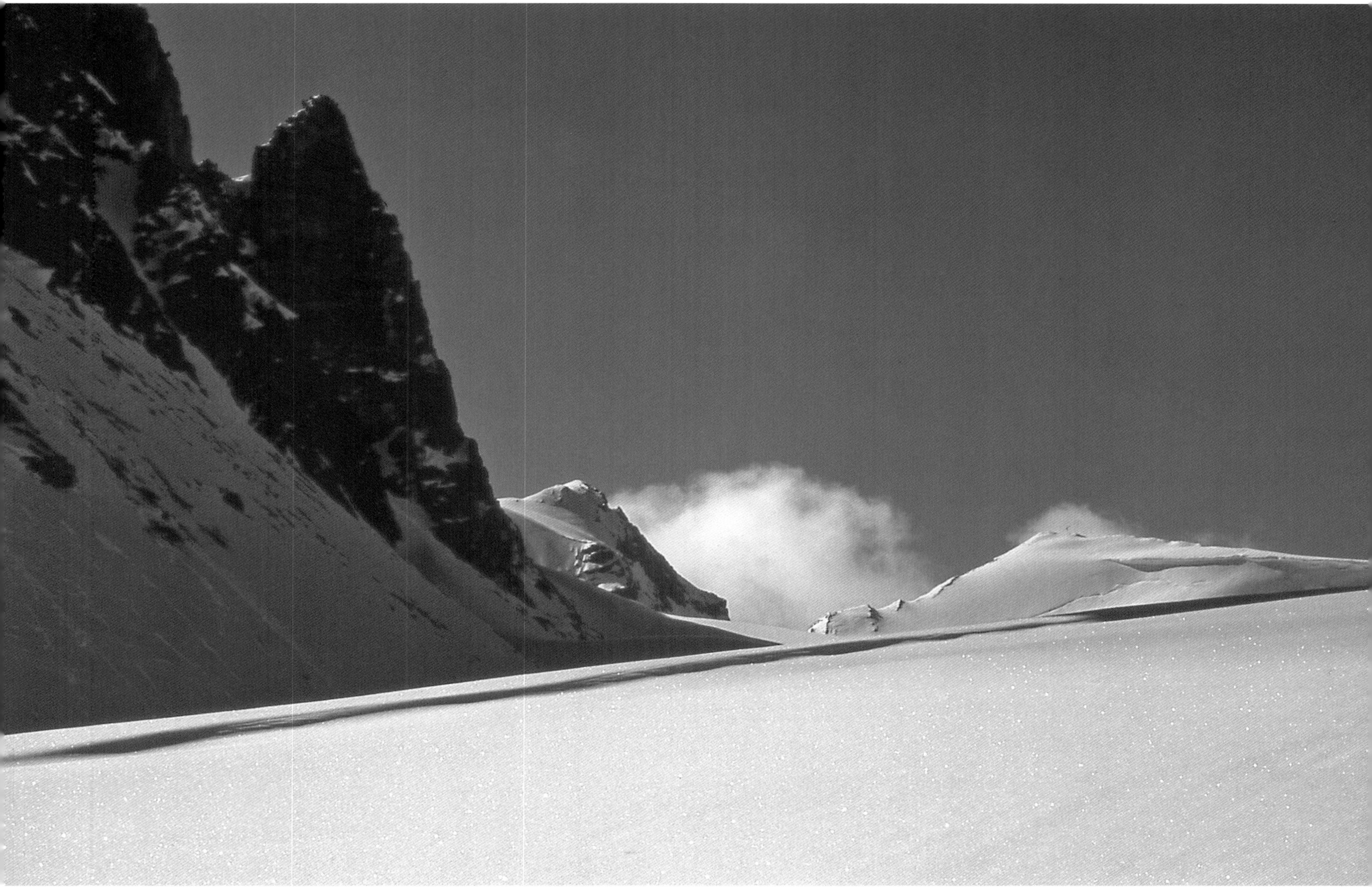

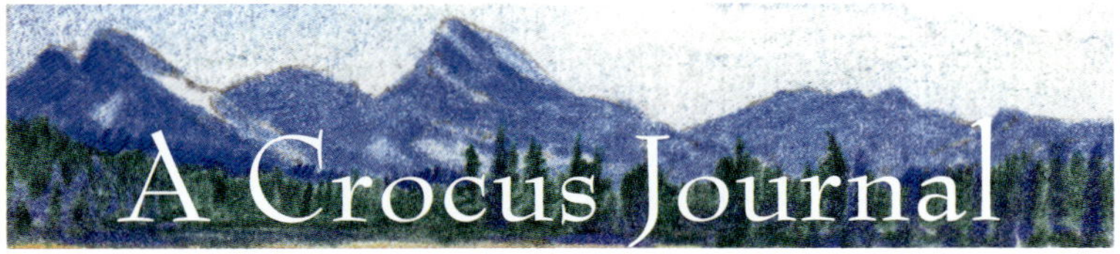

A Crocus Journal

BEHIND THE RECEDING SNOW OF LATE WINTER blooms a delicate blue-purple, six-petalled flower with a lustrous yellow and creamy white interior. The prairie crocus, a perennial that's perversely not a crocus at all, but rather a member of the anemone family, lies dormant through winter in the frosty soil. Deep inside, though, something keeps on ticking. This organic metronome speeds up as the earth warms, bursting out with a little fanfare of colour each spring.

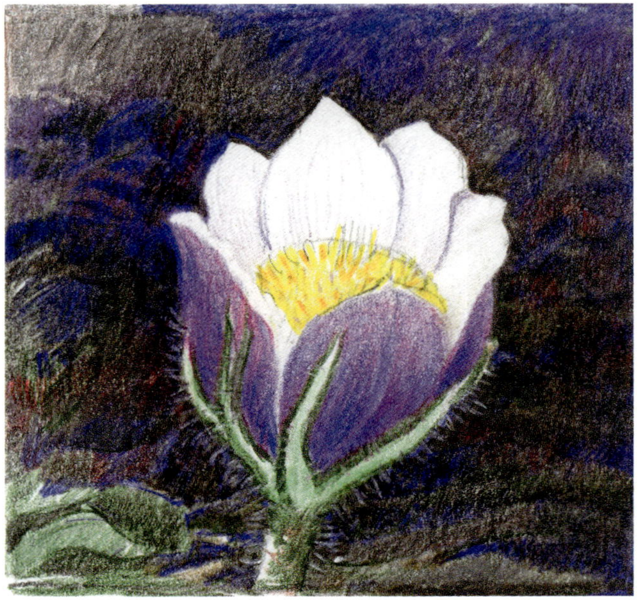

March 9, 2004

In a meadow on the south-facing flank of Grotto Mountain, Canmore

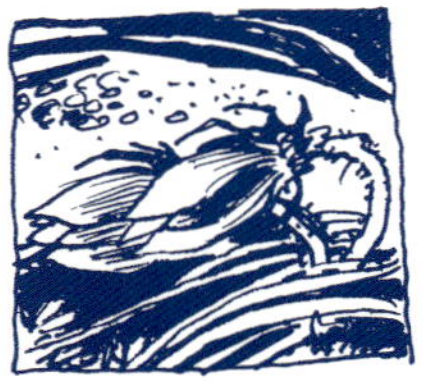

8 a.m. *"Morning begins with a quick solo hike up the mountain to catch the early morning light on the snowy peaks across the valley. The return trip brings me past newly emerged crocuses bent flat to the ground, encased in a thick coat of ice. I empathize with their struggle and resolve to record their response to the sun and the increasing warmth of the day. I'm curious to see how a vulnerable, fuzzy little structure can possibly survive in such harsh conditions. I think I will return a few times."*

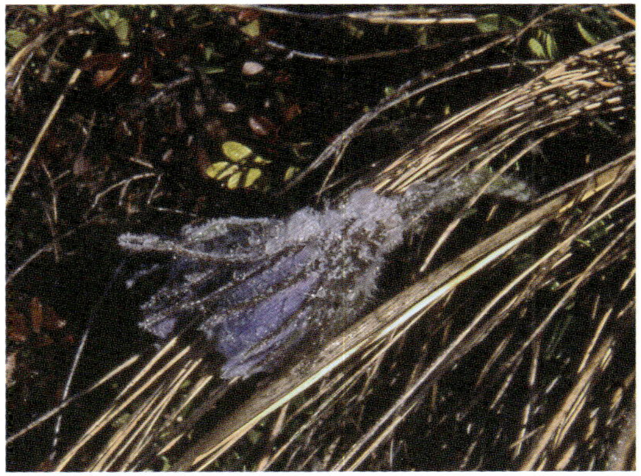
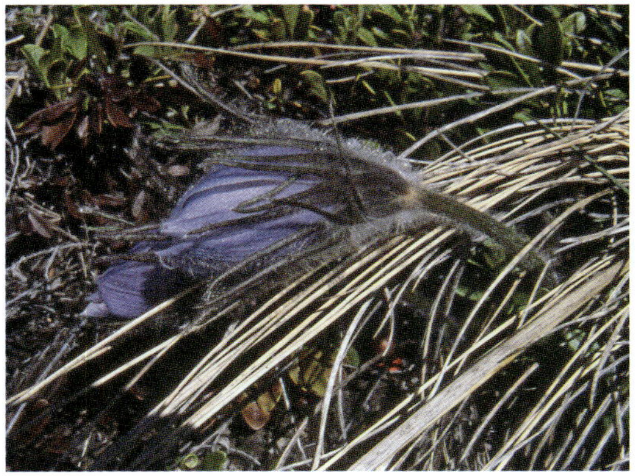
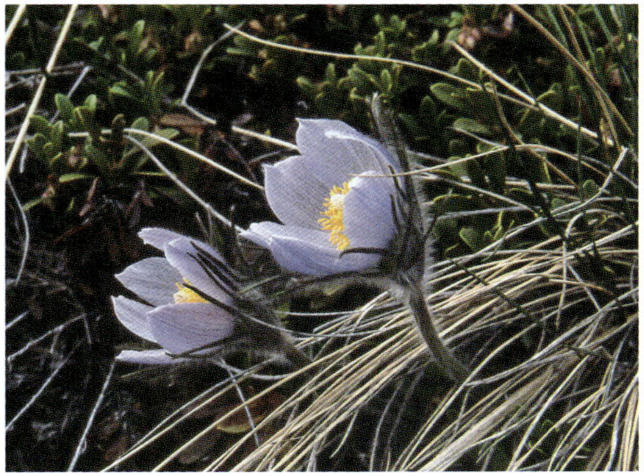

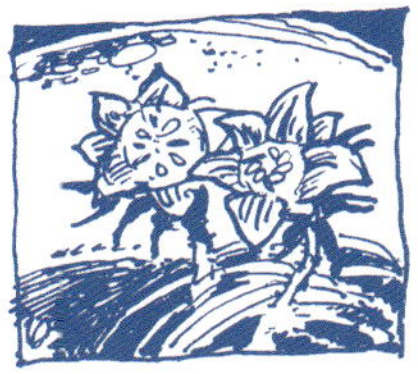

10 a.m. *"I am not disappointed. As the sun melts the ice, the tiny flower has not wilted or split apart as seems inevitable, but instead, awakes, gradually shakes off its harsh burden and rises from prone to upright. At the same time, it opens, fully revealing a delicate lustrous interior. All in an unbelievably short time, for a plant. As I sit drawing the crocus, it occurs to me there is more hereabout than just kinnikinnik and brown grass. The area is alive with life. Black ants are out foraging. A fast flying bug of some kind alights on the page of my sketchbook, skidding sideways, barn-stormer biplane style. It caroms off my eraser, arriving in a dishevelled heap against my pen-nib. Upside down on its carapace, slowly rotating like a spun bottle, its legs flail wildly. Unshaken, but in the grips of what looks like some mad mating frenzy, it rights itself, wiggles his/her bottom seductively then equally incompetently launches itself again.*

A black- and yellow-trimmed butterfly appears and flits this way and that, sketching an abstract composition in warm sienna and cool green around a small conifer. Over in the tall spruce trees, a squirrel seriously agitated by an intruder has become a rapid-fire scold. Robins, newly arrived after winter, stake their territory, and ravens with their rough caw-caw and ventriloqual interlocutions fly reconnaissance just above the treetops."

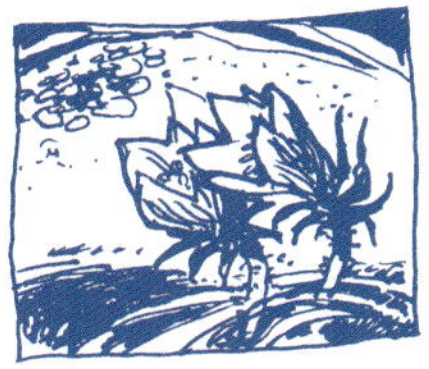

10 p.m. *"The spring night is mild. The flower's stem remains upright but the petals are closed over on themselves. Closer inspection with my headlamp reveals tiny insects inside the micro-world of stamen and petals. In their delicate world, they are protected from wind and warmed in the circular array of petals that stores the heat of the sun like a mini solar oven. No longer than a millimeter, these tiny tenants appear to be permanent residents. They wander around the soft inner petals, living out their lives, making no effort to leave. No matter how closely I look, there are more, successive microcosms, worlds within worlds, like those wooden Russian dolls."*

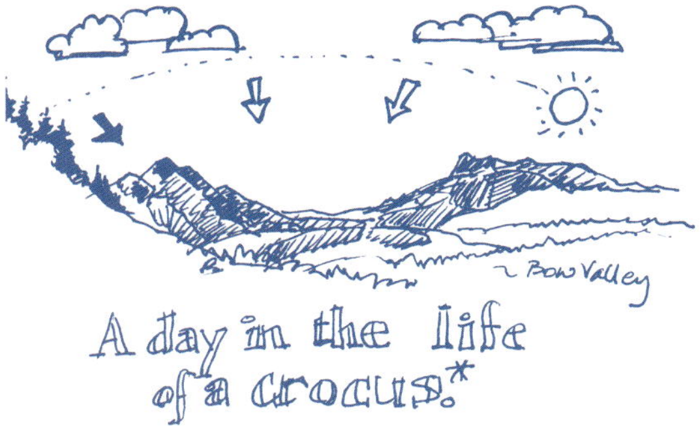

EACH DAY IN THE LIFE OF "MY" CROCUS WOULD repeat the pattern, petals opening in the sun-warmed morning, closing as day cooled into night. And its reclusive residents were probably thrips. Half the size of a grain of rice, thrips begin their lives as eggs deposited in the plant tissue. Having over-wintered in the soil, they return to the petals first as hungry nymphs consuming tiny aphids, mites and the like (dinner time) and finally as adults to mate (party time), the scene to which I had been witness.

Tools for a Vision Quest

ALONG WITH THE NECESSARY mountaineering or backpacking equipment, the construction of these images and words requires me to carry certain tools of the trade. I almost always have a camera in a carrying case strapped to my backpack bellyband. This used to be a loyal and unbelievably hardy Nikon FE, but more recently the Nikon has been callously rejected in favour of an emotionally complex but brilliantly talented Canon EOS Digital. Both are fitted with a wide angle to telephoto zoom lens that remains on the camera. Mountaineering photography is particularly challenging because I must be safely of two minds—recorder and climber. Sometimes a situation becomes precarious, as when, in the middle of a climb, I brace myself, hang on with one hand, lean out over the void, take the shot and hope for the best. I have frozen my fingers solid handling a metal-bodied camera at -30°C.

At various times I carry a selection of other well-loved items: a coil-bound sketchbook, waterproof Pilot pen, some pencils and/or pencil crayons, and occasionally a watercolour prestretched pad and paint set. Always in my breast pocket is a custom-made sketchbook, a little bigger than a deck of cards, for notes and drawings on the fly. This is so easy to use that it helps avoid the temptation to "just move on" when one is in the hard grip of fatigue and hunger.

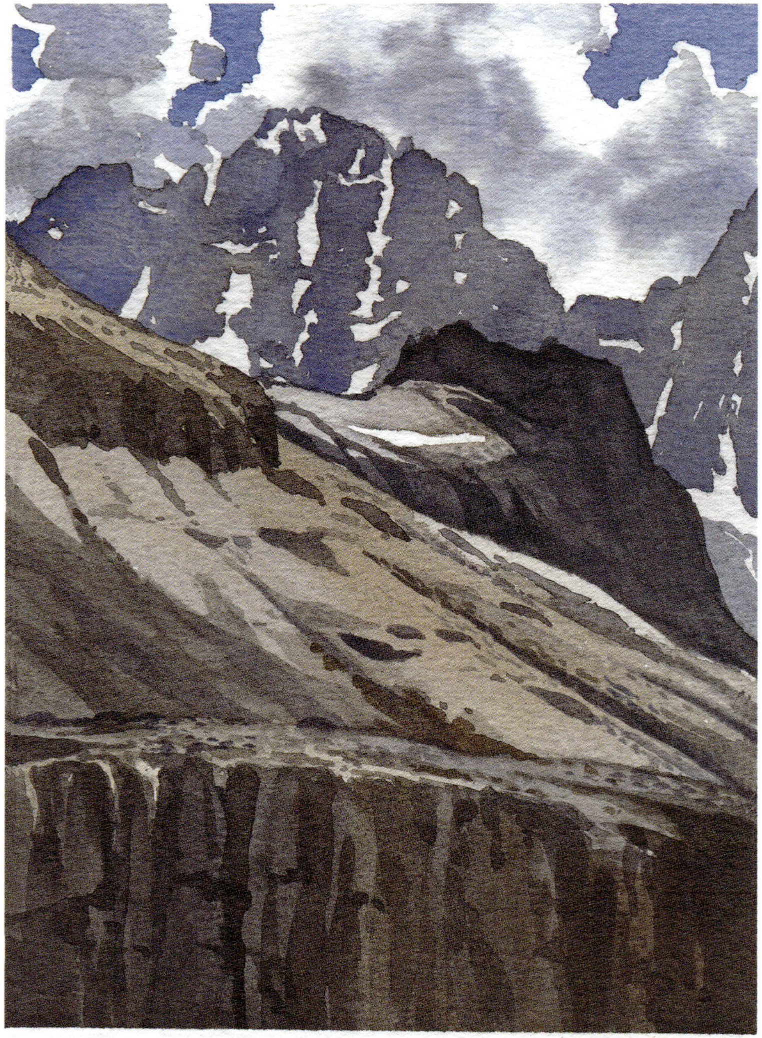

Lorne Perry · Shadows Above Lake Ohara · Aug '89

Looking up toward Yukness Mountain with Ringrose Peak behind. The dramatic play of light and dark on the mountain forms culminates in moments of crystal clarity that I strive to capture in watercolour sketches, in this case, from a meadow near Lake O'Hara in Yoho National Park.

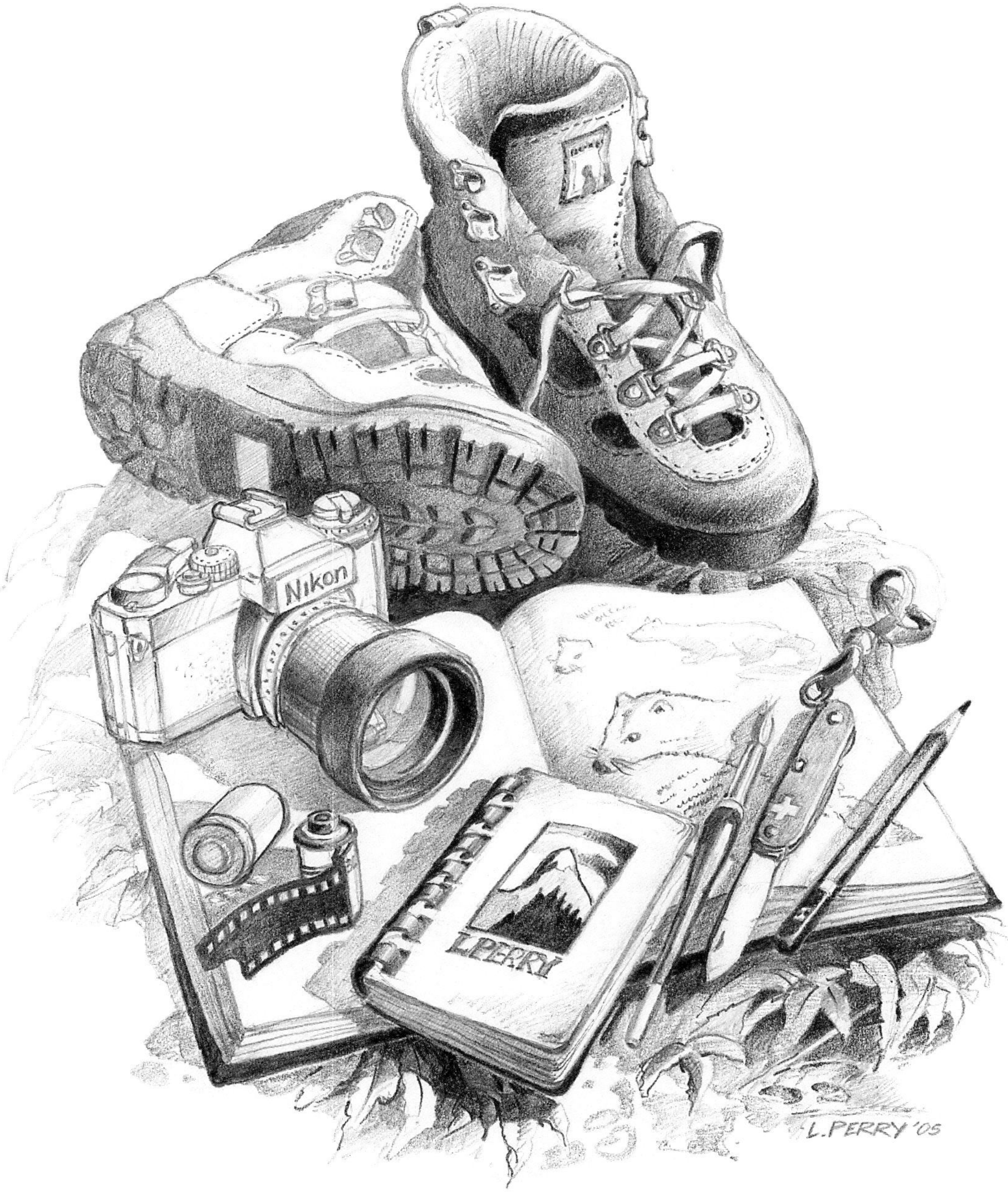
Nikon
L.PERRY
L.PERRY '05

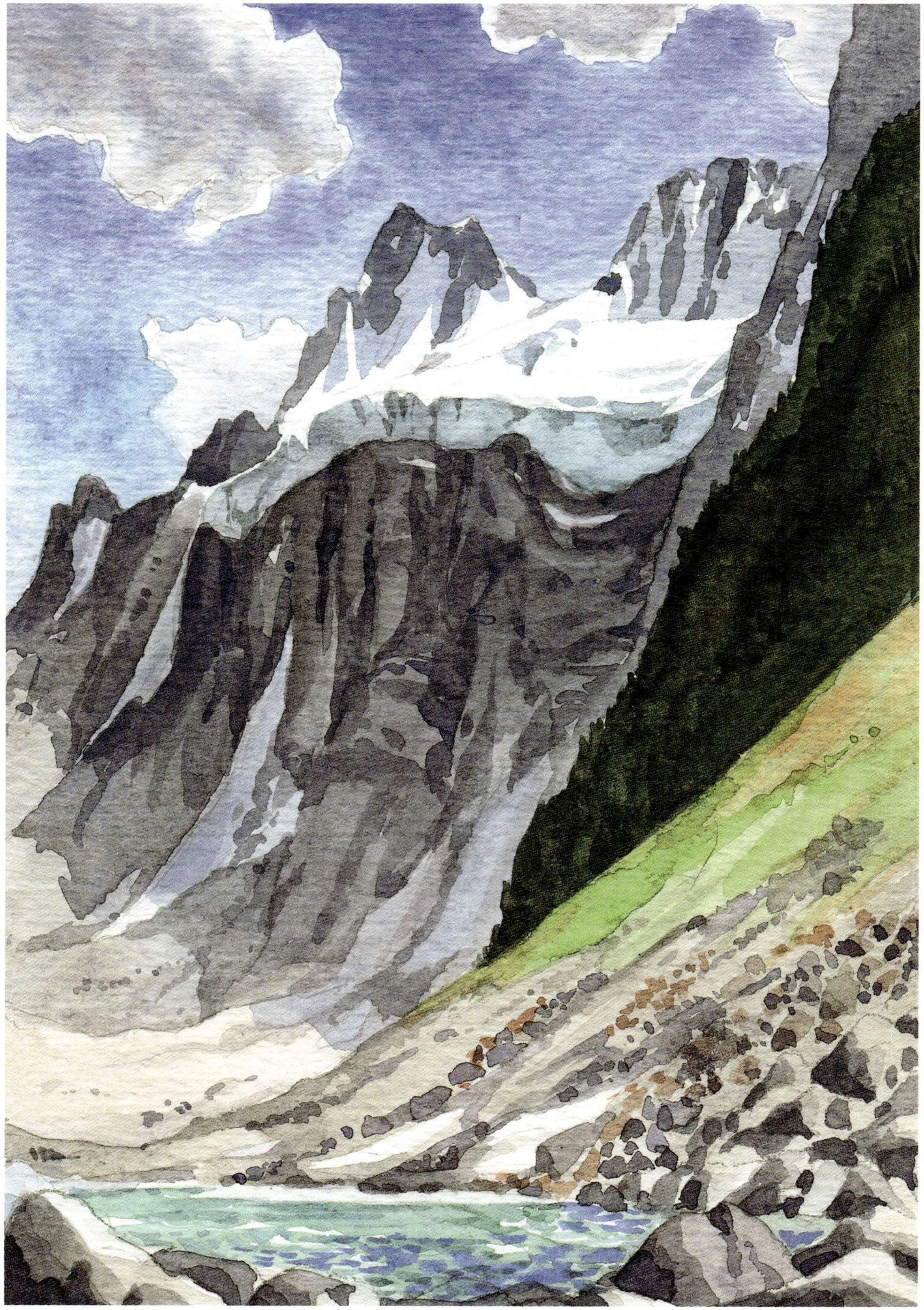

Consolation Lakes are less than an hour's walk from the parking lot at Moraine Lake in Banff National Park. On the great wall above the lower lake hung a glacier brilliant with light.

I love the light on the mountain
shapes: the contrast of light and
shadow on high cliff faces, the
subtle blue-greys and deep greens
of icefields, the hazy blue of
high peaks on a fall afternoon.

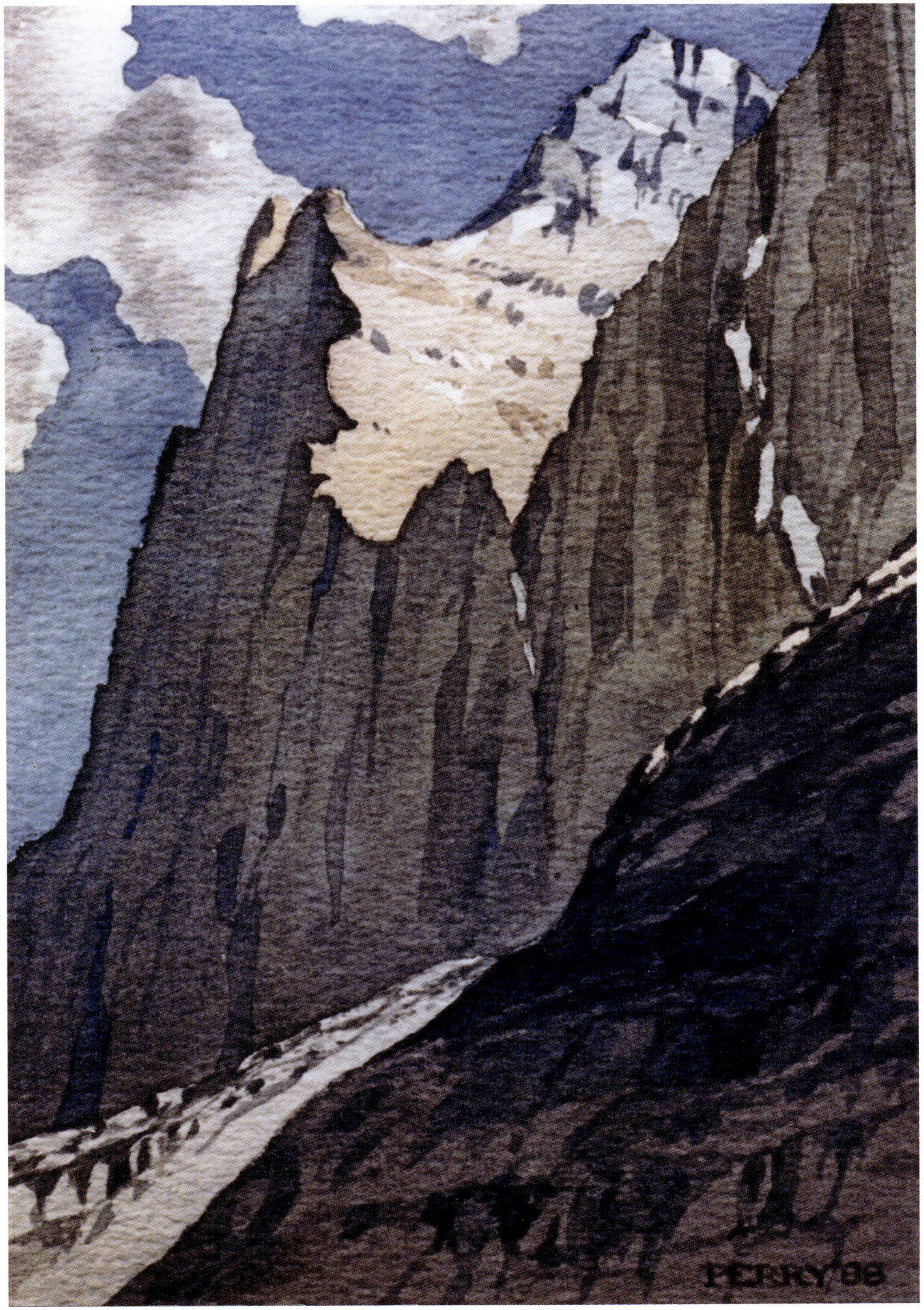

From the Alpine Club hut at Lake O'Hara, I walked up a trail toward All Souls' Prospect. The late afternoon light lit up the face of Mount Biddle, leaving its great east wall in shadow.

FROM THE COLLECTION OF G. HOYNE, CALGARY.

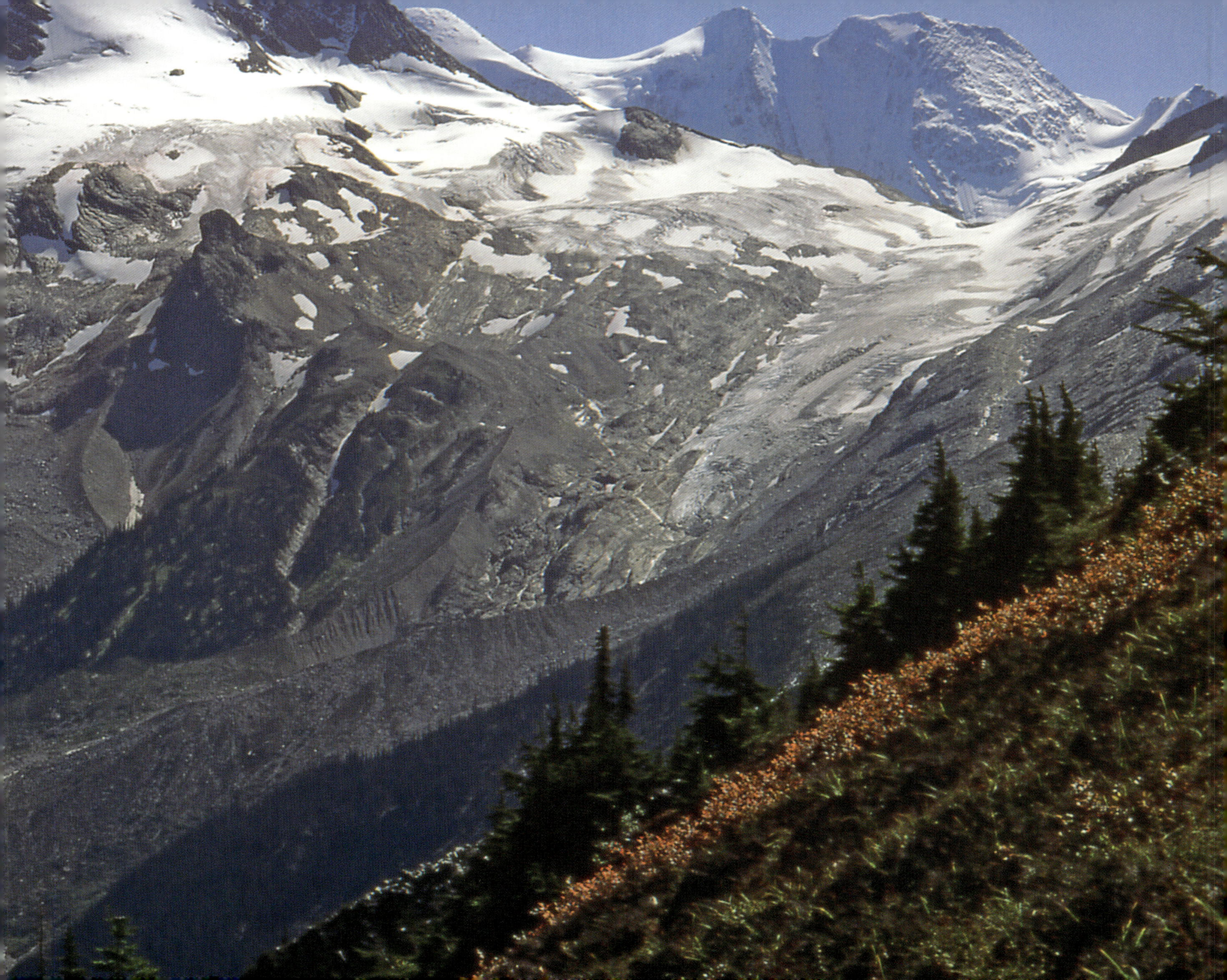

Flesh and blood

CHAPTER 7

For Patricia van Tighem, victim of a bear attack,
and for the Kamchatka grizzlies, Chico and Biscuit, victims of a man attack.

My intention was to take the August holiday long weekend to climb, sketch and paint. Exciting, daunting, this would be my first solo trip of any length. I planned to hike for several hours along a creek to its headwaters at a pass, climb a mountain and descend a second valley to Moraine Lake where I had parked my car.

Though undertaken late in life and without a great deal of forethought, my journey would evoke some elements of the spirit quest—a search for self-knowledge and strength. In First Nations mythology, one of the most powerful spirits one can enlist is that of the grizzly bear. A power not easily won, it obliges the acolyte to confront the bear directly. Not in my wildest dreams did I have any notion of carrying things that far. Nor was I in any way prepared to do so. Mountain rambles had frequently taken my companions and me through alpine meadows heavily dug up by the hungry ursus in search of a succulent hedysarum root salad or a high-protein ground squirrel sandwich. We'd followed huge clawed tracks in the mud after a mountain storm. The presence of these masters in their domain had always been more felt than seen and hence no longer an overriding worry.

I left the parking lot with its usual frenetic press of summer tourists at about three in the afternoon. My pack was heavy, loaded with drawing materials, camera and climbing gear. I soon passed the few hikers and travelled on into the wilderness. The well-trodden trail led through mature spruce stands and willow thickets. But eventually, as I left it too behind, there was a gathering solitude. The sun was setting, and the forest that had been bright with slanting rays and alive with birdsong fell silent, cold and dark. Even the gregarious Canada grey jays abandoned me, and like a small boy discovering himself to be alone in his own house, I began to look over my shoulder. The busy rush and sparkle of the creek provided the sole comfort and I instantly adopted it as a friend. As the gap between the city and me grew and the tie with the natural world deepened, it was easy to see why aboriginal peoples saw spirits in things animate and inanimate.

An old, overgrown trail I now was following appeared and disappeared frequently. Rotting tree trunks criss-crossed my path. It was low and boggy as I stepped over deadfall into deep, wet grass. Spider webs clung to my face and I brushed them away. The narrow gap in the towering trees revealed clouds touched with sunset pink and orange. Time to find a campsite.

Steadily, I moved upstream. But then, in a clearing, I was shocked to a halt. Damn it, this was definitely *not* what I wanted to see—a huge mound of bear dung. Not fresh, maybe a couple of days old, but enough to invoke book and movie images of dark, powerful predators with slashing teeth. I chided myself for my volatile imagination with a "C'mon, get a grip."

Just across the creek from an old avalanche path, the valley levelled out a bit. Shattered tree trunks were piled in heaps—evidence of another sort of violence. A white waterfall cascaded down worn limestone and disappeared into some old snow, its sound rising and falling on the soft evening wind. High above, the ridge was turning golden orange in the last light of day.

To a mountain traveller alone, each object, animate and inanimate, seems to take on greater significance, and it seems possible for life to reside in all things. How to photograph the spirit of water?

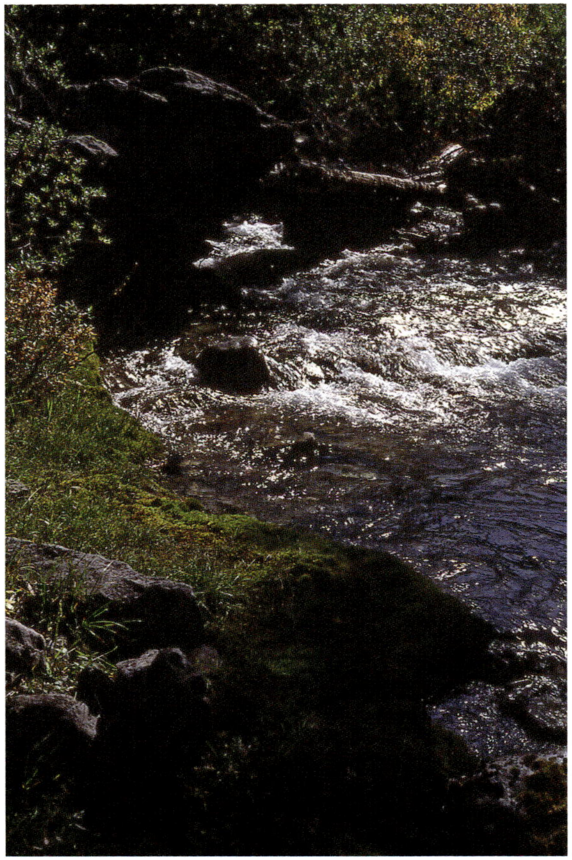

I set up my tent and watched as the stars, one by one, were revealed on a deep purple sky. My noisy little one-burner stove chuttered away as it heated the evening meal. This stove, it must be said, was the absolute focus of my undying love and affection. How attached you can become to a busy little piece of cast metal! My green pack lay open on the grass; sketchbook, camera, jacket and wind pants lay in a familiar jumble. In the solitude, these too had become my friends—my whole world, my band of brothers, everything I possessed.

After the sun had set, the cooling air brought with it dew that collected in clear beads on the tent fly, camera lens, any exposed surface. I bustled about, pulled out my sleeping bag, set it on the inflatable mat. The stove was packed up and dishes washed by the creek in a little warm circle of headlamp light. I jammed all the food in one bag, tied it up and struggled downstream over rough ground to a suitable tree, where I hung it over a high branch. I had performed this awkward and annoying task more than a hundred times on various canoe and kayak trips, as well as mountaineering adventures. Having never had bear trouble, I'd never really been convinced this time-consuming and sometimes comical stratagem really worked. With a rather more cavalier attitude, I tended to regard the chore as an annoyance. Back in my tent, I shut off my headlamp, gawked one last time at the starry sky, set my ice axe near the door of the tent "just in case" and crawled into my sleeping bag.

When I awoke, the sun was already well up and peering over the hazy green shoulder of a mountain. From inside the already warmed tent, I could hear the creek and the birds in the meadow. What a day! My nervousness over last night's bear scat evaporated with the morning dew. I apologized to the resident ground squirrel for cooking beside his doorway, assuring him humans had much higher purposes and that I would soon move on. Up on the ridges the snow was bright white against a deep blue sky.

I packed up quickly, repeating the routine I'd carried out many times before: sleeping bag first, tent next, soft stuff against my back so nothing sticks me in the ribs, climbing gear to the outside, then bags and more bags of this and that. Everything in its place. How well I knew this battered old pack and its contents.

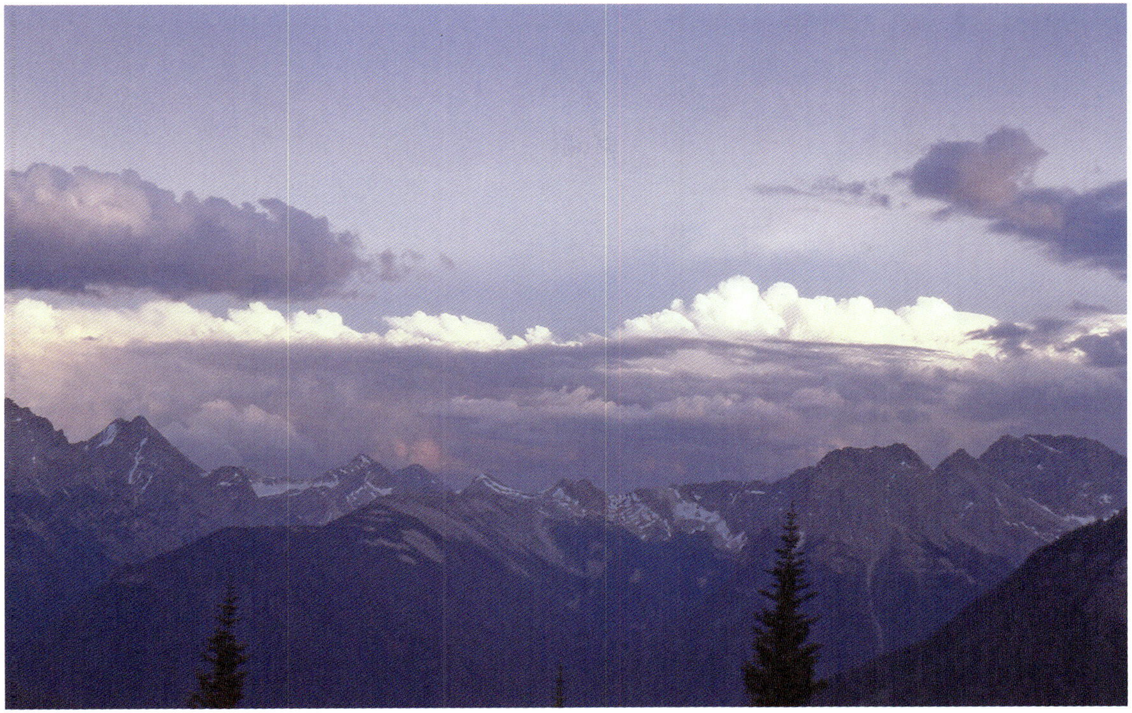

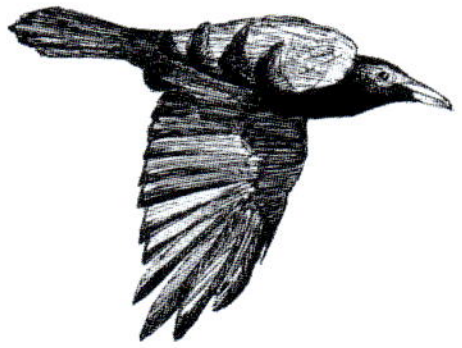

Evanescence, stillness, waiting. Clouds crowd over mountains in the front ranges at nightfall, a time of contemplation in the high alpine.

Yet unknown to me, just a short distance away, following their own ancient imperatives and familiar routines, a beautiful mother grizzly bear and her two cubs settled down in the grass of a mountain meadow. Unlike me, she was no apprentice, but a hardened graduate of the wilderness school of martial arts.

As I walked, the forest began to thin out, giving way to the occasional alpine meadow. Now I could see around, and my spirits soared. My legs carried me in long confident strides along the creek, first one side then the other, as I pushed higher. At each creek crossing I carefully removed my socks, stuffed them in my boots and tied the laces together. Very embarrassing to go for a slip, thought I, lose the boots and have to make my "triumphant" entrance down at the busy lodge in stocking feet. As it turned out, that would be the least of my worries.

Willow grew on both sides of the creek, some well over my head. Bad news for two reasons. It's abrasive on bare shins and, worse, you can't see anyone coming. And they can't see you. Add to that the noise of the creek drowning out any sound you make (including your swearing as you push through the tangled undergrowth) and you have a recipe for unexpected meetings.

I stopped and put on thick climbing pants, hot but some protection at least, and pushed on. Mindful of the dangers of that unthinkable, one-in-a-million-you've-read-about-but-can't-happen-to-you chance encounter, I began to clap and shout. My voice sounded strange, out of place, as though it weren't coming from me. The willows thinned out and now there was much more meadow than forest. My kind of territory. I strode along, grateful for the open terrain. I even undertook a professional analysis of my new contact lenses. Hmmm, right one excellent, left, well, not great. I walked into a broad clearing admiring the view…

If my life were an hourglass, and my experience the shiny, white grains rushing through its tiny neck from one bulb to the other, this is when time stops. I am riding those grains, travelling so fast there's no sense of progression at all. Fate could snap the glass neck, allow all to run free. So many events have occurred in my life before, and as fortune will allow, so many after. But at this moment, it all devolves to that tiny fast slipping stream—a falling unstoppable nightmare.

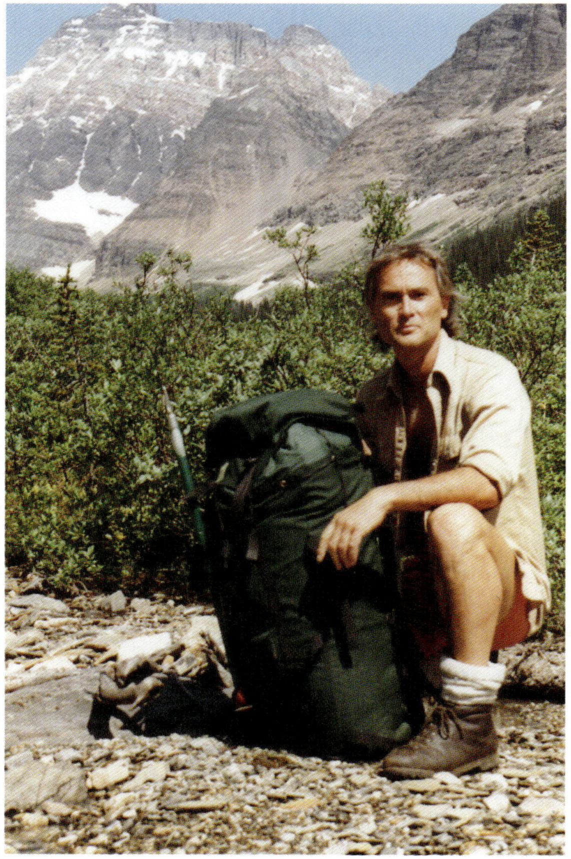

This self portrait, with backpack and ice axe, was snapped moments before I turned to cross Tokkum Creek. Out of sight, just beyond the creek, is "my" grizzly bear.

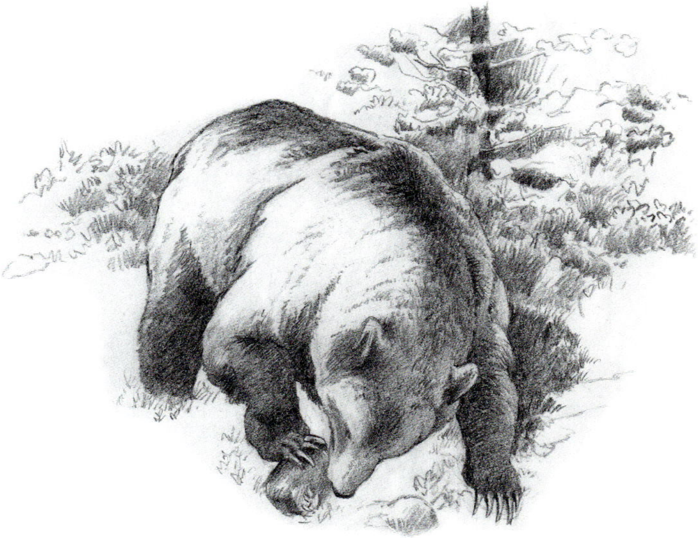

Slightly uphill to my right, about 10 paces away, a large dark form. Moving. I jerk my head around. *My Christ, a mother grizzly.* The cubs are behind. She is instantly enraged, surprised and up on hind legs. Something rises up from the pit of my stomach and my chest and throat are constricting. Total terror. Front paws apart, claws out, she snarls and woofs, swinging that great heavy head left and right. The cubs behind her halt then tumble backwards. Then she's coming; nothing will stop her. She has me. Nowhere to run. *You're alone, you're finished* says a voice inside.

My mouth opens wide. My ears tell me I'm screaming, long and agonized—a kind of slow motion. Body and mind become detached. On legs not mine, I move a few steps back. Stumbling. Hands come up. Again, that screaming, this time like a child. Me? I hear a small, small voice, "Go! G-go away, bear!"

She comes at me, shifting slightly right. Watching carefully, she hesitates momentarily, sizing me up. Unsure how to bring down my ungainly form. Dark jaws seize my wrist. Teeth puncture flesh. Claws pass before my face, right then left, so quickly I can only guess what has happened. She has taken two swings, boxer style. But I fall away and she misses. Darkness. Rolling, tumbling downhill. I know she's there. No pain. I

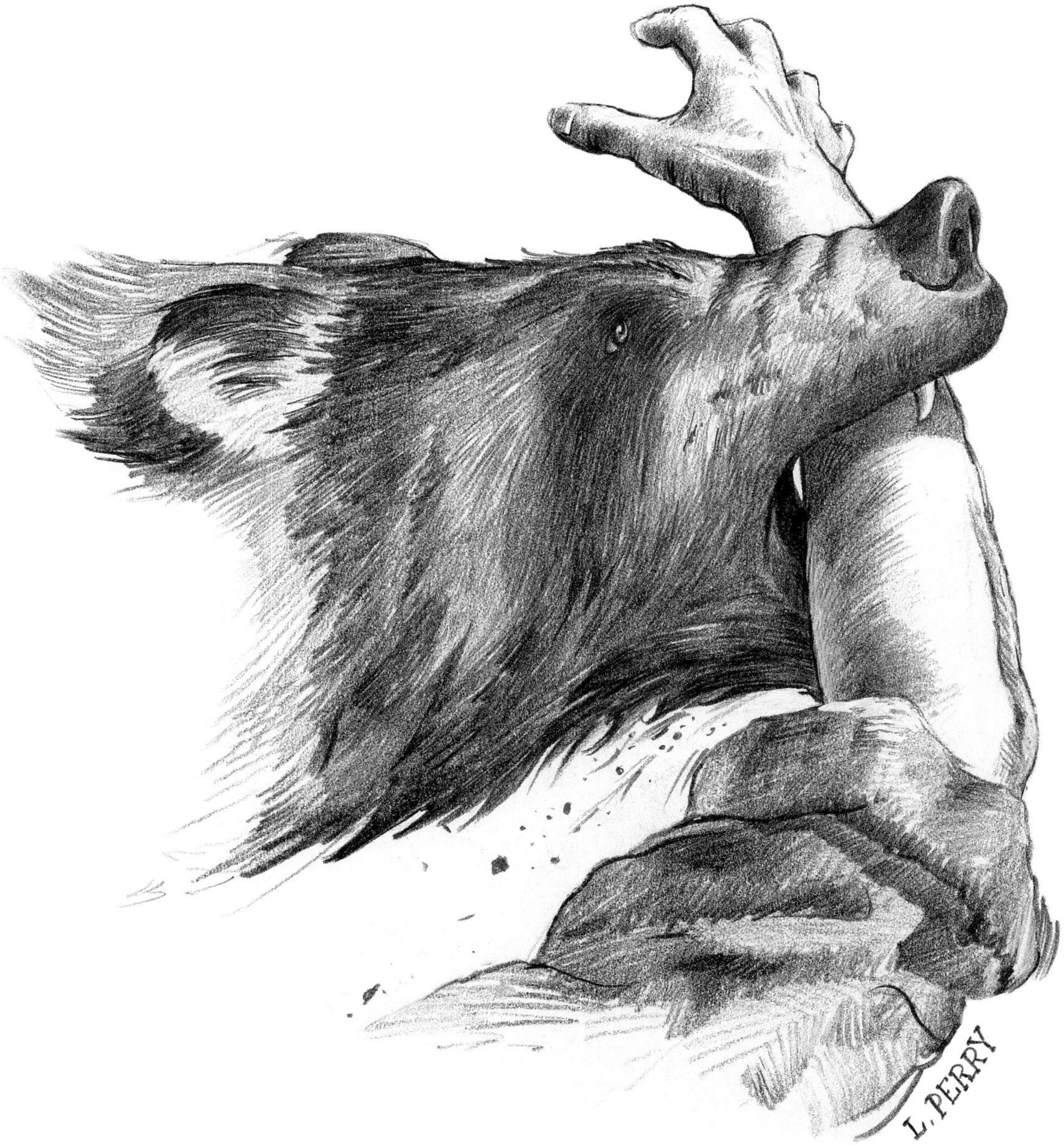

slide sideways. Where am I? Cold creek water soaks my left side, and I'm shocked from ancient instinct to conscious thought. Memory, found again, barks a frantic command: *Play dead, Jeezus, play dead, play dead!* I hear quick, desperate gasps, "Ah, ah, ah!" Bear behind me. For a split second, my head is in a clamp—jaws. Blood runs. Loud snort. My hands are in front of my face, fingers spread wide apart. Out of the corner of my eye I see a great paw. Long claws press me down in the water.

The action stops, a momentary pause. *What the hell?* She's curious, unsure of her next move. I try to avoid making eye contact. Behind the dark lattice of my outstretched fingers, I see a big black nose and two bright amber eyes set wide apart in thick, dark fur. Desperate to convince her I'm no threat, I make the most unthreatening noise I can think of, like a whimpering puppy. She hesitates.

I am now lying on my side in the creek, my elbow protruding above my body. She lunges, teeth slicing through muscle. Crunch. A chip of bone sheared off. Pop, pop go the ligaments. The sky fills with a spray of blinding lights. A cry comes roiling up out of my guts but I disallow it, swallow it down. No. *Shut up,*

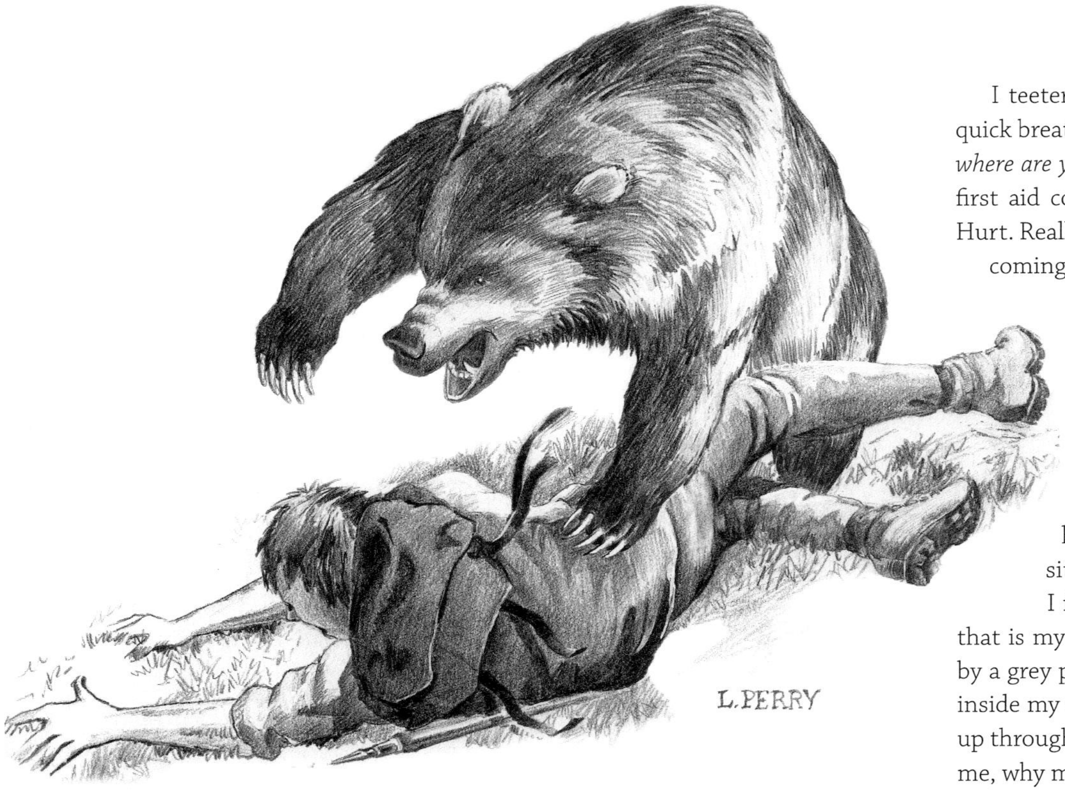

damn you! Play dead, play dead! All is quiet. She pushes away from my body and vanishes up over the bank in a cloud of flying gravel and dust. She'll be searching for the cubs that retreated when we crashed into the creek. Since the bear and I first startled each other, just seconds have passed. I stay still on my side in the water, face turned down. Waiting. How long, maybe two minutes. Then the pain, an unbelievable, silent shrieking. An agony of burning.

The strange inner dialogue continues. There's me, and there's the voice in my head. The voice seems to know what to do.

Me (out loud): "What happened? What in the hell happened?"

The Voice: *You've been attacked by a bear. Yes. Attacked by a bear.*

(A sound of sobbing.)

The Voice: *No, none of that. Get yourself under control. Stop that! If you don't play your cards right you may die right here.*

I teeter on the edge of an abyss. Control. Yes, that's it. My sharp, quick breathing slows. I'm drawn back from the brink. *That's better. Now, where are you hurt?* I run a point-by-point inventory as I was taught in first aid courses. Legs: okay. Feet: yeah they're okay. Hands...hands? Hurt. Really hurt. Seems bad. Head? Sort of okay, but where's that blood coming from? Jaw: numb.

My thoughts jump. Damn. The bear. Where is that god-damn apparition from hell? I slow my breathing and listen. All is quiet. Oh please, I beg. Oh, please, no.

Blood mingles with the water. Things are serious. I am alive, clawing my way from despair to action. Round one is over, but now what? If I stay here, I'll die for sure. Decisions must be made. *Right now.* I recall that bears are reported to have returned to the scene. I know I cannot face her again. If I sit up, the bear may see me. If I remain where I am, I'll freeze.

I find myself up on my knees, looking down at the sorry sight that is my arms and hands. Each tooth mark is a pink orb surrounded by a grey pucker of fat. It is somehow obscene and embarrassing to see inside my arm. Flesh and blood, that's what I am. A wave of pain sears up through me and ends in a sobbing cry: "This can't be happening. Why me, why me?" No reply.

A pale, flat disc of sun hangs motionless in a colourless sky. Wild-eyed, I raise my head, half twist one way then the other where I kneel in the stream. Seeking comfort where there is none. My affable companion, the creek, that only moments before was rippling and jumping, is a still life of blue-black waves and weak reflections. I'm searching for help, but of course none comes. Tricked. Abandoned. Double-crossed. How can everything be so strange?

My right forearm oozes blood from the elbow down, and judging by the terrible pain centred there I know it is badly cut, maybe broken. It will not move. My wrist is a mess of bleeding holes, swollen stiff and black with dirt and coagulated blood. I try my fingers, which move a little. Maybe not broken. I breath through my mouth to avoid gagging.

The forefinger on my left hand is ugly and misshapen, dislocated, bent out to one side at an impossible angle. Well, I'm going to need at least one functioning hand. Cognizant that I must act now, while I am full of adrenaline, I grasp the finger with my right hand as best I can, and press it in to my stomach. Bent at the waist, I simultaneously exhale sharply and wrench it hard back into position.

Stop. *Where's the bear?* I crouch so my head cannot be seen above the riverbank. Bloated fingers fiddle with plastic buckles, and my big pack is swung to the ground. It's far too heavy to carry now. No time for second thoughts; the bear might roar back over that bank at any moment. Holding the top flap open with my teeth, I pull each item out. *Hurry, hurry.* I know exactly what I need and where it is. The absolute essentials. This bag stays, this stays. *Jeezus hurry.* I must have this. My travelling companions—sketch book, camera, tent, stove—lie forlorn in a little heap. Say goodbye to good friends. Sleeping bag, tent fly, pile jacket, a bit of food and matches are stuffed back in. I glance up at the riverbank. *No time, no time left. C'mon. C'mon.* Frustration, swearing. My right hand won't work the way it should. As I close the pack with my teeth and good fingers of my left hand, blood drips onto the top flap. Is this where the lifeline ends? In a valley by a river? *No. Time to get up.* Time to find out how this life-and-death story ends. *Time to go.*

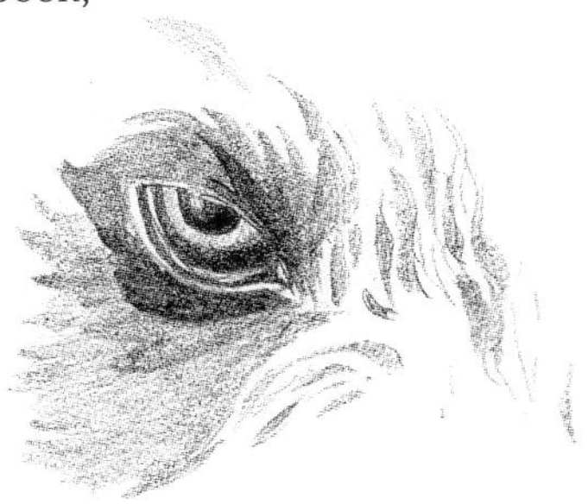

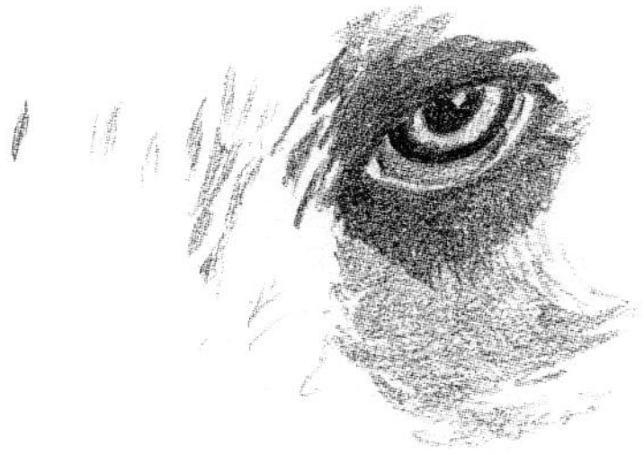

But which way? Downstream, back the way I've come, is a long way. Also the direction in which the bear vanished. Unthinkable. Upstream, toward the open alpine meadow, I must climb a pass. At the top of the pass is the terminus of the busy Moraine Lake trail and hope of help. Through the hourglass, the sand and I are rushing. The choice is unfortunately clear. And I absolutely must not dawdle. Arrive too late at the pass and the day hikers will have gone home: I'd be left to my blood and pain in the cold alpine night.

The Voice gathers spirit and body, and cautiously we rise to meet our fate. *Nothing. No bear. Up or down the valley. Gone.* So, ice axe in hand, dislocated finger flopping uselessly, arm swollen and full of holes, I half crawl, half walk out of the creek. My back is turned to where she disappeared. I don't look back; I simply cannot face her again. Boots slide hopelessly backward in the steep gravel of the bank. At any moment, I expect to feel the claws and be dragged back. But somehow I find myself above the creek, in the grass and going. *No stopping now. Move on.* The side zippers of my pile pants flare open and catch on every branch. Infuriated, I curse them as accomplices in this murderous plot—"Damn and god damn you to hell!"—and rip my legs free. Next, I start up a chant, with every second step, a loud shout. Meant to sound intimidating, the noise is really just a hoarse cry: "Huh, huh, huh!" Stumble forward. Every now and then I stop at a boulder, raise my axe and bring it down several times. With each thudding impact, the dislocated finger sends a stab of pain. Through a false bravado, I yell, "I'm coming! Look out, you bastard, I'm coming through!"

Everywhere in the meadow, the grass is torn up—bear, searching for food. At the base of a dead tree, a huge hole in the ground, earth moist, tells me that activity here has ceased only minutes ago. Panic tightens my throat, dries up my mouth, I can no longer shout. The thought dawns—*Jesus Lord Christ, there's another one.* I glance over my shoulder. *Somewhere down below me. Coming or not?*

Blood continues to ooze, my dislocated finger throbs mercilessly, my elbow is a ball of fire screaming for attention. I blunder through the creek again and again as the terrain demands. The Voice keeps talking, warning: *Be careful, don't fall, you're too tired to fight.* The rushing torrent could easily carry me away. Dimly, I note the beauty of the creek sluicing down over gorgeous rock forms.

Above treeline now. Meadow gone. Still no sign of the bear and I begin to slow down. Weary, lonely and frightened, I simply put one foot in front of the other to gain the upper valley and then the pass. The question I have not dared ask now looms large. Will there be people when I get there? I engage the Voice in a debate: Am I justified in shouting for help? A solo trip could be construed as unnecessary risk—get yourself into shit, better get yourself out. In addition, my climber's ethic demands one call for help only in dire need. Am I there? Will anyone think less of me? What would my climbing buddies say? Yes, I finally decide, I think it's okay to ask for aid.

I can now see the high, rock-strewn route to the pass. No trail—looks like hard going. Well... no problem. After all, I'm a climber; it'll just take a bit longer than usual. I raise my good arm to shield the sun. Anyone up there? I squint and stare. Yes, yes. Yes! People, I see people! Tiny dark shapes move around, silhouettes on the blue sky... and disappear. *Don't worry; there'll be more.* I feel lighter and stronger, and for the first time dare to hope.

It is about noon. I must reach the top or at least come within hailing distance before two or three o'clock. By that time, the last hikers of the day will reach the pass, turn around and head back down to their cars by the lake. By the creek, I gather myself for the push. I'm so thirsty. Lowering myself onto the soft moss I slowly lean down until my face is in the clear water. So cool, wonderful. I try to ease my throbbing elbow in as well, but the pain, far from soothed, intensifies. I fill my water bottle, take a long drink, and awkwardly push up. As they have so often, my eyes find a route up through the rubble. I set off.

It's hot. I'm bleeding. Adrenaline is wearing off. It doesn't take long to recognize this is going to be very hard. I take a few steps, rest, carry on, taking advantage of snow patches that make for easy solid walking. Kicking steps, I progress slowly upward, pain dogging every step. Heat and fatigue wear me down, and, too often, I give in to the need to stop. I stuff handfuls of snow in my mouth, rub more on my cheeks to extinguish the fire there. Then I sink down. So good to stop. My forehead rests on the cool metal ice axe. Unsteady on my knees, I sway, watch the drip, drip, drip in the snow. Glance down the valley: Where is the old bitch anyway? Would she follow me this far? I see no real sign, but my mind plays a cruel game, making stalking bears out of every odd-shaped rock.

My mouth opens, and a real voice emerges. "Help," I hear this voice shout. "I'm hurt! I'm hurt!"

Up at the pass, people still come and go. How thankful I am! Push upright, carry on. Step, step, step until at last I believe I might be close enough. My mouth opens, and a real voice emerges. "Help," I hear this voice shout. "I'm hurt! I'm hurt!"

High on the pass, two hikers have been idly watching a lone figure far down in the valley. They comment, lose interest and turn their attention to the incredible view. How can they not have heard? I wave my ice axe above my head in panic. The dislocated finger makes it difficult to control and it swings back down against my leg. I watch in despair as the two figures disappear. I call out again, and keep walking.

Then I notice a figure coming down the steep scree toward me. When my call went floating up on the wind, two women, seated a bit closer, had in fact heard and raised the alarm. *They're coming! They're coming!* I'm saved. I lick my dry lips. A spasm in my stomach may gutter into a laugh or cry. There is no doubt now. *I have been heard.* The distant figure moves steadily downward. For a terrible moment, it looks as though he is going to go right on past. I call again. He's coming. I alter my course a little and go to meet him.

How different are our solitudes: me bloody from the battle of my life, him casual in light-coloured shorts and T-shirt, a crumpled khaki sun hat perched on his head. Nonchalant, still enjoying the beautiful day, he glances at me curiously. But when he comes closer, his expression is instantly changed. Immediately self-conscious, I round on myself. Perhaps I shouldn't have called out, should have walked out on my own. What am I doing? Climbers don't whine for help.

"What happened?" His voice surprises me. The distance between us is smaller yet. Now the second man is on his way down, approaching quickly with water and medical supplies. Tears well up in my eyes, and I wipe them away with a quick brush of my hand. Collecting myself, I straighten up and speak in a voice intended to be level and matter of fact. "I'm hurt."

A steady, gentle hand takes me by the shoulder. With that touch, the long internal dialogue ends. My separate selves merge into one. I ease the fierce grip on myself. The world is sane, and time, the time I understand, moves on again.

THE TWO GEOLOGISTS WHO CAME TO MY ASSISTANCE were well prepared. Out of their first aid kit came gauze bandages, a large triangular bandage to support my arm, tape and beautiful pills—pain-relieving codeine. Applied immediately, together it all made me feel reborn. I rested, even commented on the beauty around us. Uncomfortable with the possibility of a helicopter ride, I tried to talk them out of calling one. They would have none of that and signalled the people at the top of the pass to go down to the lodge at Moraine Lake and call in the rescue unit. We walked slowly back up the pass, reaching the summit at about four. It had been six long hours since the attack. After some discussion, we walked further down into the Moraine Lake valley where helicopter pick-up would be easier if the wind came up or darkness overtook us. After a long, pain-wracked wait came the familiar whine and the helicopter arrived with its smell of fuel.

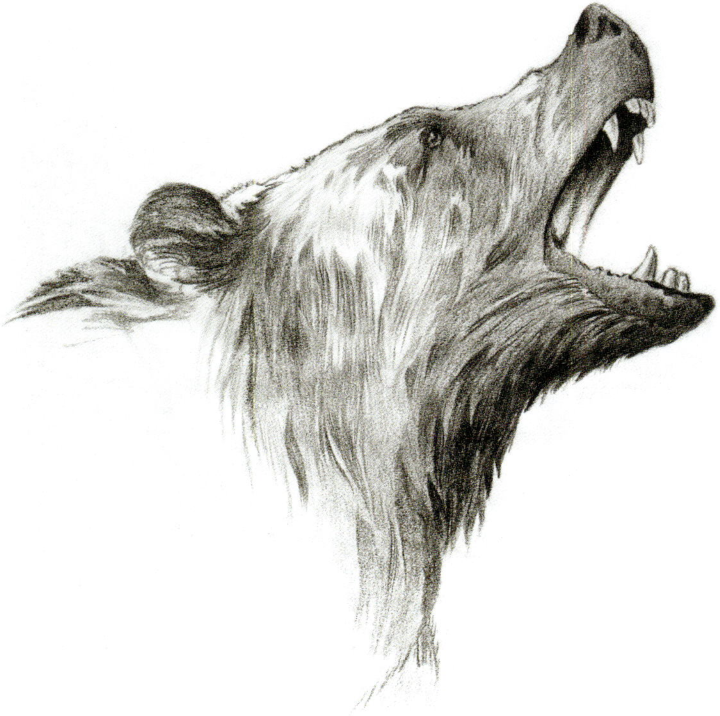

In emergency at Mineral Springs Hospital in Banff, I groaned in pain as a young intern tried twice to reset my dislocated finger. A doctor then took over for a third, successful attempt. Three and a half hours of probing, cleaning and stitching later, brown Betadine solution flowing into my arm and dripping out, the nurses guided my aching, exhausted body into bed. Next day, to no one's surprise,the wounds became infected, and I was informed that the successful treatment of bite wounds is not a foregone conclusion. It was possible I might lose the arm, my right, the one upon which I depended to earn my living as an illustrator. For two restless nights I wrestled with that prospect, thrown right back into the fight.

Eventually, with further work at a Calgary hospital, the infection was brought under control. The plastic surgeon—experienced in repairing bear damage!—commented that although the grizzly jaw is powerful and teeth large, the teeth are not sharp in the sense of a knife. When she bit in, the theory ran, ligaments and blood vessels had rolled out of the way. Consequently, I would likely not lose any fine motor skills and, therefore, would retain my ability to draw.

Six months of physiotherapy brought my arm to the point where it would move more or less normally. After a year, the nerve damage finally healed and my hand no longer felt as though it were being held in boiling water. I still carry some baggage though—my chipped and scarred elbow doesn't quite straighten out. The canine tooth scars, pasty callouses on my wrist and elbow, are all but gone.

There remain, unfortunately, scars and calluses of another kind. Now and again, I'll be startled by some amorphous, dark shape high and right in my peripheral vision—someone in a dark coat, for instance. Dogs, sensing the fear I'm trying to conceal, become instantly aggressive. Those open, mountain meadows are no longer the Elysian fields of my youth. Alone in the backcountry in summer, if I can make myself do it at all, I travel with a fear of some kind of darkness. I make enough noise to drive the game from entire mountain valleys as I pass though. Like the returning homeowner who discovers his house has been broken into, I've had to face up to the reality that the world is not the friendly place I thought it should be.

IN THE FIRST FEW DAYS AFTER NARROWLY ESCAPING WITH MY LIFE, I sought to file the attack in its proper place and, flattered by media attention, agreed to write an article for the local paper. Rereading it now only confirms how unaware I yet was of just how deeply such an event can burrow into the psyche—and how shallow was my understanding of its long-term effects. Ignoring my own instinct regarding the respect the bear was due, I chose instead to aggrandize the bloody confrontation, Man-vs.-Nature style.

Bears have been part of our mythology for a very long time. The Great Bear constellation circles above our heads every night. Nanuq, the Inuktitut word for polar bear, was believed to have great powers far beyond that of mortal man. The Nakoda people of western Alberta maintained that the strongest personal spirit quest and, it would seem to me, about the riskiest one could undertake, was that of lying down beside a den to confront and thereby absorb the power of the grizzly bear. I now have some sense of what that would feel like. The symbolic value bears hold differs among cultures and between men and women: power, sexuality, courage, aggression.

In Jonathan Waterman's disarmingly honest account of his harrowing 3,200-kilometre solo kayak trip through the entire Northwest Passage, it is clear he also wished to come to terms with his fear, a fear represented most obviously by the great spirit bear, Nanuq. The search, he points out, is made more difficult because he, and we, have lost contact with the land. Waterman describes our modern selves as not much more than bad tenants, knowing little more about our world than is necessary to heat our houses and run our televisions.

In this environment of dissociation, we see bears as plush animals stuffed and comfortably at our side through childhood. Or as the shambling, discoloured, displaced ramblers of the tiny jails we call zoos. As the targets of deadly, testosterone-charged hunting parties in our local wild lands. As overweight, cross-eyed mascots for various commercial enterprises or walking, talking characters in cartoons. And perhaps worst of all, as the raw material of big business, herded like cattle into pens or shot from helicopters, slaughtered for their gallbladders.

Fortunately, sometimes bears are the subject of carefully researched, beautifully photographed documentaries that reveal a wonderfully adapted animal, sometimes deadly, sometimes disarmingly playful, imbued with great strength and courage. A truly courageous example of such work is that of Maureen Enns and Charlie Russell on the Kamchatka Peninsula in the former Soviet Union. Having rescued three orphaned grizzly bear cubs, the two Albertans named the cubs, fed them and set them free to live as they should in their own environment, returning each summer to spend time with the bears as they grew up. The pair literally lived with the bears, fishing, sitting by the lake, exploring, even sleeping with them in the meadows, living the Edenic existence I'd dreamed of. The two books they produced from that experience reveal in word and photograph some of the most astounding examples of human/ursine harmony ever recorded. Unfortunately, in the end, Russell and Enns also endured the bears' destruction at human hands—shot, probably from helicopters, for their gallbladders. The organs were found nailed to the walls of the couple's tiny cabin.

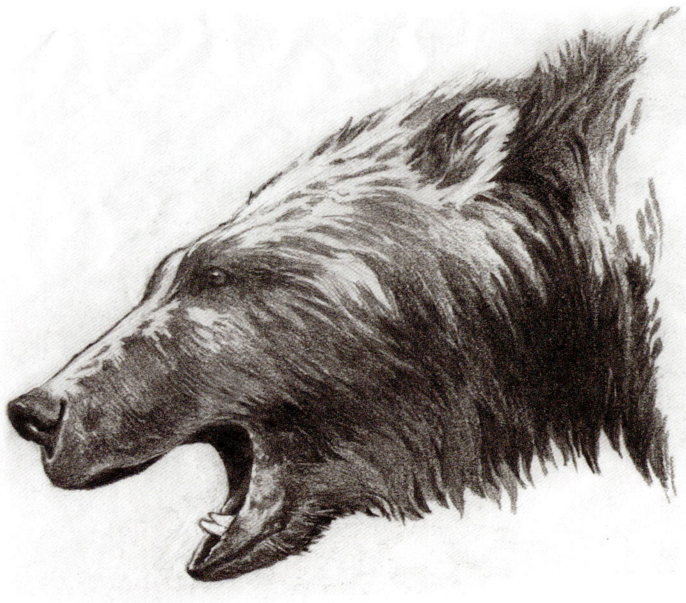

Grizzly in territorial argument (a discussion involving different points of view).

The human/bear interface is a difficult one. Although I've always been afraid of bears, at the same time I liked them. And though rationally I knew otherwise, somehow I expected *them* to like me. Experienced eco-tour guides describe how their clients demonstrate an innocent-verging-on-self-destructive attraction to these powerful animals. Wouldn't it be great to scratch their heads behind those round fuzzy ears and playfully goosh their noses? Maybe even roll around in the long grass or slide down a snow slope together? But of course, bears are not pets. They are not harmless. There are cases of grizzlies that have deliberately hunted and killed humans (which, of course, we have done routinely to bears for some time). The late Patricia van Tighem's horrific encounter with a bear defending its kill (poignantly captured in her book *The Bear's Embrace*); the recent death of Canmore resident Isabelle Dubé, attacked while jogging; the tragedy of the well-meaning but unbalanced Timothy Treadwell, who was finally attacked and eaten after several seasons in the wild, are ample proof of that.

Regardless, my car proudly sports a bumper sticker perhaps not quite so familiar to Albertans as that other one to which it refers. I Love Alberta ... Bears.

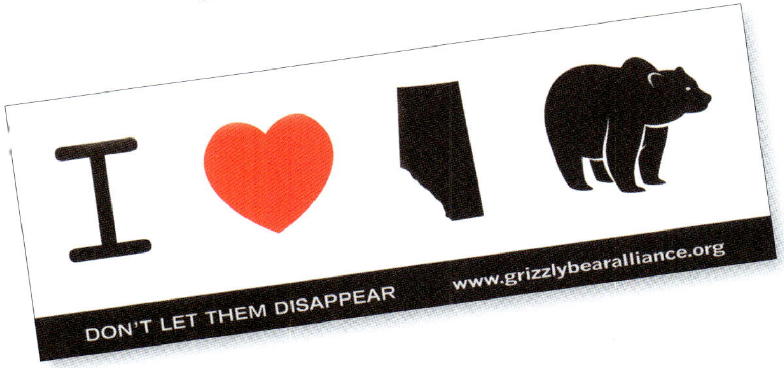

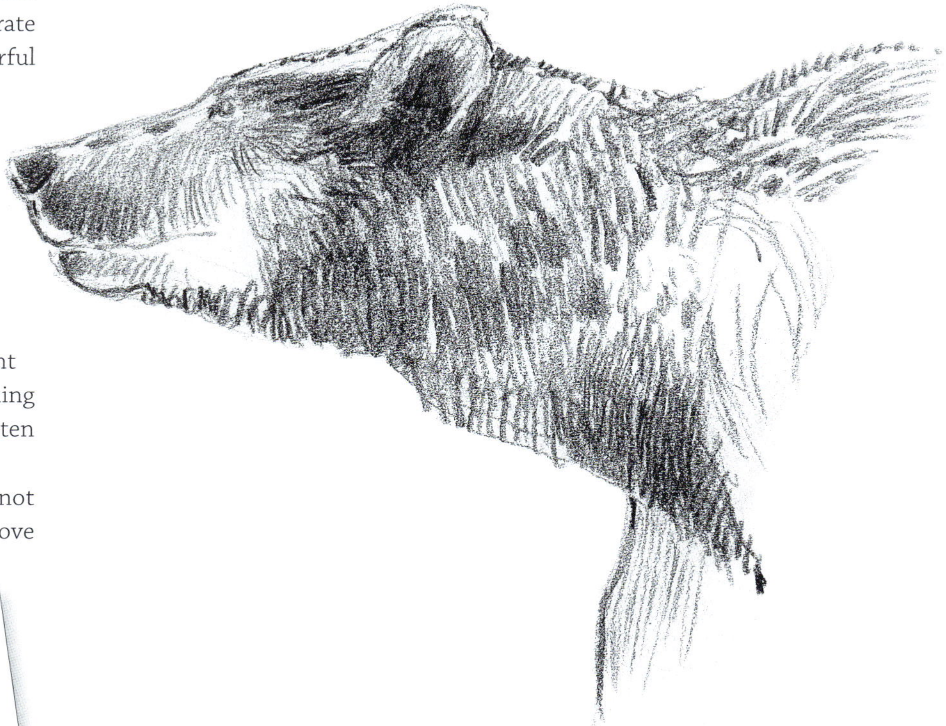

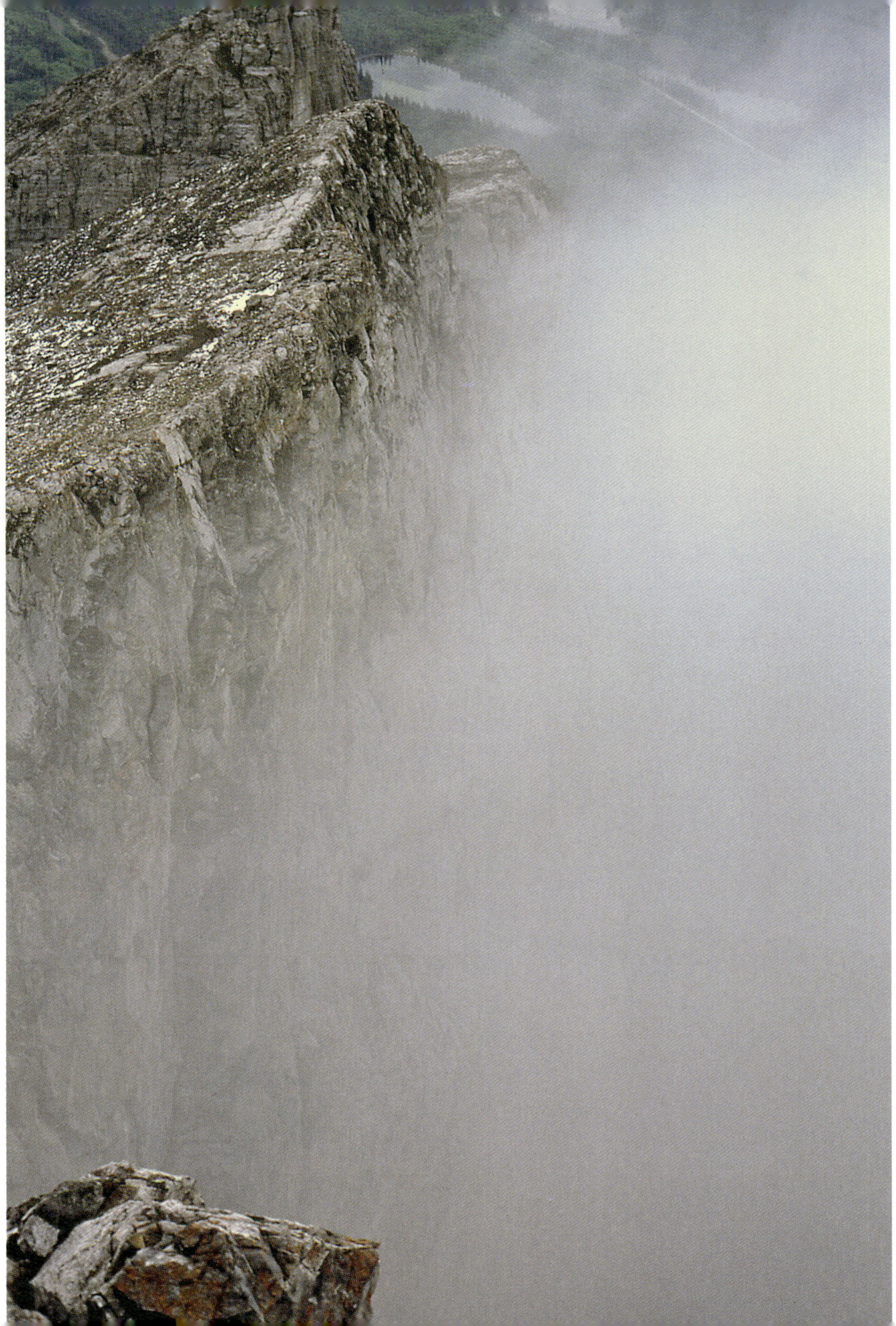

On a cold day, Jim and I traverse the long ridge of Mount Yamnuska as mist rises to envelope the spectacularly steep south face. This is rock-climbing central for many Calgary climbers.

The gift

CHAPTER 8

Better shoes, fixed points of protection, improved training, new techniques: all have helped young climbers surmount overhanging rock on a regular basis.

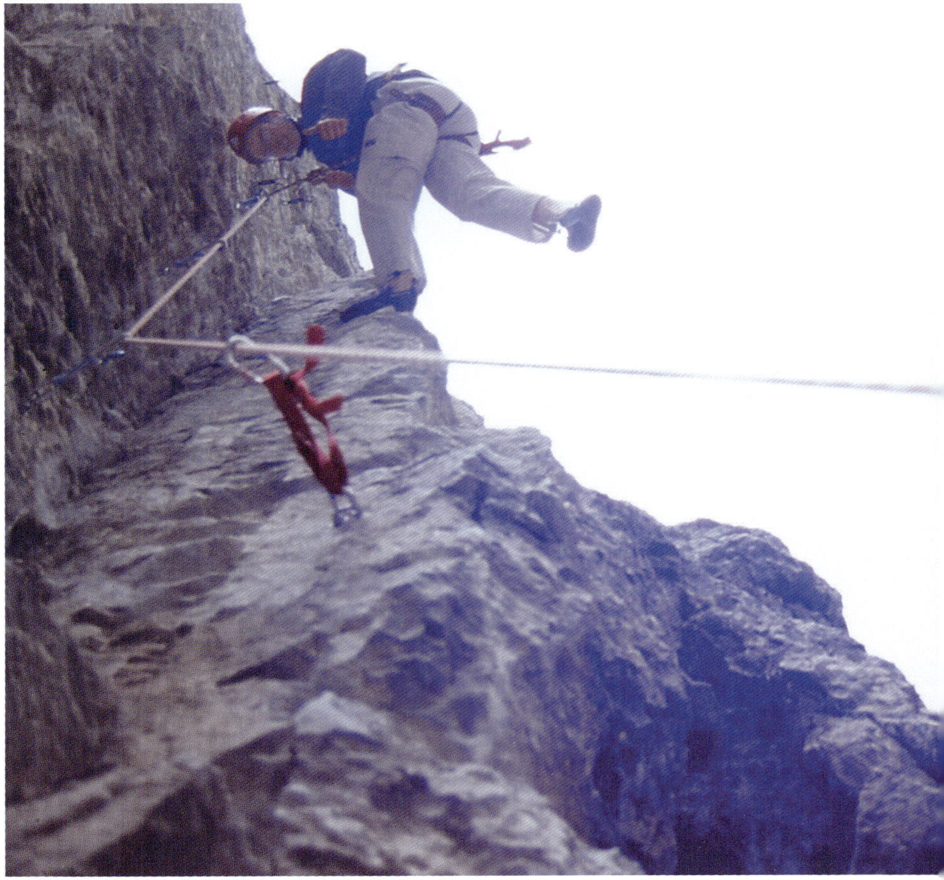

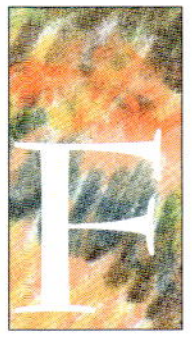

From the time he was 8 years old, I had taken my son Laurence to The Stronghold, an indoor rock-climbing gym in Calgary. As a result, by 17, he climbed at a technical level far surpassing mine and, in fact, seemed capable of feats of levitation. During that time, however, he obtained little real mountaineering experience. As a result, there was a deficiency in his curriculum, that piece you might describe as an opening door, silent music, soul experience. Missing was that moment of summit clarity whose alchemy makes a drink from a mountain stream more satisfying than a finished wine, a chunk of limestone more precious than gold. Ineffable, hard won, that elusive state of mind was one of my most valued possessions.

Historically, First Nations people, employing only interpolation and intuition along with their five innate senses, navigated accurately across vast stretches of flat prairie. To us today, whose stereotypical routine consists of a numbing daily commute to and from an all-consuming computer terminal, their accomplishments seem almost beyond belief. Small wonder when, having submitted to what has been described as a kind of sensory deprivation, the same senses in us have wasted away almost to nothing. As a university student I'd seen the damage drugs could do. Since then, there had become available successive generations of increasingly accessible and highly addictive drugs that beckoned to those adrift in a sensory and spiritual wasteland. Male teenagers in particular seemed to crave the opportunity to test themselves physically and so find their place in the world. What had I to offer? The answer was this gift of seeing mountains. A gift I was determined to pass on.

There may have been a time in history when necessity dictated otherwise, but fatherhood in affluent Calgary did not include voluntarily exposing one's offspring to death, especially for what might superficially seem an arcane, temporary nirvana. In a litigious society desperately intent on eliminating risk, I was haunted by the spectre of father-and-son as portrayed in an endlessly banal culture of TV. In such a world, when some kid finally manages to get out in the backcountry and an accident occurs, parental response leans toward lawsuits seeking solace and restitution in a hopeless attempt to compensate for real life.

Without risk, there could be little adventure, self-reliance or self-discovery in young lives. But there was a catch. All things come at a cost—in mountaineering, it was bone-grinding hard work, the possibility of injury, even death. A serious matter, and infinitely more so because my gift's recipient was to be my son. The accepted father/son bonding activities—teaching him to fish, rag the puck, swing a golf club or the like—carried little threat compared to what I had in mind. Only a madman would destroy what he loves. How could I possibly justify that kind

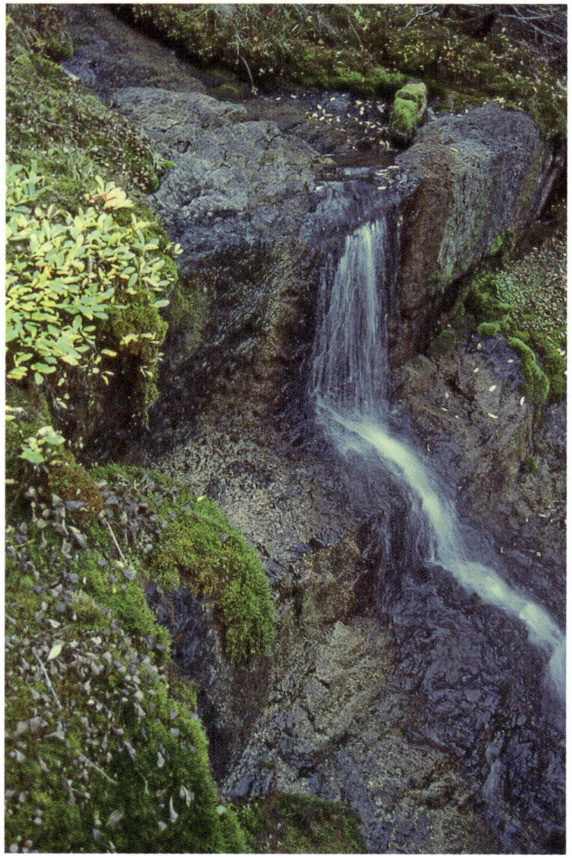

A small creek pours over ancient limestone ridges just above a lake in the Rockies' front ranges.

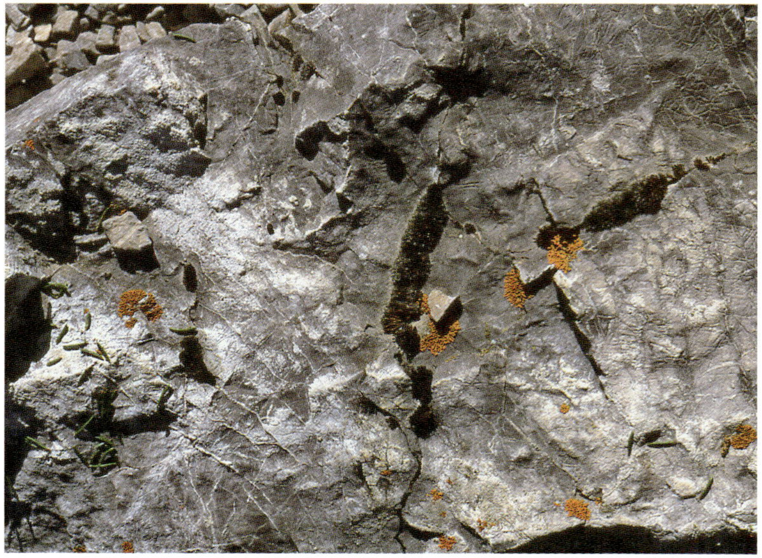

At the moment of discovery this shard of limestone seems very beautiful. Take it home and it becomes just another dusty knick-knack on the shelf.

of risk? In darker moments, I worried I was passing on my own selfish addictions, my gift just another drug for personal devils. In a waking nightmare I saw my son's body silently tumbling down an endless, grey wall. But in the end I could not accept that he might not glimpse what I had seen in the soul of the limestone crags. And so we went climbing.

SWEAT SOAKS THE SHIRTS UNDER OUR PACKS as we traverse open meadows and zigzag through rock bands and gnarled pines. The steady three-and-a-half-hour slog up the lower slopes of Castle Mountain, a grand citadel of towers and battlements that juts into the Bow Valley, has finally brought us to the base of our intended route. Once here, a clear delineation sees you virtually step up onto steep rock from a talus slope. Beneath the rough shelter of a small overhang that will deflect rock falling from above, we stop and take off the packs. We will enjoy a few minutes rest, put on harness and helmets, gear up and start up. We pause in our steady patter while I think over a delicate point, which, on reconsideration, might have been more thoughtfully approached elsewhere. Still, the vast ramparts above us lend urgency to the discussion, which goes something like the following.

Me to Laurence: "Um, y' know, what we are about to do can be lethal, and I don't think it's going to happen, and you're probably safer here than on the highway, and I don't want to scare you, but... if I die, it's okay." Which, as soon as it is out of my mouth, sounds absurdly melodramatic. I soldier on, "I mean, if I get hit by rock fall, or fall and hit my head, or whatever, that's the way the game is played. Okay? It's the price of admission, and it's okay." Serious stuff. I pause to see how that has gone over, and in the absence of significant response, which I'll admit is a bit of a letdown, continue. "If it looks like you can do it safely, rap back down (reverse the route by sliding down the rope with a metal friction device), walk back to the highway and go tell somebody."

Implicit in all of this, of course, is that he may suffer a similar fate. I pause again to gauge the effect. Laurence seems unperturbed, maybe even a little bored by this awkward monologue. I feel a little like I've been

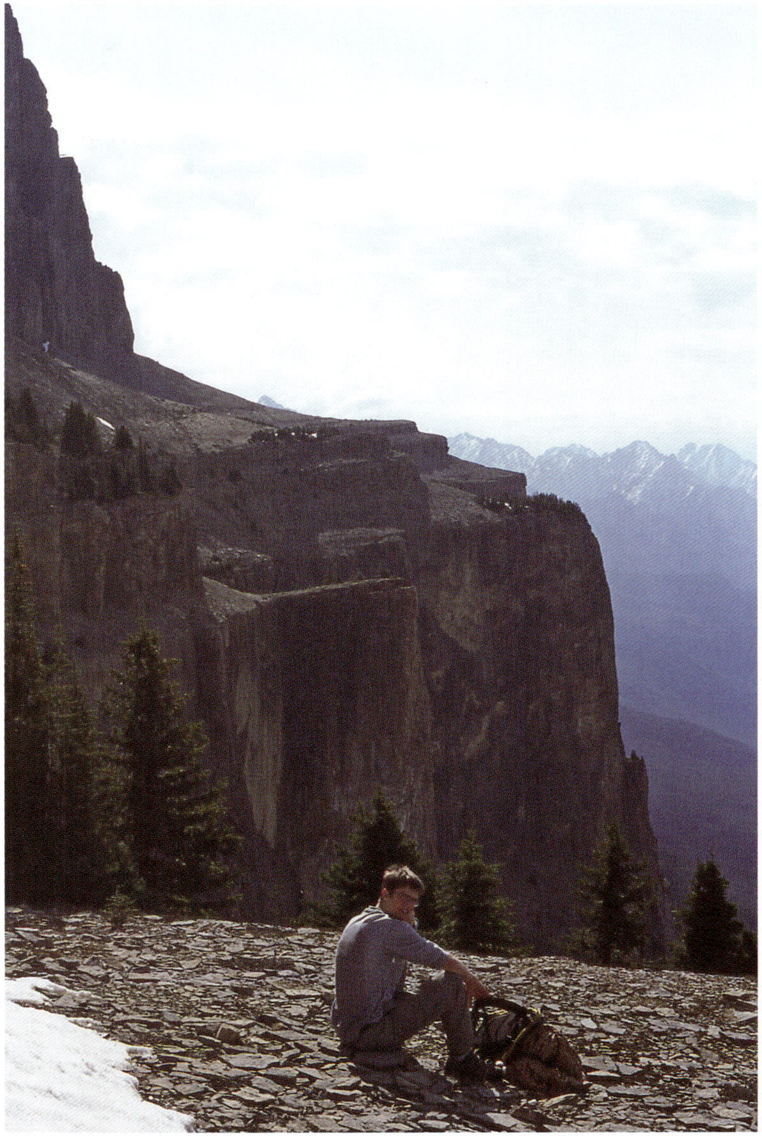

Laurence takes a rest on a big shale plateau halfway up Castle Mountain. This is the abode of mountain goats, which pass through here from time to time.

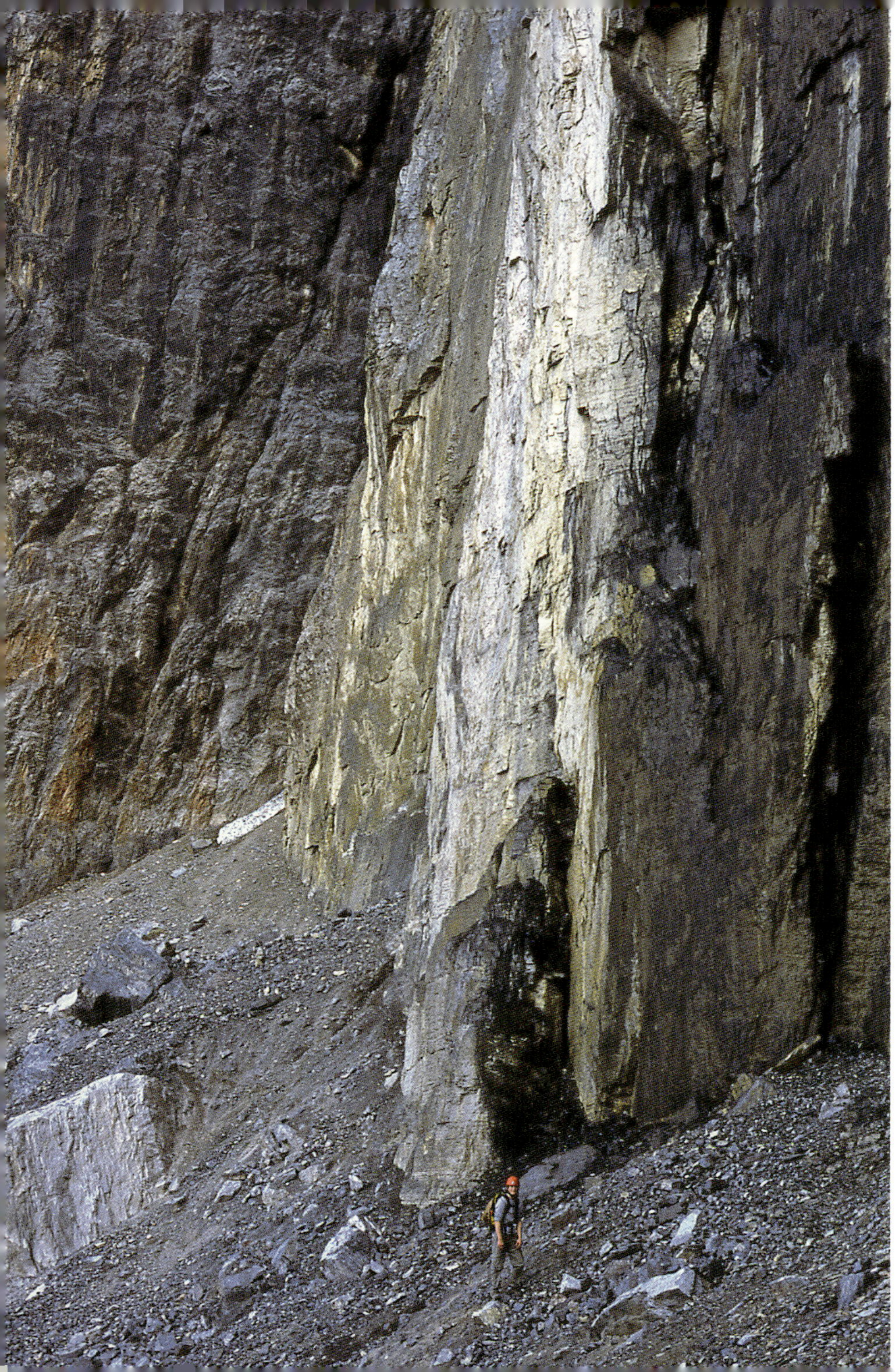

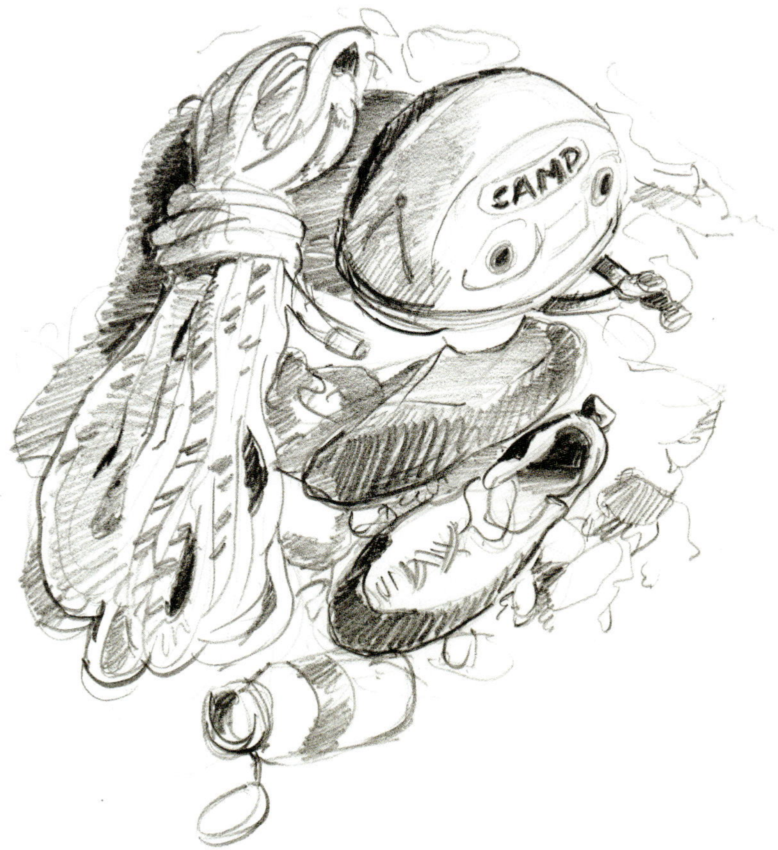

Walking beside one of these huge walls can be intimidating, like discovering yourself shaded by the colossal knarly leg of some unthinkable creature.

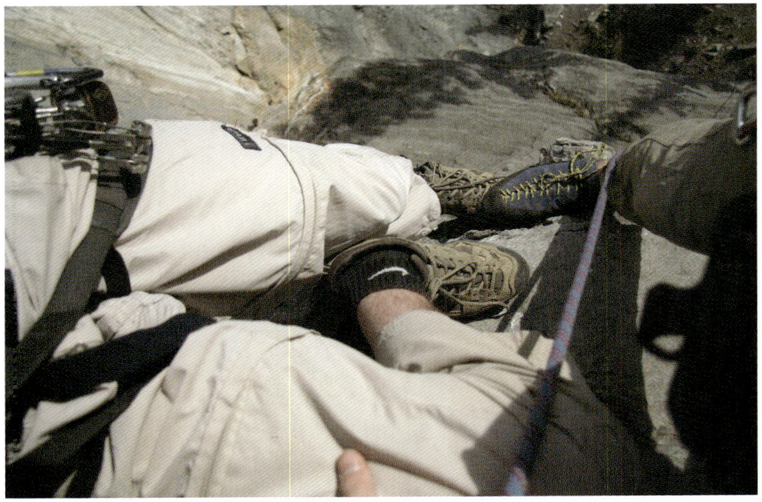

edging up to that *man-to-man* talk only to discover he already knows it all. Which turns out to be the case here, and I wonder if this fatherhood business ever gets any easier. Several years ago on a minor peak, as a storm bore down on us, I told him if I were struck by lightning he was to leave me there and go down on his own. What I did not know and was humbled to discover is that when we got home he'd lain awake in the darkness long into the night thinking about that, trying to put things in perspective. So, by himself, in his own way, demonstrating at once the grace of youth and maturity beyond his years, he'd already faced his own mortality, acknowledged the risk and embraced the vision.

Conversation thus turns to the challenge at hand. Since I've been here before I lead first, up vertical limestone to a ragged inside corner, clipping into protection I've placed in crevices. Then I belay Laurence. Face-to-face on a small ledge, teetering as though in a telephone booth 10 storeys up, we exchange the hardware rack. We crane our necks back, decide on the best line, and then he leads off, literally stepping up past my head. One of his bright blue, precisely fitted shoes almost in my pocket, the other at my cheek, I see the soft black rubber sole flex—and then it's gone. I hear the clank of metal above. From time to time the rope that lies coiled

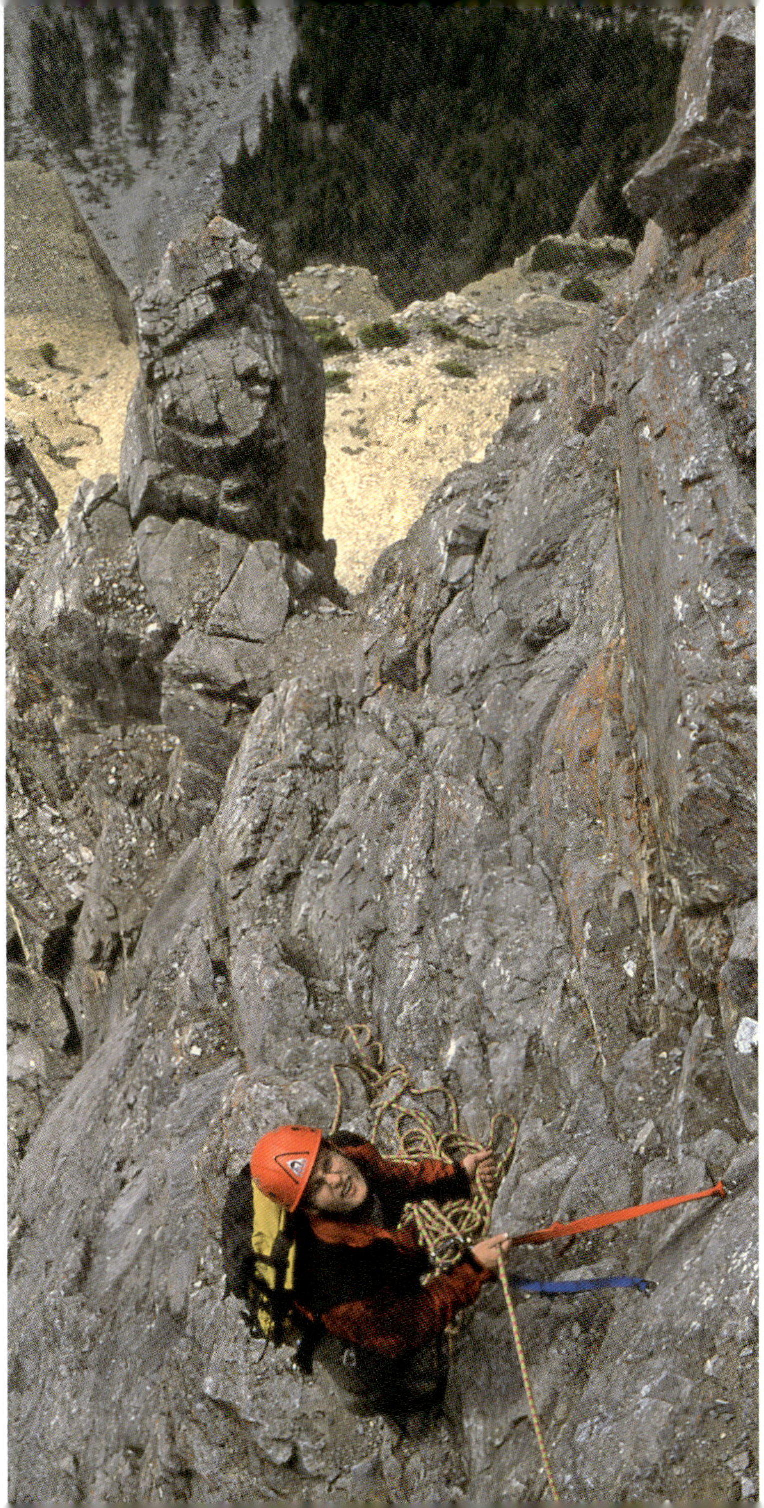

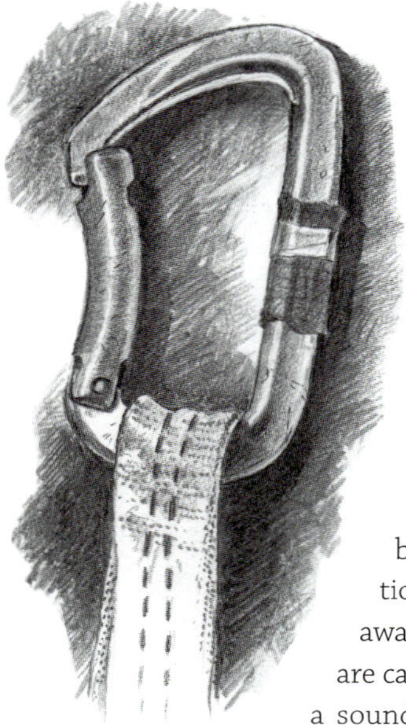

just at my feet rasps the side of my helmet—*zzzt, zzzt*—as it snakes upward. We will continue to alternate leads this way, leap-frogging all the way to the top. Along the way, the leader will secure various types of equipment in cracks and secure them to the rope with a carabiner (an extremely strong, alloy snap link). The second climber will retrieve the gear as he comes, and the process will be repeated. It's a fascinating mode of connection with another human being, who, for the moment, may as well be on the other side of the moon. No body language, no meaningful glance, no conversation. Most shouts are blocked by rock bulges or carried away on the wind. For this reason, climber's exchanges are carefully scripted such that if direct articulation is lost, a sound's cadence and intonation carry the meaning. "Up rope" is two short syllables. "On belaaaaaaaaay!" Two short, one long. "F***!!! Falling!" Well, unmistakable.

The rope in my hand transformed to eyes and ears, my son transmuted in the movement of a length of bright nylon rope, I feel him advance, thinking his way upward, hold by hold. Then a retreat. The loop of rope sags then rises, and I know he is searching with his fingers, trying another way. The black halfway mark on the rope slides past in fits and starts, then disappears. As I pay out the rope in one hand, I feel vibrations caused by wind. Which means he's on steep stuff. If the rope moves slowly, hesitantly, halts for too long, then goes slack I'll know he's in trouble, maybe coming off the face altogether, and my mouth will go dry as I wait for his shout and brace for his fall. But the rope starts to move steadily upward again. He's reached

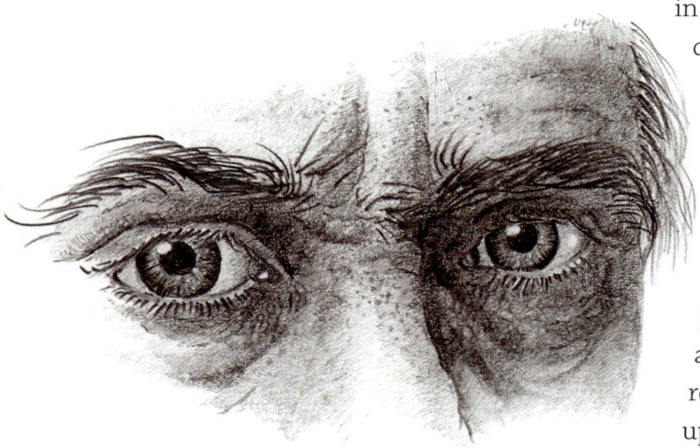

easier terrain. His strength and agility on the far end of the rope has me imagining a gecko scuttling far above. Now I rush to pay out quickly enough. With one hand I struggle to clear snarls and kinks that writhe around my legs; with the other I feed the rope through a bright green friction device.

At the moment, I'm sitting on a ledge about the size of child's stool, legs dangling over the Bow Valley. The rope sways in the light breeze far above the green forest. A little yellow hover fly, wings ablur, helicopters up and down the rope, landing occasionally, attracted, I think, by its warmth and colour. To a heavily laden climber intent on staying alive up here, its busy nonchalance is impressive.

And so the day passes—in silent leads, animated conversation at belay points, the occasional shouted communication ebbing and flowing on the wind. The valley falls below as summit clouds draw nearer. Freed from the urban crush by the simple goals and total focus of mountaineering, life is delightfully reduced to slow, length-by-length measures of yellow rope. Our journey through time is measured by the sun as it rises up the sky, describes an arc, then sets. Later, when the climb is finished and we are hiking back to the car, our time will be again literally circumscribed, this time by the moon rising, floating, traversing west. So strong is my consciousness of this magnificent clock that I sometimes feel a resonance like music, a kind of dance of hours set to the rhythm of the universe.

THE SHADOWS ACROSS THE ROCK GROW first shorter then longer. Finally, in the late afternoon, we have no more rock to climb, no more up. Fittingly, this Father's Day, my gift is not breakfast in bed or a new tie or tickets to the game, but instead this shared moment on a lofty esplanade. We celebrate with our dwindling supply of fruit bars and spring water, pack away the climbing gear and descend the more gently sloped back of the mountain. It has been a cold June and snow still lies thickly on the slopes that face away from the sun. We are soon soaked to the armpits from repeatedly falling forward in the chest-deep, waterlogged drifts. Laurence has frozen his toes; I can't feel my fingers. We drop through a narrow cleft, leaving snow and cold behind to enter a remote hanging

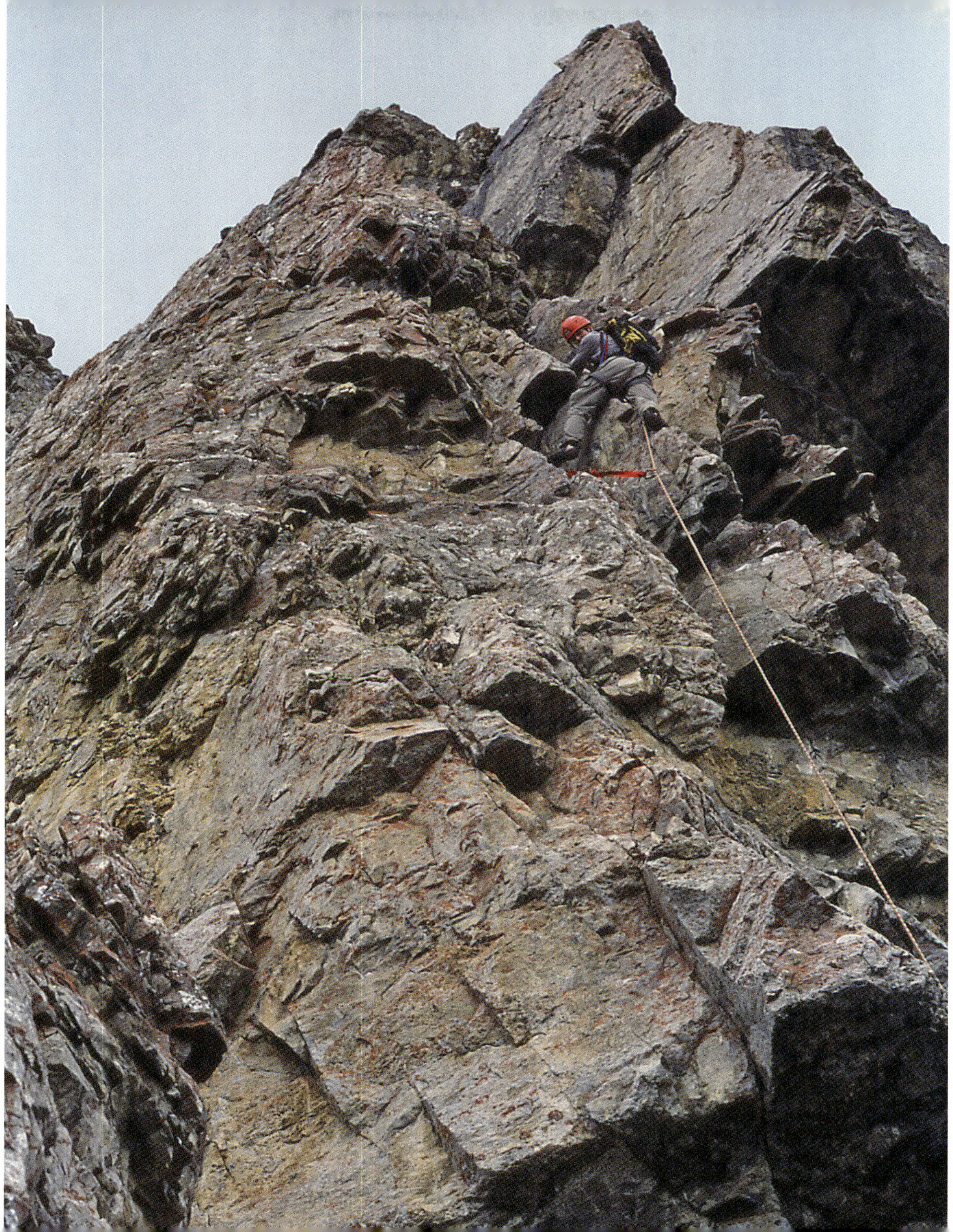

On the Castle Mountain climb, Laurence leads up one of the easier sections. Visual foreshortening, here evident, makes it difficult to judge upward distances.

I sometimes feel a resonance
like music, a kind of
dance of hours . . ."

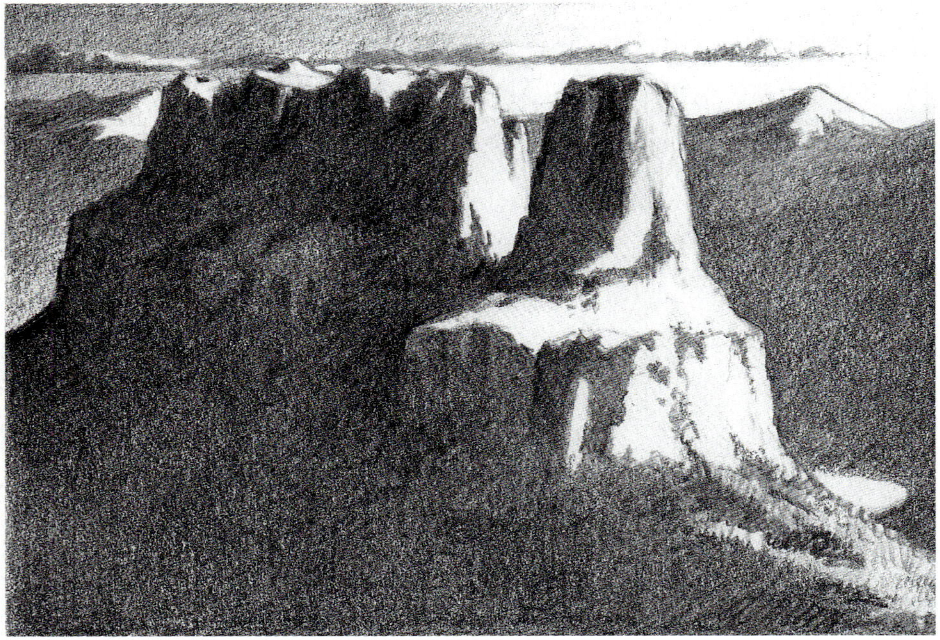

first light

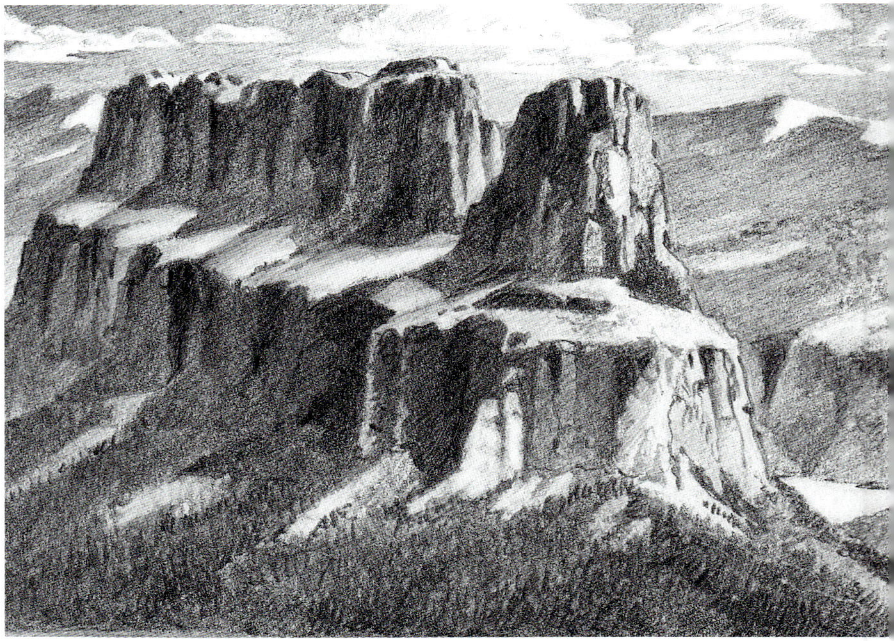

morning

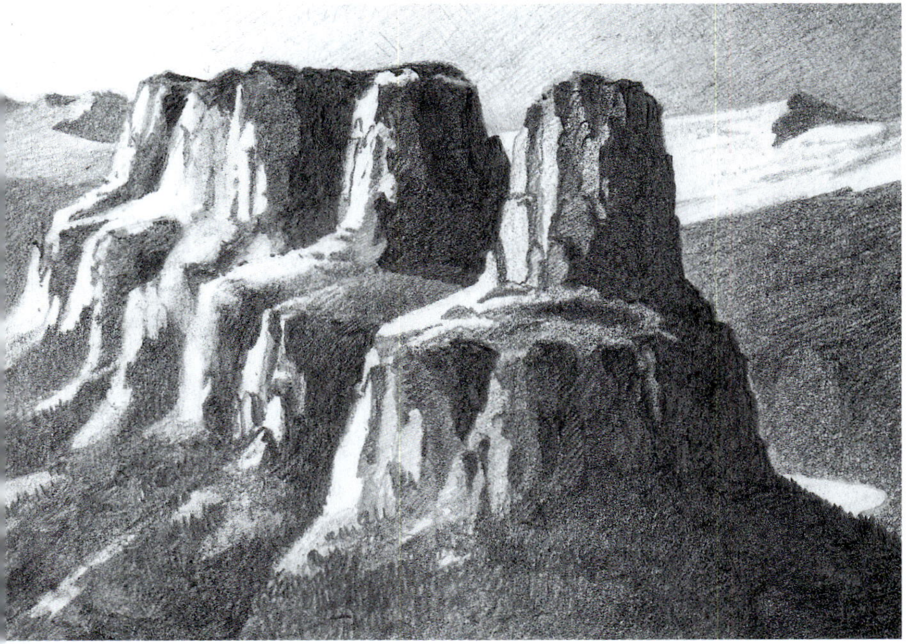
dusk

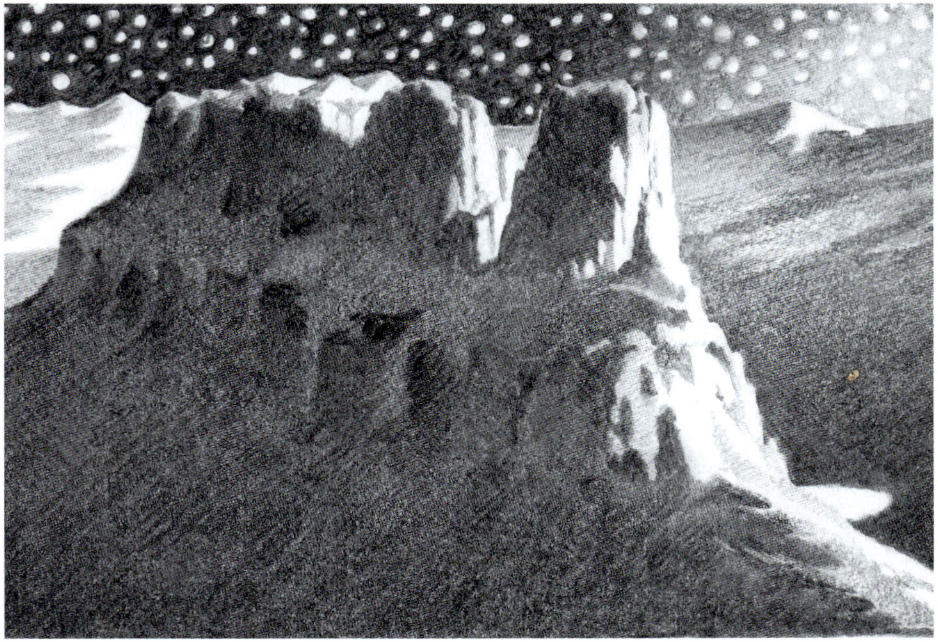
moonrise

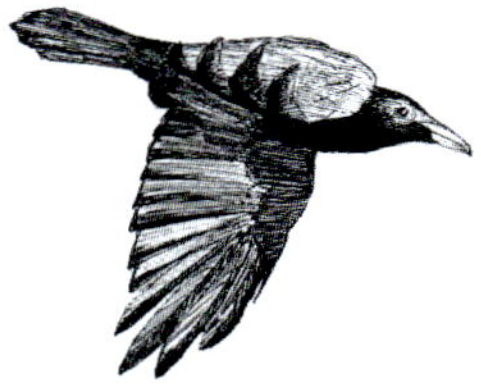

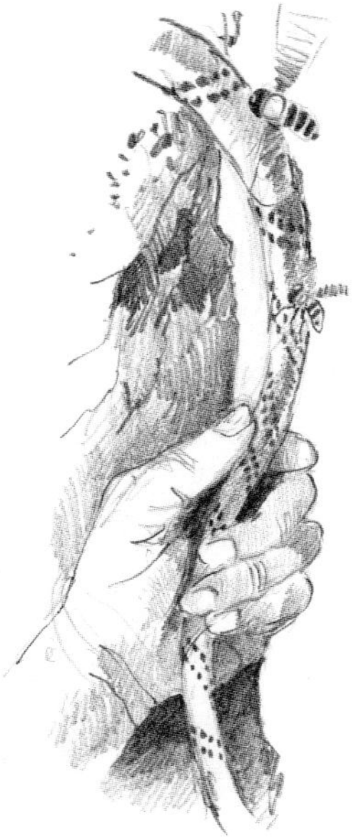

valley, which, rarely visited, reveals only the faintest of trails. Under our feet the grass and thick moss are soft. Larches turn gold in the low light. Before me, a creek burbles and leaps, rushing out first as a spring from the base of a cliff, coming from nowhere. It winds across the meadow and tumbles over a precipice, vanishing in blown spray and a flash of reflected light. A single marmot whistles. This valley we've entered seems simply to float in space.

The sun is descending over the western peaks. Those above our heads just catch its last light. The air is still, and shadows are beginning to stretch to the eastern horizon. I narrowly miss crushing a tiny nest containing the speckled tan and cream eggs of a white-tailed ptarmigan. The hen must be somewhere nearby, superbly camouflaged, pacing in excited circles, first one way, then the other. Just out of harm's way, in the grip of her avian ferocity, she'll be swearing: *chrrrr, chrrrr!*

No longer on guard for myself or my son, I'm still worried our discomfort will make him impatient and cold. But that is not the case at all. Despite circumstances that would leave many wondering why we're not soaking in Banff's hot sulphur springs—it's definitely crossed my mind—to my great relief Laurence is delighted to be here. He's obviously captivated by his grand surroundings. At the same time, something in his gestures tells me he does not see the world the same as I. He has his own vision and, as I should know, that's as it should be. He may not continue climbing, but that's not important. Part of me, in fact, hopes he won't.

This is as far as I can take him. My mission

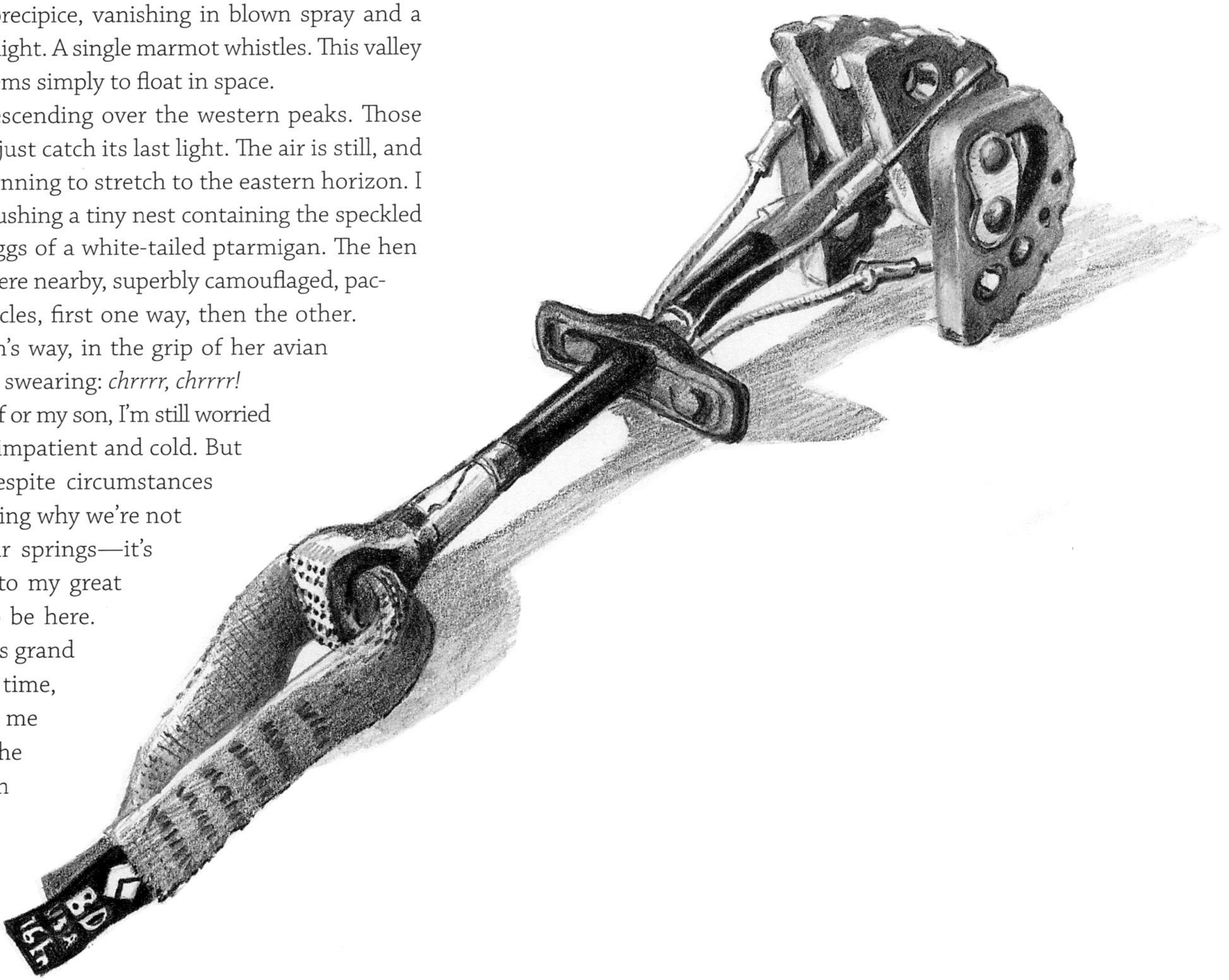

Last pitch. The climb's finale is made more challenging by the cumulative fatigue of an early drive from town, the long approach and sustained climbing through the day.

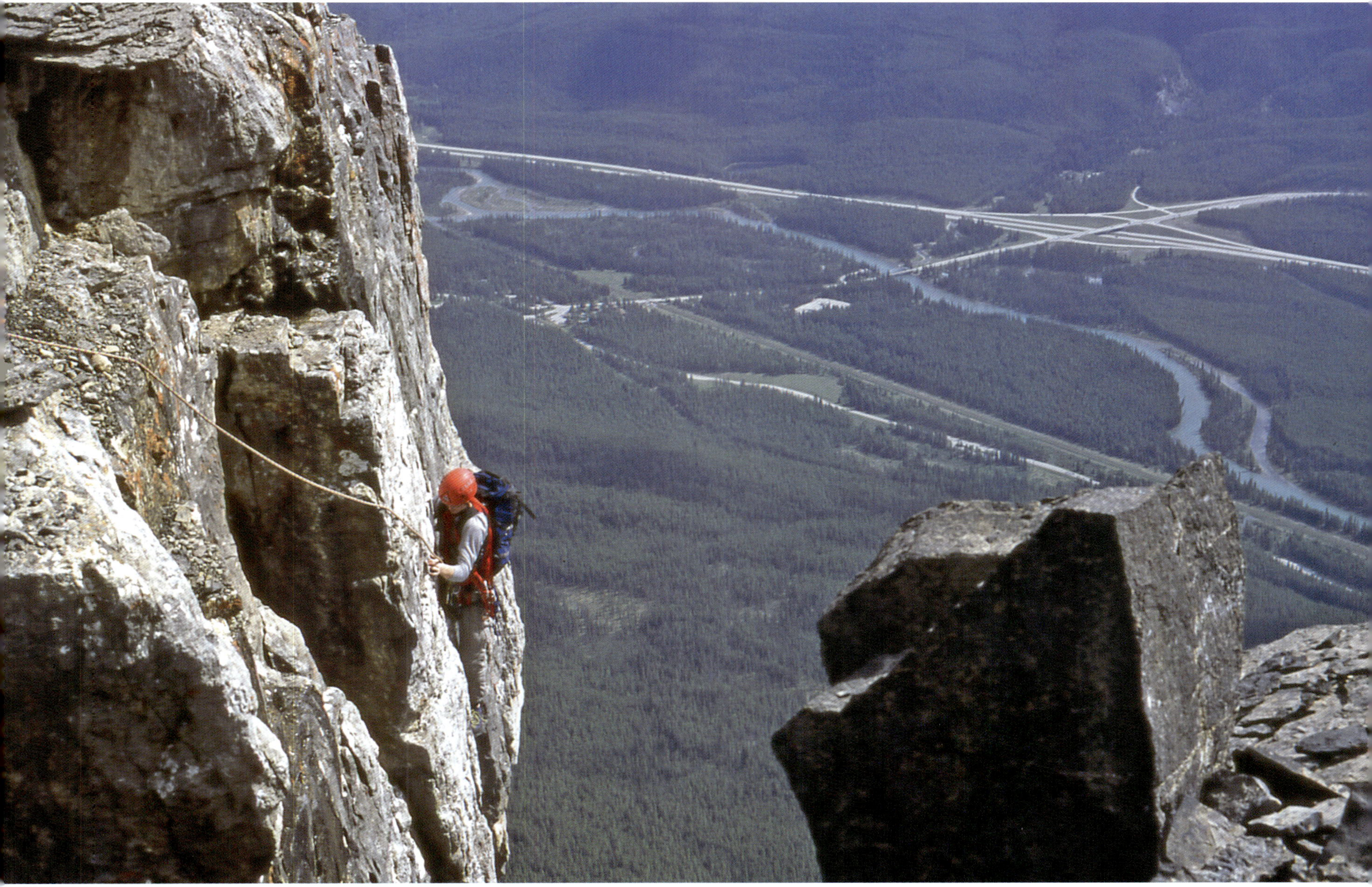

Kings of the Castle: An unusual celebration of Father's Day sees Laurence and I achieve the summit of Castle Mountain, easily visible to the Trans Canada motorist, together.

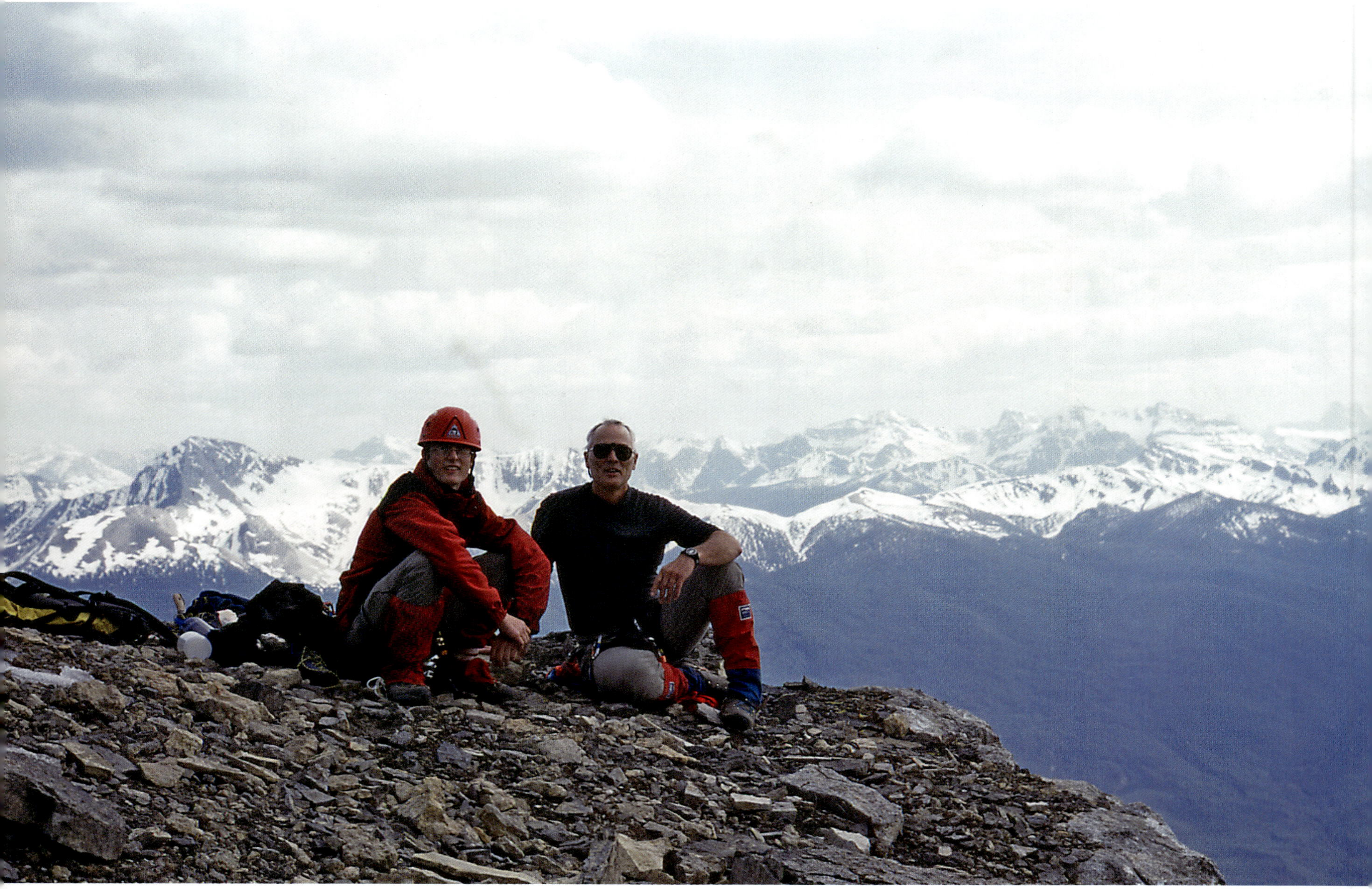

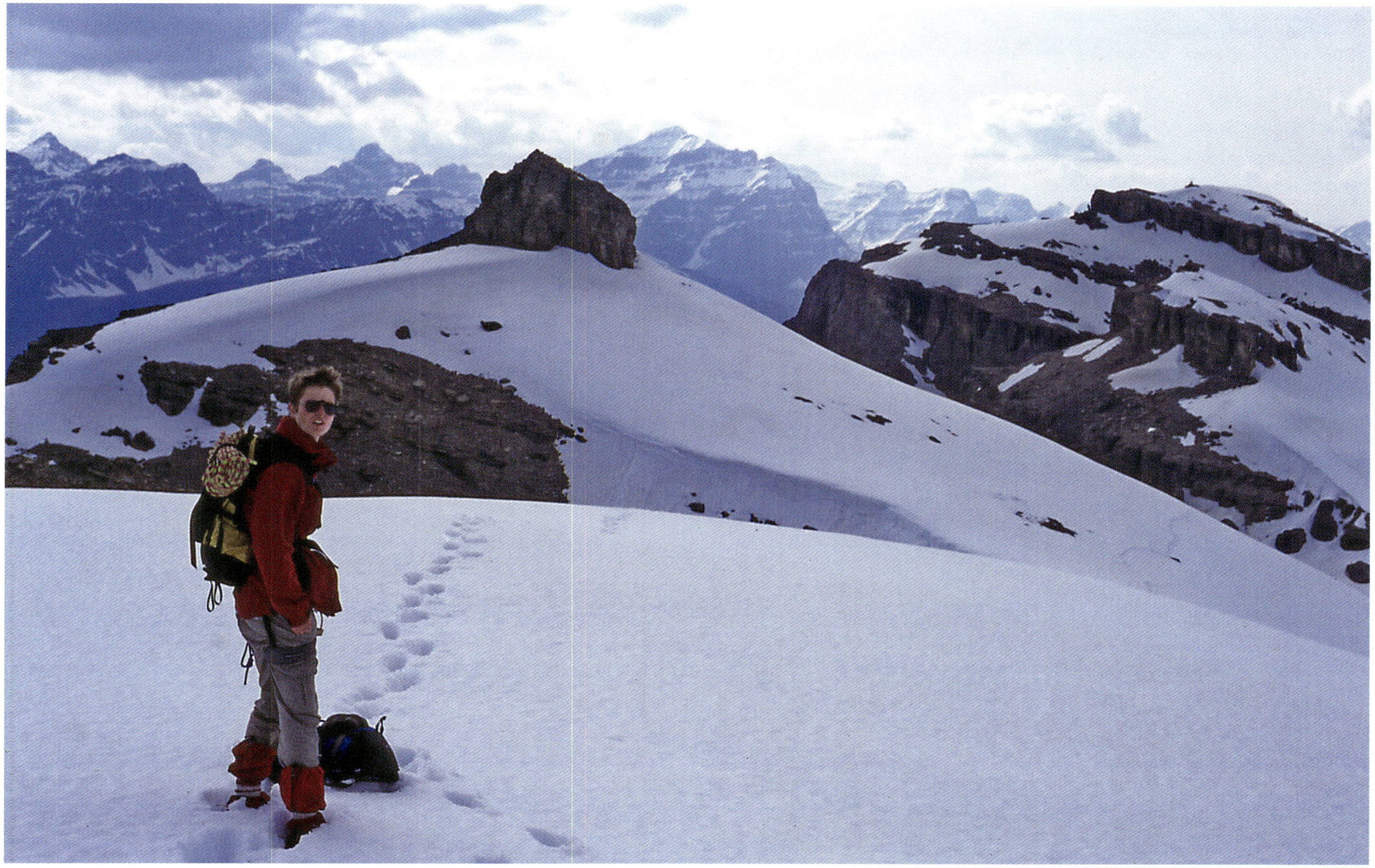

has not been accomplished quite the way I'd planned; still, his journey has begun. This is the little kid for whom I built a tiny set of wooden ski poles with red plastic baskets, for whom I bought a diminutive blue guitar. I nearly fell out of the bleachers cheering when he scored his first goal in hockey. I saw him offer his hand to his first girlfriend. He was transformed by that gesture into a khaki-and-T-shirt-clad Sir Galahad, she to Lady Guinevere of the pierced belly button and purple hair.

Deep snow on the back of Castle Mountain makes difficult walking until we reach the meadows below.

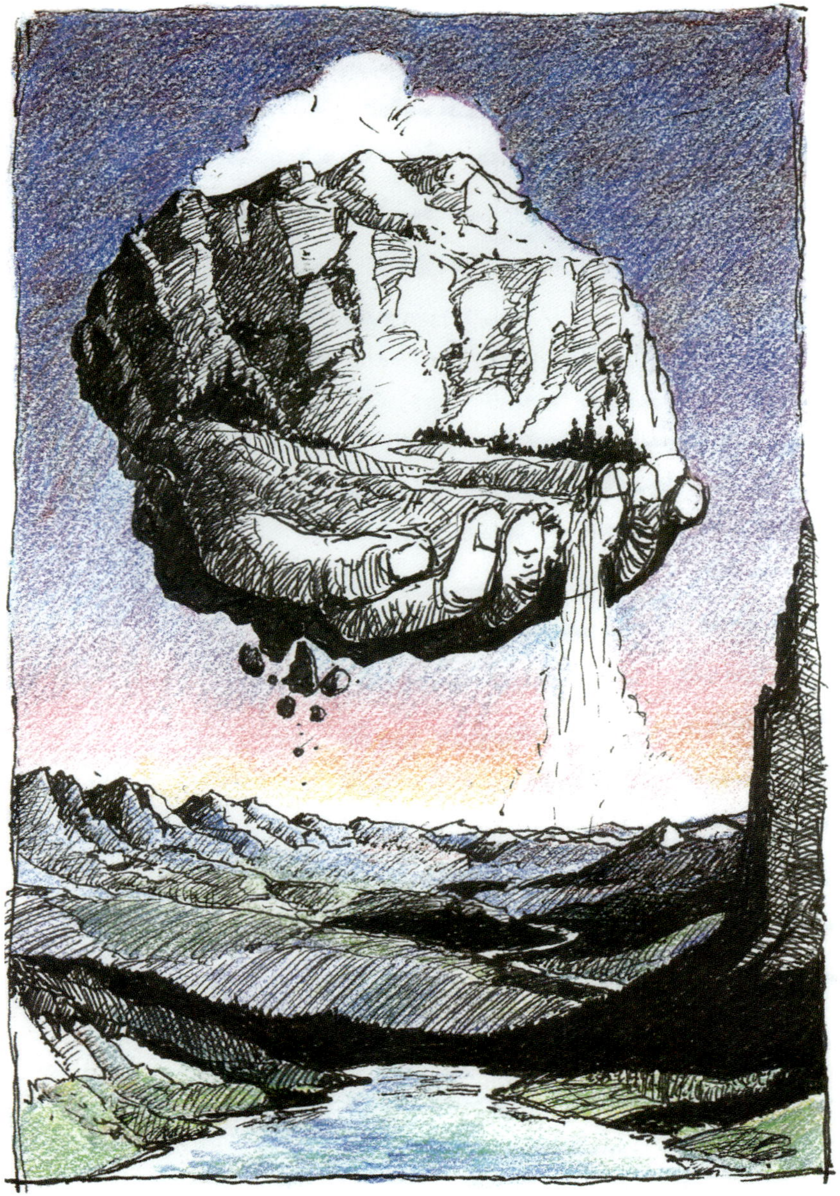

Our paths have come together and now they will begin to move apart. Letting go is a hard thing for a father. But Laurence has sensed the mountains' resonance, and that is the most valuable gift I can give.

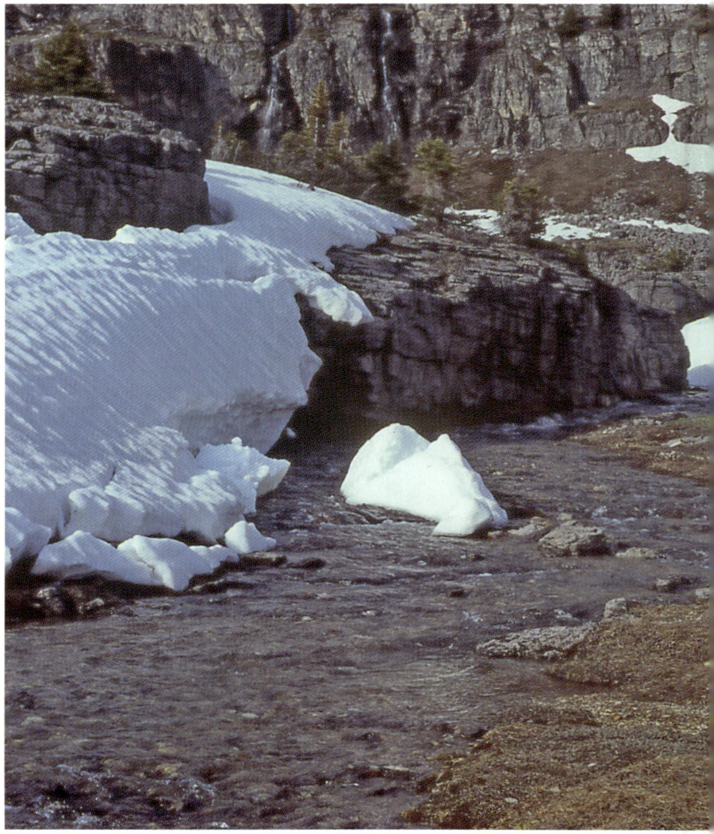

A creek is still partly frozen. Twigs, grass and bracken are glazed in a delicate purl of ice.

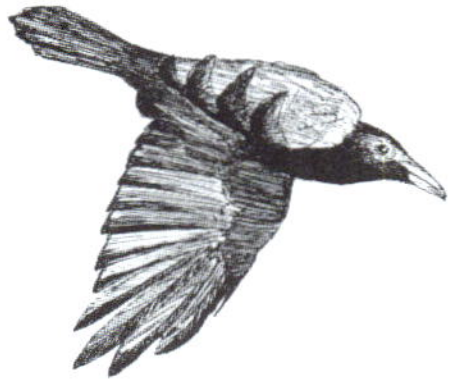

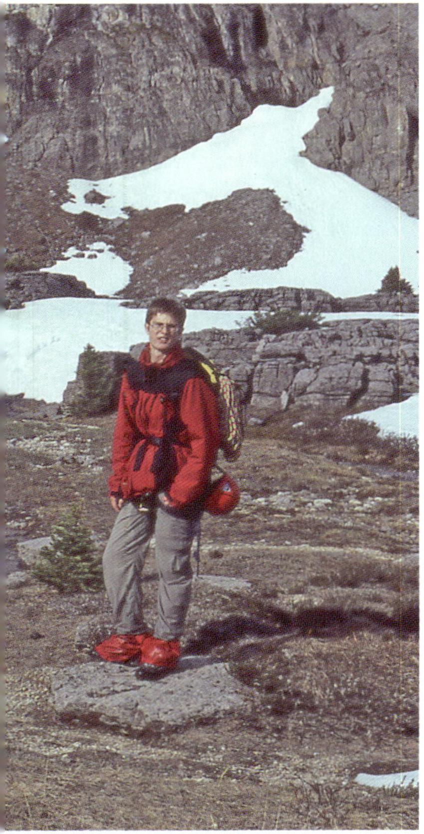

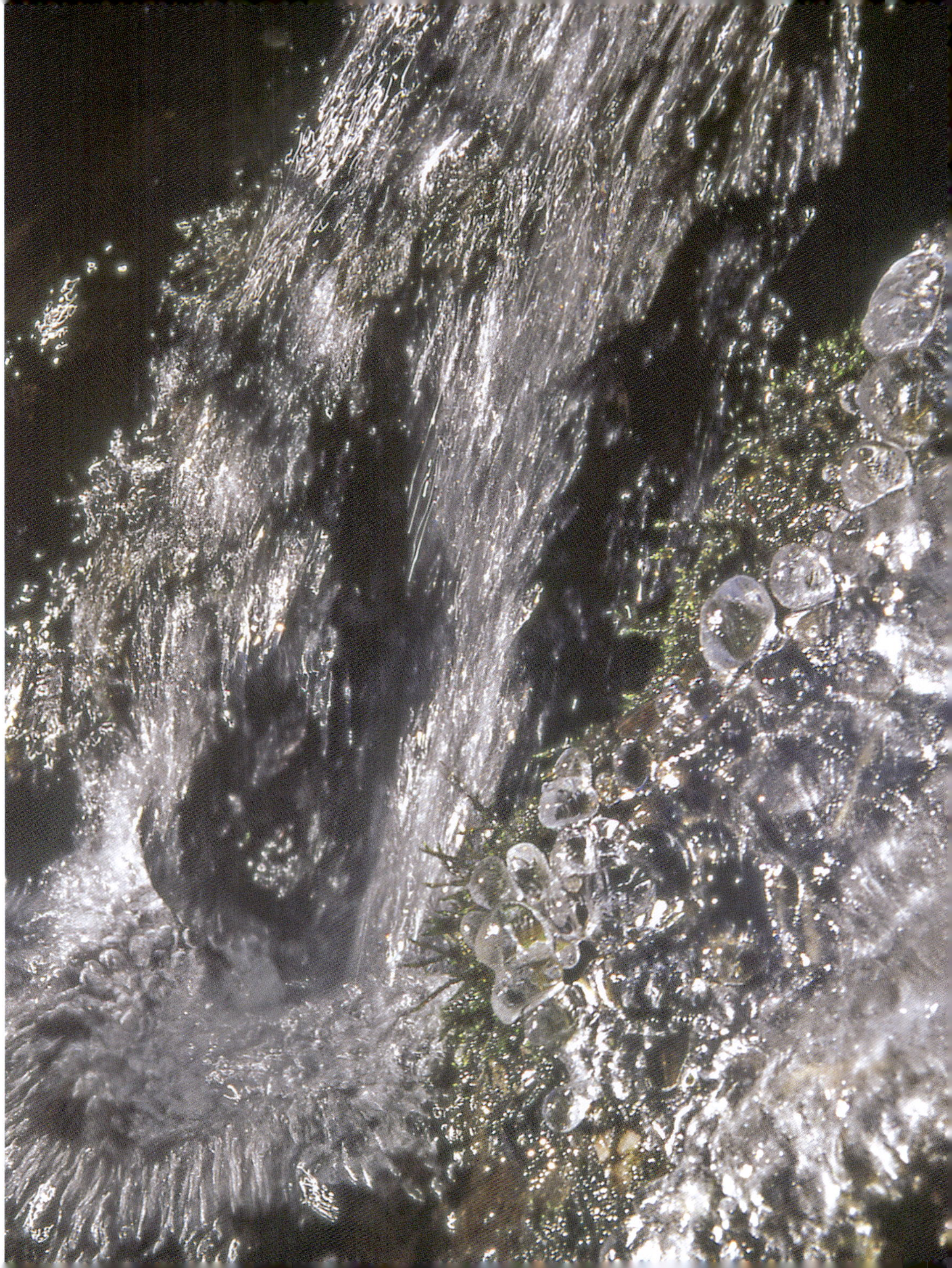

Two families stand atop the east tower of Castle Mountain between Banff and Lake Louise.

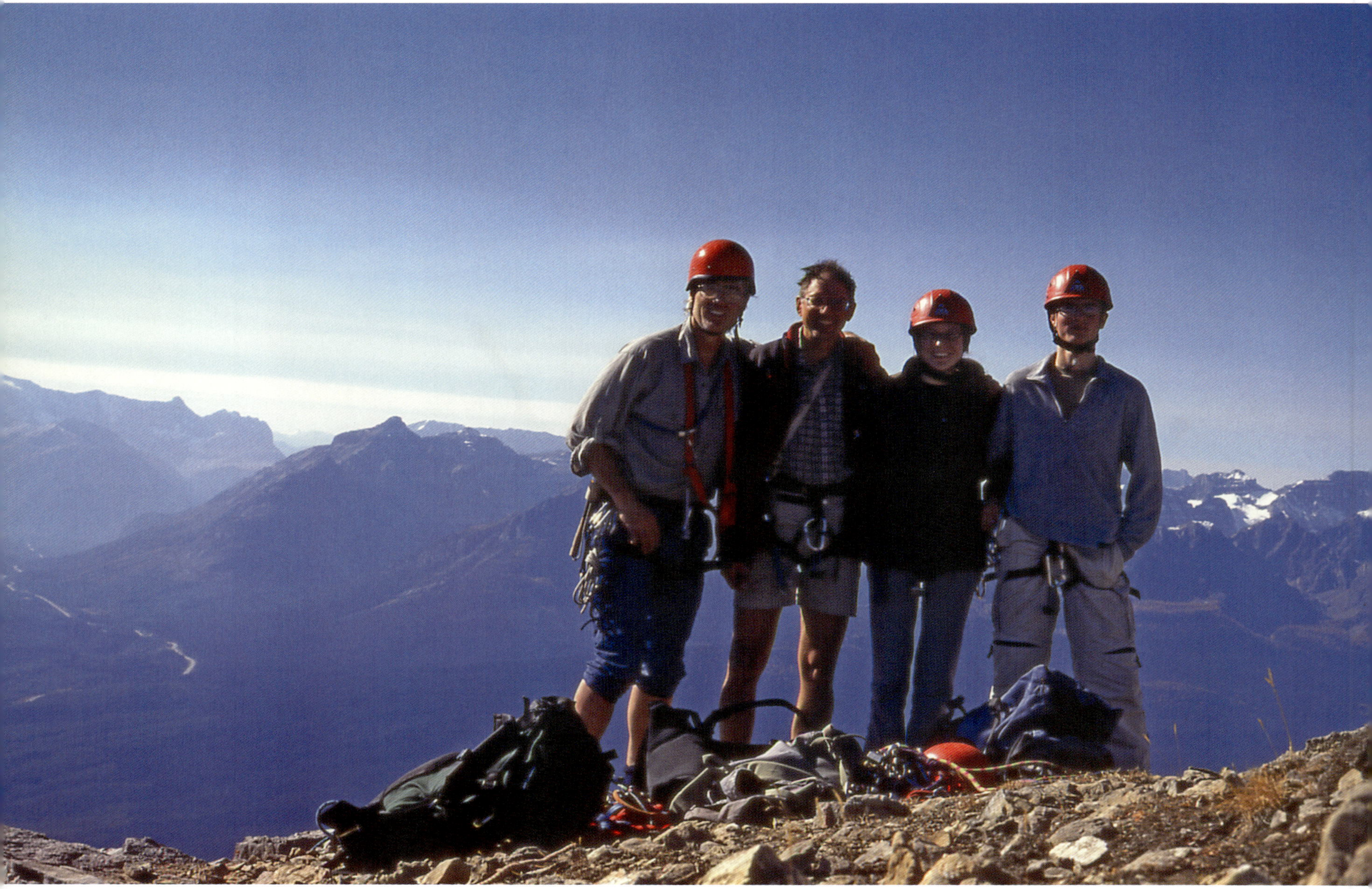

Epilogue

Bob and Susan Saunders head home along the high plateau. All is windless, quiet. The climb and nerve-wracking rappelling is over. Now they need only put one foot in front of the other all the way down.

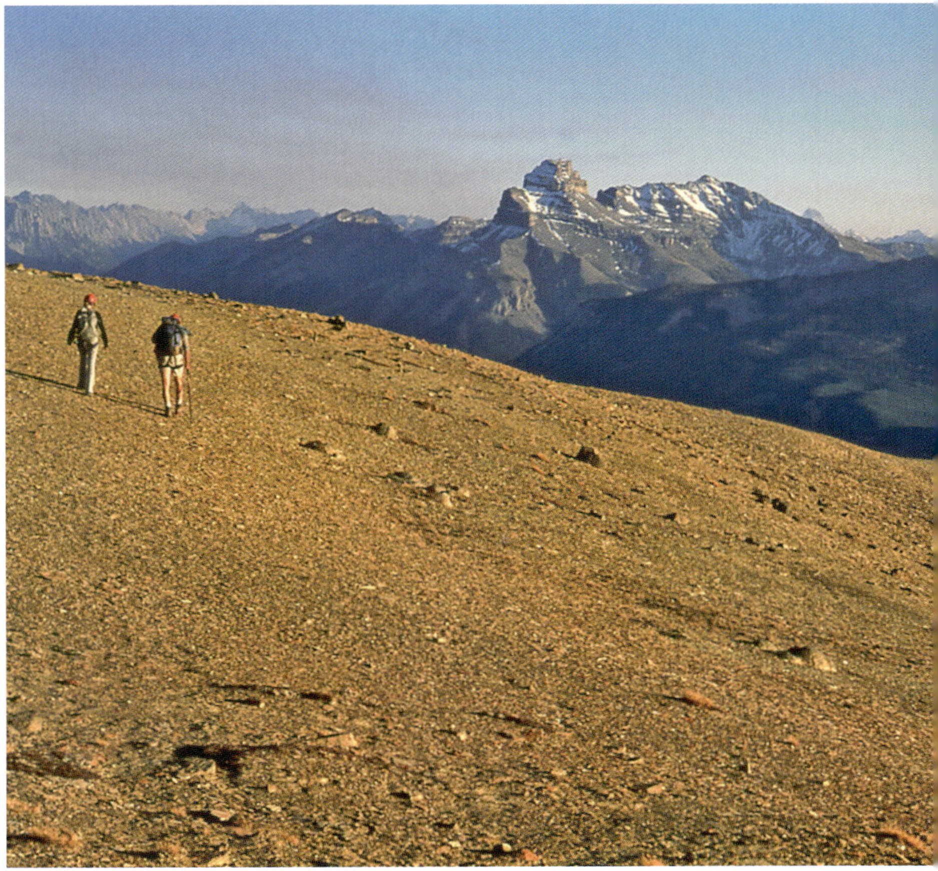

Sculpted and scattered, pieces of limestone lie all about, encrusted with circular patches of orange lichen. I stop and pick up a fragment. Looking closely, forgetting my place and size, I imagine tiny alpine routes in the fissures, as though the rock itself were a mountain. I would carry this gem home, but I know now it wouldn't be the same.

Yet its touch brings a flood of memories. I see the boy that played in the creek, the youth that ran out the door and climbed at Lake Minnewanka under a long ago summer sun, the young man who set out to slay dragons on the ramparts, gazed enraptured at a tiny snow crane fly, got far too close to a grizzly bear.

I recall the happy hubbub as a group of climbers—family and friends—at the end of a long day, consume the remains of lunches and snacks. But their voices are changed, as is mine; there's a veil through which I must speak. Warm in the sun, out of the wind, the climbers pack up their gear; hikers cram jackets into packs and tighten bootlaces. Now they are moving off down the mountain, leaving. I'm afraid of leavetakings and hesitate. Drawn to join them, I sense something stopping me—a sense of panic whose cause I'm at a loss to explain. Then I understand: part of me will be staying, will never leave.

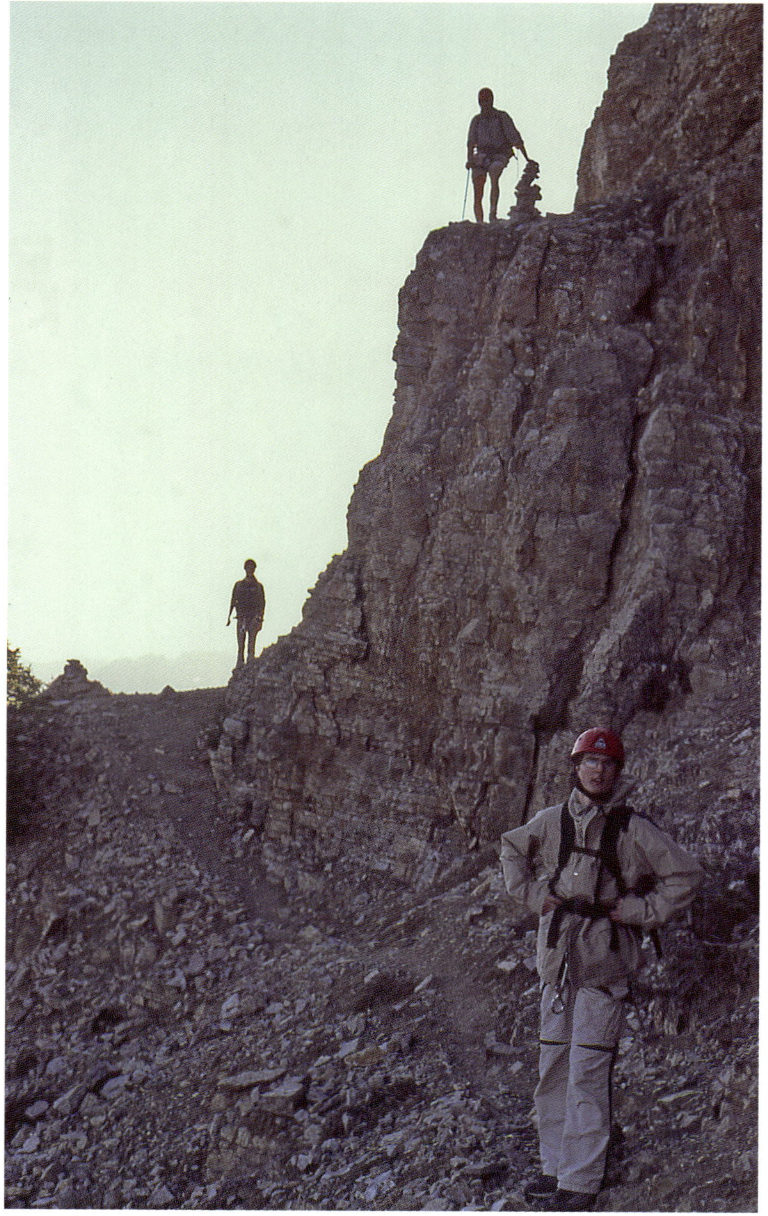

From the hanging valley at the top of the cliffs, I watch my son, our friends, then myself descend into the valley, skirting a viridian lake. Boots thump on the hard-packed trail. An exhausted climber stops by the glassy water for a drink. He looks startled when his outstretched hands touch liquid so clear he's misjudged its distance from his face. Just then, a solitary duck bursts from the translucent green surface into flight. Describing a rising arc on the deep valley, its excited calls breach the stillness of the violet dusk. The two events—climber drinking, bird rising—are somehow connected; time has momentarily collapsed.

The group moves on in laughter, jokes, talk of a great hike *just over there,* the next climb. In a few minutes it is dark. A pale rising moon casts long silver bands across the trail. The climbers, now just dim figures in the darkness, travel in a happy little train along a pale forest track. They are exhausted but elated, thirsty but satiated. After hours of effort, fatigue, fear, adrenaline push and elation, senses are tuned, ultra sharp. The soft wind carries the scent of alpine flowers and Jack pine. The night air cool on their faces, they can sense where elk have lain, hear rivulets that before would have passed unnoticed. At each bend in the trail the little train twists and turns. Arms swing back and forth, shoulders sway, packs with helmets and ropes bob in the soft, silver light. Thump, thump, thump. Slosh of water as someone takes a quick swig. Quiet words, mumbled thoughts. Then silence.

The moon has climbed higher in the blue-black sky. Northern constellations dance their great circle. Above a ridge of trees, the black mountain looms. Soon another rosy dawn will warm its ramparts and—up in the valley—that small piece of lichen-coated limestone only just returned to its place. Down deep in the valley, the striding figures' giant, gangly shadows appear briefly on a moonlit glade, flicker out in darkness, appear momentarily again. Then they are lost, and vanish altogether in the resin-scented forest.

On the descent, climbers take a moment's pause on the ridge just where the steep rock ends.

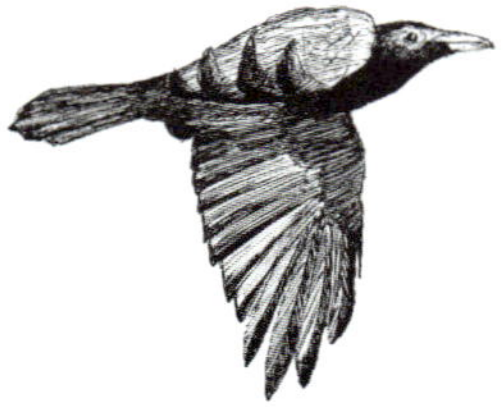

On a dark ridge high above me, larch needles are outlined in crystal brilliance by the sinking sun.

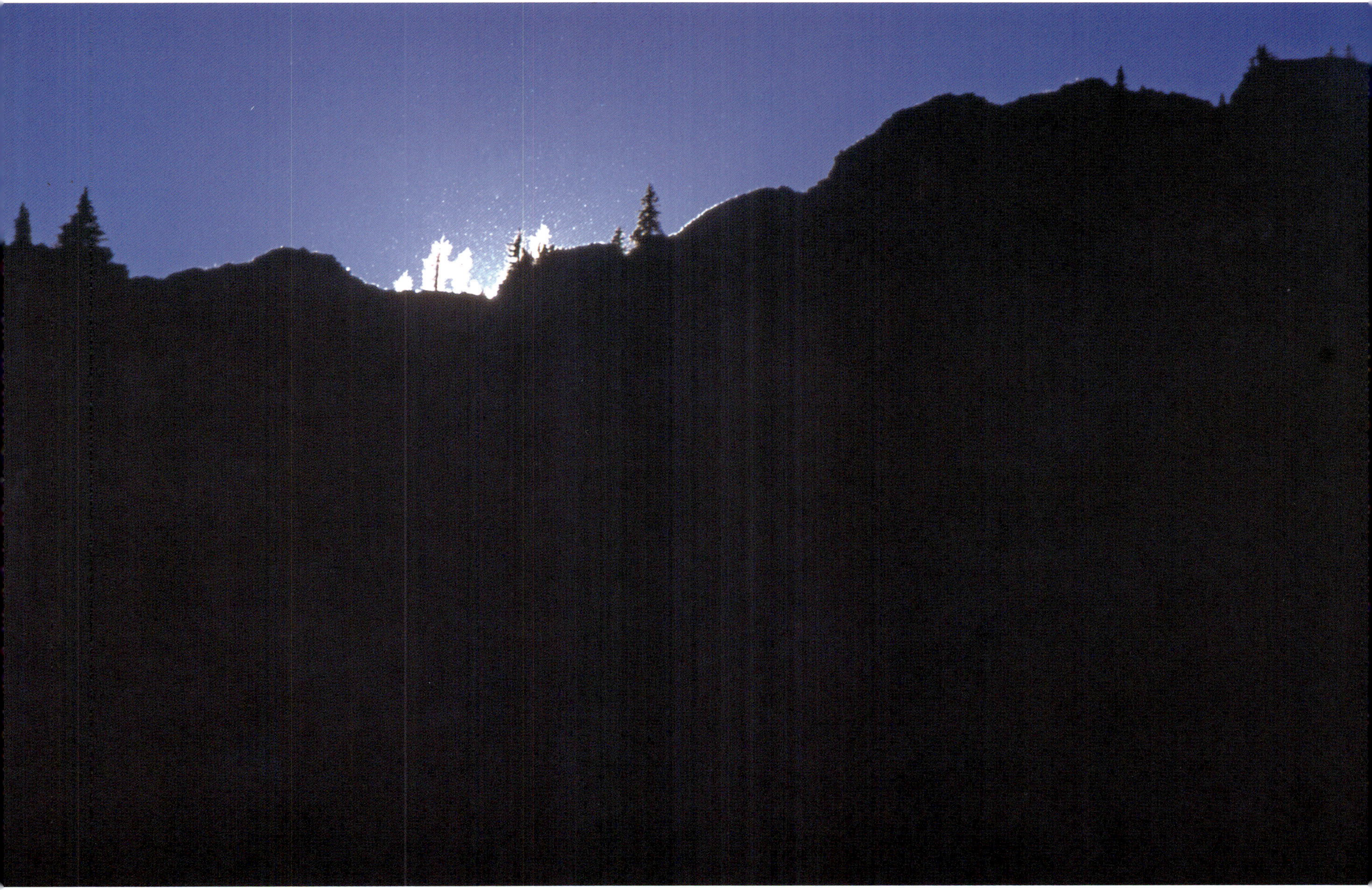

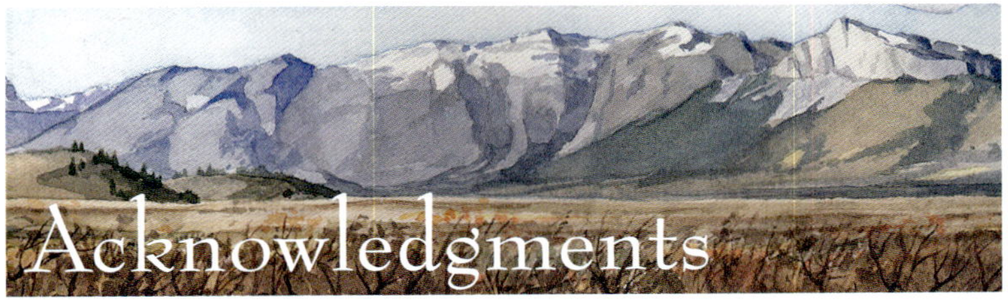

Acknowledgments

FOR THE ABRUPT TUG ON THE ROPE TO GET ME STARTED, I am indebted to Michael Mott: designer, tireless builder. Heartfelt thanks also to my life's climbing partners in order of appearance: my parents, George and Alice Perry, who took me on that first hike in the Yoho Valley under the summer sun such a long time ago; Donald Campbell, teacher and mountain lover for saying one day to a startled physics class, "Hey, who wants to go climb a mountain this weekend?"; and Charlie Locke, climber, mountain guide and entrepreneur, who understood perfectly that adventure and challenge were everything.

I also pause and tip my climbing helmet to Patrick Clarke, Ron and Joe Robinson, Bob Saunders, Susan Saunders, Bill Hoyne, Nick Krishanowski, my son Laurence and all the "weekend warriors" for sharing the sharp end of the rope, and especially to Jim Tanner, who ran across that ragged alpine ridge at midnight, clad only in undershorts, in the middle of a violent lightning storm.

He, Bob Bragg, Susan Cannon, Danita Maslankowksi, Joanne Ramondt and later Bill Hartman in Tucson, Arizona, inexplicably agreed to put up with innumerable questions and read my illuminated ravings, and thus was convened an informal editorial board. Their tolerance, support and effort are a debt that cannot be repaid. Dr. Jim Stewart provided all-important scientific accuracy; Denis Chalifoux actually understood how computers work. And to paraphrase from one of Bill Putnam's books—for the errors that inevitably accumulate in a work like this, I would very much like to blame someone else.

Bouquets to the staff at Rocky Mountain Books for their commitment to the publishing task. Judy Millar, editor, achieved the miraculous in transforming my notes into a real book. Thanks to the rest of my family—Alissa Avens for insight beyond her years and to my wife, Dale Lamont, for enduring it all and being my first line of defence in the preservation of truth and beauty.

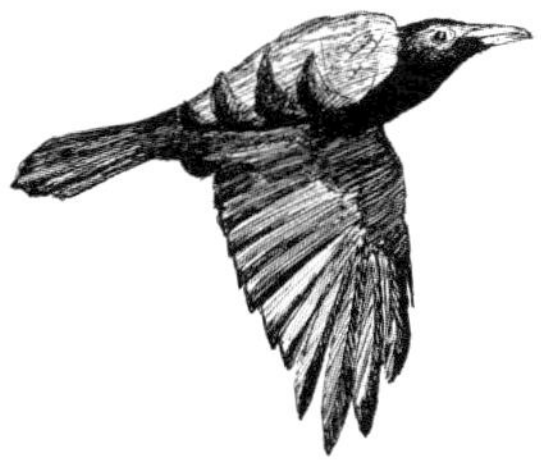

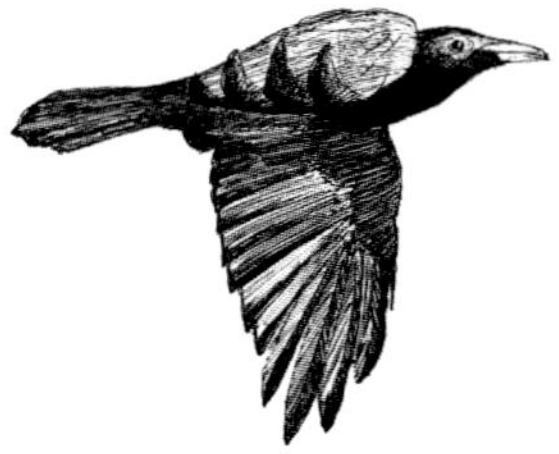

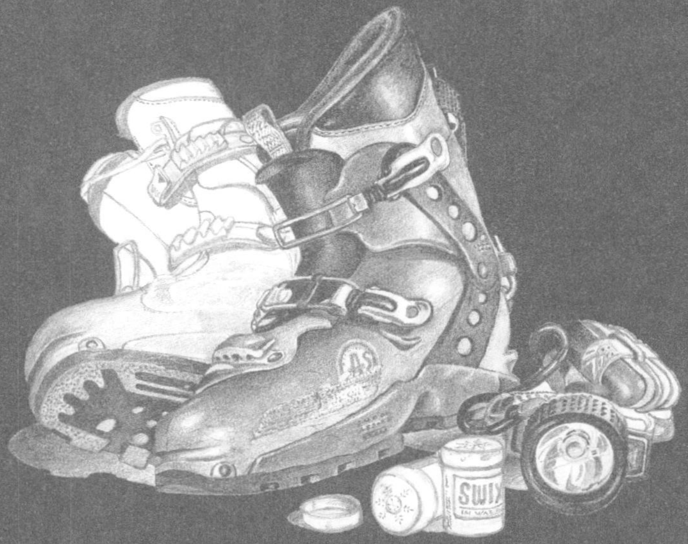
SWIX